Praise for **Wordstruck!**

Janssen's crisp, elegant prose leaps off the page. Her skill in weaving humor, etymology, and cultural insights will make her a hit with fans of Lynne Truss and Karen Elizabeth Gordon. Each paragraph has the playful, wry humor of your favorite linguistics professor and the grace of a tango dancer. This gem is not to be missed!

—**JODY GEHRMAN,** author of *Bombshell* and *The Truth About Jack*

Facts made fun! I'm *wordstruck* by Janssen's tell-all truth about lies, time, money, open kimonos, and godly goodbyes. I want a classroom set!

—**E.HALE,** High School teacher and author of *Birthing Orgasms, Time, & Money*

"It's hard to imagine 'A gram of prevention' becoming worth 'A kilo of cure' in one's lifetime."—True, but it's fun to try, aided by Susanna Janssen's light-hearted (but fundamentally serious) and experience-based tour of global culture and language. Pack it in your old kit bag, and smile at her anecdotes, etymologies and wit.

—**JONATHAN MIDDLEBROOK,** columnist ("It's All Good")

Susanna Janssen has been writing about language for the Ukiah Daily Journal in California and our readers have come to look forward to her fun plays on words, her personal stories, her travels and mostly, her vast knowledge of our language and how it gives us myriad ways to express ourselves. Get ready to be delighted at what you'll learn. You're in for a treat!

—**K.C. MEADOWS,** Editor, Ukiah Daily Journal

My interest was "peaked" "peeked" "piqued" in the first paragraph of this intelligent, high speed and frequently zany romp through the alternately charming and mind-boggling babel of our language. From personal anecdotes to Shakespeare creations, Susanna has crafted a page-turner.

—**LAURA FOGG,** artist and author of *Traveling Blind*

What a delightful and insightful book! Susanna Janssen's *Wordstruck!* unveils fantastic aspects of language, all across the spectrum from the linguistic perspective to the bilingual brain. Your awareness of the significance of words and how the inner and outer worlds are affected by them will certainly increase as you enjoy her reader-friendly and fun style.

—**RICARDO STOCKER, PH.D.** Professor of Communication and author of *Our Compassionate Kosmos*

Anyone with an interest in language and culture will enjoy and learn from this book. *Wordstruck!* presents an amusing, eye-opening, and well-informed array of anecdotes, examples, historical vignettes, and observations about the history, usage, and even the neuropsychology of language. Placed at their elbow and lifted for just a few minutes at a time, *Wordstruck!* will give readers a stream of tidbits and insight into how language works to reflect upon and share with others.

—**H. STEPHEN STRAIGHT,** Professor Emeritus of Anthropology and of Linguistics, Binghamton University of New York

With wit and wonder Susanna Janssen lures and captures the reader into her world of words in *Wordstruck!* Her passion for origins, historical context, metaphors and hilarious adventures is infectious from one memorable passage to the next.

—**HEIDI CUSICK DICKERSON,** author of *Roots & Ridges: Wine Notes from Mendocino and Soul & Spice: African Cooking in the New World.*

Wordstruck!

Wordstruck!

The Fun and Fascination
of Language

SUSANNA JANSSEN

ISBN: 978-0-9983048-0-9

Book Design: AuthorSupport.com

To my father, Friedjof Johannes Christie (Fred) Janssen, and to my mother, Caterina (Kay) Crai Janssen Bowman. Their multilingual, multicultural union is to blame and bless for all that follows.

CONTENTS

FOREWORD

Half a lifetime ago, I saw the famed semanticist S.I. Hayakawa hold a dictionary over his head and proclaim to a gaggle of undergraduate poets and writers, "This is a history book. If a word is already in it, it's old. It's well-established. But it's also ready for play."

Instead of memorizing rules, he further suggested, creative writers had to take competence for granted and practice word-play, thought-play and venture into new fields of knowledge (thus into new vocabularies) that would stretch meaning and moods. I never forgot that lecture, and I've tried to reflect it in my own writing.

I suspect that Hayakawa would love Susanna Janssen's book. I know I do. It is rich with anecdotes, full of unexpected chunks of knowledge charmingly presented, as well as controversies placed in perspective. For example, on the evolution of *goodbye* from *God be with ye*, she writes that the loss of *God* in *goodbye* "did not sit well with many people who viewed it as a trendy and degenerate utterance popular only among certain slices of society." To that I can only say, "Far out...!"

The author comments on notoriously (and often intransigently) monolingual Americans, but reports on studies that indicate significant behavioral and structural enhancements in the bilingual brain, noting that speakers of more than one language show improved memory and focus as well as "increased brain size in the hippocampus and cerebral cortex structures." S.I. Hayakawa, raised in a bilingual (Japanese-English) home in Canada, a bilingual (French-English) nation, would endorse the author's viewpoint. Quite simply, it's better to speak more than one language.

Language is as mobile as our minds, yet as rule-governed as our breath. When our 6-year-old daughter told my wife and me that she wanted a pet bunny "wabbit," I replied that our house was "uninwabbitable," but that she *could* have a kitten. She knew exactly what I meant, and settled for a kitty. Today, a mature woman with children of her own, she occasionally winks at me and says, "Is the house still uninwabbitable, Dad?" It is a secret word between us.

Janssen explains such lexical strategies and histories in a light style that makes this book's genuine wisdom readily accessible. Prepare for an enjoyable ride. "Fun and funner," as one of my students used to say.

Gerald W. Haslam, Ph.D.
Author of *In Thought and Action:
The Enigmatic Life of S.I. Hayakawa*

PREFACE

Wordstruck! It's not a disease or a mental imbalance, but certainly a lifelong condition of which I hope never to be cured. Of all human creations, I rate words and language in top place. There are some forty-six alphabets in the world today, but let's take just our Roman (also called Latin) one, and consider how many different alphabet soups have been concocted throughout the past three thousand years with a couple dozen letters. The number of letters varies slightly among the over five hundred languages that use this alphabet (mostly in Europe and the Americas), but basically everything that ever has been and ever will be written with it is just various combinations of twenty-six (give or take) symbols linked to specific sounds. If one is speaking, then well-placed pauses and inflections round out the meaning. If writing, then a dozen punctuation symbols are all this alphabet soup needs for clarity and flavor. Endless possibilities for construction and communication with so few building blocks and tools—what a miracle language is!

One could make a similar claim to supremacy for the creation of music out of a mere twelve basic notes and their endless combinations. Chapter Five, "The Wonders of the Bilingual Brain", explores how the brain is strengthened and many cognitive abilities are enhanced by learning foreign language. It's worth mentioning here that studies of the effects of music on the human brain have uncovered similar enhancements and labeled them "The Mozart Effect."

Words and music. I would not want to be without either. My appreciation of music is huge but my personal accomplishment in that field is limited, despite a decade of piano lessons and the conviction I was born to sing opera, though not gifted with the voice. Banish me to a desert isle, but let me have words and music. If I must choose between the two, I'll take words because Nature creates her own music, and, in solitude, I can screech out opera to my heart's (if not ears') content. Whenever I think about solitary confinement, it's the horror of being with nothing to read that floods my mind and grips my heart. I do seem to be able to generate a lot of words of my own, but what if in my cell, I had neither books to read nor tools to write with? That is a fate that gives me nightmares, while an abundance of words is always a promise of sweet dreams.

I did not set out to write a book, so I think I should tell you how this came to be. As a child, I wanted three things: to have a pet monkey, to play the harp, and to be a poet. I was perhaps ten years old when we took a family trip to the San Diego Zoo and I was smitten at first sight by a golden marmoset monkey, as enchanted by the velvety sound of its name as by the hairy little mammal itself. The family toured the zoo while I clung to the monkey cage. I begged and cajoled for what I was sure was my birthright. We got a dachshund puppy instead.

I knew becoming a harpist was my destiny, and I was convinced I was meant for a starring role in the orchestra with that huge, graceful instrument rocking in my arms. I made it clear to my parents that *that* was the musical instrument with my name on it, and...I got ten years of piano lessons with Grandma.

And poetry? Well, at least I had more control over that dream. I wrote goofy, rhyming lines about the Easter Bunny, Mom's routine of routing us all to bed, and what a meanie my big sister was. I thought brushing my teeth, disliking liver and onions, and watching my little brother belly flop off the high dive were verse-worthy inspirations. In adolescence, I poured out the requisite righteous angst over self-discovery, social woes, and unrequited infatuations. During the middle years, my creative pen was mostly still. I wrote an occasional poem, essay, and impassioned letter to the editor, but mostly and daily, I wrote lesson plans, homework and composition corrections, to-do lists, and birthday cards. Oh, and musings on scraps of paper about what I might write—someday.

One day, that *someday* came. It was not long after I retired from teaching college Spanish that I retrieved that pile of scraps. On a yellow pad, I wrote one topic idea at the top of each page. All were things related to words, languages, and cultures that I thought might be article-worthy: what I was fascinated by, knew a lot about, had an inkling of and wanted to explore, found hilarious, found deeply moving, wanted to share. Off the top of my head and down to the bottom of that pile of scribbled scraps, there were dozens of topics like:

- Captivating word derivations
- Crazy English pronunciation

- Collective terms for animals, like "a murder of crows." (I didn't know then that these are called terms of venery.)
- Sputnik and the lingo of the Cold War
- How Shakespeare's originality changed English forever and for better
- The Word of the Year
- Untranslatable words from other languages
- Arabic words in English
- Translations gone hysterically awry

Well, you get the idea. These and several dozen more are in the table of contents.

I willed myself to emulate the dedication of master storyteller Isabel Allende, who graciously declined my invitation to speak at Mendocino College, adding that she closets herself in her studio in early January of every year and writes daily with as few interruptions as possible until she finishes the project. Perhaps if had a turret manned by a jailer to repair to, or if a friend insisted I take over his Italian villa for six months. But no, I lacked Isabel Allende's focus and discipline.

My solution was to propose a column on words, language, and cultures, called "A Word in Edgewise," to the local newspaper editor, and once accepted, write an article of nine- to twelve-hundred words for publication every two weeks. This became a huge and hugely satisfying part of my life, and as such, I never missed a deadline, writing the better part of Friday-Saturday-Sunday twice a month. My social life dwindled as my number of published words grew. When I wrote an article about prepositions (*to, with, for, in, out, on,* etc.) that readers found funny and worthwhile—more to the point, that people actually *read*—I knew I had found firm ground as a writer.

These essays, originally launched to readers of my local newspaper column, now are released to a wider audience—that's you—in book form for your enjoyment and entertainment. In the writing and publication of them, I had more fun and satisfaction than I ever thought I had a right to. I hope you will smile a lot, laugh too, nod in resonance, and come across things you find wondrous, compelling, annoying, provocative, moving—whatever. Most of all, I hope you come away loving words and language all the more.

Susanna Janssen, October 2016

CHAPTER ONE

Life and Language in the USA

The Tower of Scrabble Babel

The official Scrabble lexicon of playable words recently grew by over 5000 entries. Even if I memorized and strategized every single one, I still couldn't beat a certain formidable opponent at the game. Experience and treachery will always overcome university degrees and a big vocabulary. In Scrabble, that is.

You Say Goodbye and I Say Hello

Is there "good" in *goodbye*? Is there "hell" in *hello*? The origin of these words goes deeper than you might think. And why *do* we answer the phone with "hello"?

The US and "Them" View of the World

Besides our non-use of metric, there are about a half dozen more areas in which the U.S. operates differently than most countries, including how we write dates and numbers, how we tell time and eat our food, and even how we do bathrooms.

Minding the Metaphor, Part I

Am I opening a can of worms, a box of chocolates, or reaching for a forbidden fruit? Metaphor engages the imagination through the five senses and can create an unexpected jolt, a deeper understanding, or simply a fresh way of perceiving a well-worn subject.

Minding the Metaphor, Part II

Herein are metaphors on love from some superbly creative writers, metaphors that motivate us to part with our money, and mixed metaphors that might have you "burning the midnight oil from both ends."

Let's Play the Dictionary Game

This word game costs nothing, but builds biceps and brain cells, critical thinking skills and funny bones, and lets you practice making friends and influencing people. (Author not responsible for split sides or busted guts.)

Pants on Fire

The statistics on how many times a day a lie comes our way are hair-raising. Herein will be revealed a baker's dozen of verbal clues that can tip you off when someone is lying to you.

How Are You Fixed for Time and Money?

There's so much energy invested in suffering over the scarcity of these two "commodities." What if they aren't absolutes but creations following the mold of cultural conditioning?

The Tower of Scrabble Babel

Well, it's about time. I've spent years "chillaxing" on Sunday afternoons, "mojito" in one hand and "Sudoku" puzzle in the other, pausing now and then to snap a "selfie" for social media self-promotion, yet only recently has America's leading dictionary publisher canonized these as bona fide words in the English language. Merriam-Webster's youth-friendly update to the college dictionary with thousands of new, trendy words created nary a ripple. But after that publication, M-W's next dictionary release created a tsunami of interest and media attention. As soon as new words appear in a standard dictionary, they are already fair game in Scrabble, as long as they are not abbreviations, capitalized words, or words with hyphens or apostrophes. Merriam-Webster's Fifth Edition of *The Official Scrabble Players Dictionary* was published on August 6, 2015, and its more than five thousand new words became fair game for official club and tournament matches as of December 1, 2015.

With my sweet mother's birthday coming up, it crossed my mind to gift her this dictionary, the first new edition in nearly ten years, because she is an avid Scrabble player. And a ruthless one. I have accused her of cheating more than once when she plunks down two tiles to connect with two existing words on the board, and then counts out her score for that move both horizontally and vertically, increasing her lead over me by about forty-eight points. Or when she plays one tile (usually a *J, Q, X,* or *Z*) to make a two-letter word that I would have bet money didn't exist.

SJ: "Mom, what does 'zu' mean??"

Mom: "I don't know, but it's a word."

SJ: "But Mom, it's not among the bazillion words in my *American Heritage* dictionary."

Mom: "No, use the Scrabble book."

SJ: "...Oh, of course—it's 'a monetary unit of Vietnam.'"

To add injury to insult, she played that *Z* for a triple-word score: 33 points. Grrrrrr!

There are only a few tiles left in the bag. I am playing with a mixture of anticipation for my suffering to end and ardent effort to lose by as few points as possible. There are seven tiles in my tray, and all I can manage to do is add a *T* under an *A*: "at." Score two points.

Mom's turn, and she pops a *Q* in front of my meager move.

SJ: "*Q-a-t*? *Qat*?? That's not a word!"

Mom: "It's a variation of *k-a-t*."

SJ: "That's not how to spell 'cat'!"

Mom: "No, nothing to do with that. It's *k-a-t*."

SJ: "And what does that mean?"

Mom: "I don't know—you look it up."

And she pushes the fat *Merriam-Webster* paperback my way.

This isn't the first time I have felt deep hatred for *The Official Scrabble Players Dictionary*, and I refuse to take it in hand. I look up "Qat" and "Kat" in every dictionary in the house. Nothing. I look online and...oh, but of course: "*qat*—the leaves of the shrub *Catha edulis,* native to the Horn of Africa and the Arabian Peninsula, which are chewed like tobacco or used to make tea; has the effect of a euphoric stimulant." I'm not a happy player; I could use some of that qat right now. Game over. She has beat me not by dozens of points, but by over a hundred.

According to the rules of the game, Mom is playing fair and square. Nowhere does it state you have to know what a word means before you can play it. She's not cheating. I, on the other hand (it pains me to confess), cheat often and abundantly. The rules are clear: "Consult the dictionary for challenges only," yet I troll the *M-W* Scrabble bible at practically every turn for clues of what to do with my tray of letters. This has provided me with no advantage.

Embarrassingly, there is no correlation between my performance at Scrabble with Mom and my university degrees plus over four decades in academia. In my final attempt at self-justification, I will reveal my adversary's most potent secret weapon. Mom has created her very own Scrabble "dictionary" consisting of 2"x 2" tiny pages stapled together and containing every playable two-letter word in the universe alphabetized *A* through *Z*. She rarely consults it, for nearly every word is committed to her crafty memory. It's enough to sizzle my cerebrum.

I don't know that I'll ever be a Scrabble fan, let alone approach Mom's echelon of skill (and did I mention cunning?), but I am fascinated by the five thousand-plus new words that have been inducted into the game's official dictionary. The four in my first paragraph are known even to terminally "unhip" me, so they must be known to you, too. (I suspect anyone who uses the terms "hip" or "unhip" is terminally in the second category.) I originally had to google the meaning of these additions to the *Scrabble Dictionary*, but now they pop up everywhere:

- **Beatbox**: A form of vocal percussion primarily involving the art of producing drum beats, rhythm, and musical sounds using one's mouth, lips, tongue, and voice.

- **Bromance**: A close, nonsexual relationship between two men. (This might be so rare that someone felt it needed a name. Female friendships, on the other hand...)
- **Catfish**: A person who sets up a fake social media profile.
- **Frenemy**: Can refer to either an enemy pretending to be a friend or someone who really *is* a friend but also a rival.
- **Geocache:** An outdoor recreational activity in which participants use a GPS and other navigational techniques to hide and seek out containers anywhere in the world. (Unlike Pokémon Go, you are hunting for an actual cache deposited by a real live person.)
- **Quinzhee**: A shelter made by hollowing out a pile of settled snow. This is in contrast to an igloo, which is made from blocks of hard snow. (This word has been in our language since 1984 but absent from the *Scrabble Dictionary* until now, proving, at least to me, that said tool is capricious and unreliable, though official.)*
- **Vlog**: A blog whose content primarily consists of videos.†

In addition to these, fair play on the Scrabble board includes the interjections "oof," "yessiree," " aiyee," and "meh," that last being a verbal shrug of the shoulders. Just don't breathe a word about any of this to my mom. I rejected the thought of buying

---

* This makes me think of my all-time favorite Far Side cartoon by Gary Larsen: Picture two polar bears standing next to an igloo, and one says to the other, "I just love these things: crunchy on the outside, and chewy on the inside."

† And if they seem already stale as you read this, ponder a moment the breakneck speed at which English precipitously adopts and, often, abandons neologisms. In a recent interview, a radio talk show host asked me which slang words meaning "great" have survived the test of time. After discarding boss, bad, bitchin, jake, righteous, tubular, wicked, sweet, on fleek, slaying, and snatched (by the time you read this, more will have come and gone), we agreed the survivor is "cool". Not only does it have many shades of meaning, it leaps socio-cultural fences and has been around for several generations—so long, in fact, that we don't even think of it as slang anymore. But we decided it passed the test because it's still cool to say "Cool!"

her the new dictionary. She'd have no use for any of these new words in her vocabulary anyway, and as for her Scrabble game, she doesn't need any more ammunition! She's already a lexical savant—as long as she doesn't have to produce any definitions.

You Say Goodbye, and I Say Hello

If you can get through a day without ever saying "Hello" and "Goodbye" (or the variations, "Hi," "G'bye," "Bye," "Bye-bye," etc.), you might be a hermit in the desert or a nun committed to a life of silent prayer. Where do these words come from? Did someone once decree that they were to be the official American formulas for our greeting and leave-taking? Is there "good" in "goodbye"? Is there "hell" in "hello"? No and no to those last two questions, and the country western song with those lyrics has already been written.

Let's start with "goodbye" because it's simpler, and because Paul McCartney *didn't* in his catchy song, "Hello Goodbye" ("You say yes, I say no. You say stop, and I say go go go..."). The original phrase was "God be with ye," an archaic way of wishing one well as you took your leave. Folks in the fifteenth century said every syllable of that sweet expression, but by the later sixteenth century, it had contracted to *Godbwye* (and I've no idea how that jumble was pronounced). With everyone already saying, "Good day" and "Good evening," it was inevitable that the phrase would soon become completely secularized to "Goodbye." Losing "God" to "Goodbye" did not sit well with many people who viewed it as a trendy and degenerate utterance popular only among certain slices of society. But as is our human bent, one year's scandal becomes another year's status quo, and we've been saying "Goodbye" ever since (though the argument whether it should be written "goodbye" or "good-bye" persists).

I am struck by the similarity of "God be with ye" to the archaic, but still widely known Spanish parting phrase, *Vaya con*

Dios ("Go with God"). God has also survived in the standard Spanish goodbye, *Adiós*, commending one *to God* for safekeeping. I suppose this is why *Adiós* is sometimes reserved for more permanent or meaningful partings, while *Hasta luego* works for "Bye, see you later." *Hasta la vista* is less common in Spanish speech, but about as familiar in America as Cinco de Mayo and enchiladas, thanks to Arnold Schwarzenegger in the action flick, *Terminator 2: Judgment Day* (1991). "Ahhnold" made $15 million for this movie role in which his entire dialogue consisted of seven hundred words. Let's see ... that comes out to $21,429 per word and $85,714 just for saying, "*Hasta la vista*, baby." One stunning linguistic accomplishment!

In parts of South America, it's common to say *Ciao* as a goodbye, but there it's spelled *chau* or *chao*. In Italy, it's both a greeting and a goodbye, and came into the language via medieval Latin as *s-ciàvo/schiavo*, "I am your slave," a rather weighty commitment to proffer when all you really mean is *"Hi" or "See you later."*

"Hello" is a somewhat newer word than "goodbye," but its roots do go way back. According to the *Oxford English Dictionary*, it first appeared in print in 1827, but its usage then was not as a greeting, rather as a way of getting someone's attention ("Hello, look what you just did!") or showing surprise ("Hello, Tom! Your dog can shoplift??") In its many variations throughout time and place (beginning around 1400 in Old High German and also in Old French), it was a shout to attract attention, especially to hail a ferryboat: *halloo, hallo, halloa, hillo, holla, holler, hollo, hollow, hullo, holà*, and so on. Yes, the Spanish word for "hello," *hola*, comes from this lexical lineage as well.

Let's now examine the history of how "Hello" became our formula for answering the phone, for these things rarely just happen by chance, and there's almost always a good back story.

Alexander Graham Bell and Thomas Alva Edison were both born in 1847 and leapfrogged each other through the US Patent Office with their world-changing inventions. Among his many patents, Bell is credited with inventing the metal detector, the hydrofoil boat, the harmonic telegraph, and in 1876, the telephone. Edison invented the phonograph (imagine what it meant to replay sound!), the motion picture camera (and movement!), the incandescent lightbulb, and the microphone that made Mr. Bell's telephone into an apparatus that quickly revolutionized business communication. The early telephone was used exclusively in commerce, and the line was open on both ends at all times.

For the caller to be able to get the attention of someone on the other end, several strategies were considered. The president of the Central District and Printing Telegraph Company of Pittsburg was pondering the merits of a call bell, but Thomas Edison convinced him that the perfect word, spoken "cheerfully and firmly", could be heard ten to twenty feet away. Alexander Graham Bell was adamant that word should be "Ahoy!" and stubbornly used it the rest of his life. ("Ahoy" is used to answer the phone in parts of Eastern Europe, spelled "*Ahoj.*") Other early contenders were, "What is wanted?", "Are you there?", and "Are you ready to talk?" Thomas Edison's *perfect* word won out. The first telephone books recommended this word in their instructions to users. "Hello" became the official way to start a telephone conversation and soon became the most popular way to greet people as well, altering forever the proscriptive nineteenth century etiquette of not speaking unless you had first been introduced. "Hello" or a variation close in sound (as "*Aló*") is used to answer the phone in nearly forty languages as diverse as Arabic, Cantonese, Danish, French, German, Hungarian, Hebrew, Hindi, Japanese, Persian, Polish, Russian, Thai, and Vietnamese.

The Greek philosopher Heraclitus said, "The only thing constant in life is change," and now we have the game changer of caller ID. While we're not yet saying "Goodbye" to the telephone greeting "Hello," for many of us, it's become rare to answer the phone if we don't know who is calling. When I do so, I tend to say a rather questioning, suspicious, and totally unsatisfying, "hello?" So, in honor of the amazingly inventive duo, Bell and Edison, who pioneered the electronic revolution that has progressed beyond wild imagination, I hereby resolve to make all my future hellos "cheerful and firm", and perhaps even throw in an occasional "Ahoy" for colorful good measure.

The US and "Them" View of the World

Not only is American English the fastest-growing language on the planet, but for better or worse, we are exporting our culture to the world's insatiable appetite for American music, movies, cultural trends, fast food, and big-box retail. What they want *nothing* to do with is our measuring system. In the US, the metric system is consistently used in the scientific, military, and manufacturing sectors, but in everyday life, we stubbornly cling to our ounces, gallons, acres, and 212° boiling point, unable to think any other way than miles per hour, tablespoons of sugar, and 102°F on the Fourth of July. So here we are, a huge island of ten-gallon hats in a sea of metric-users, wearing the 37.8541 liter version.

Ah, but we are not entirely alone! Myanmar and Liberia don't use the metric system either, though both have declared its future adoption. Our nonmetric system was inherited by the thirteen colonies as a legacy from the British Empire. Today, the United Kingdom and Canada use the metric system, if not exclusively, at least dominantly. In 1971, the US National Bureau of Standards proposed that metrics be phased in over a period of ten years. But when lawmakers took action, they legislated out "deadline" in favor of "voluntary adoption." Since shifting to metric would be like everyone having to read, write, think, and speak a foreign language, there were obviously few "volunteers."

Like most of us, I can't think in metric. If a pancake recipe calls for 200 ml of milk and 180 g of flour, I'm having scrambled eggs and toast for breakfast. When my aunties used to exclaim over the extremely rare 35 degrees of heat they were having in Northern

Holland, I had to get out the calculator and do the math: 35°C x 9/5 +32 = 95°F. I never got a speeding ticket driving Aunt Vena's car along the Dutch canals because going 80 to 100 seemed plenty fast to me. Of course, that's kilometers per hour, and only 50 to 62 in miles per hour, but those bigger numbers made me feel like I was flying toward the next quaint, steepled village at Grand Prix racing velocity.

With water freezing at 0°C and boiling at 100°C, the elegance of the metric system is inarguable. And it truly is a *system* because there is the same ratio (1000:1) for millimeters to meter, meters to kilometer, grams to kilogram, and kilograms to tonne. Our American way does not even have an official name, let alone any regularity of measurement. It can be referred to as the US Customary System or the inch-pound system, and includes more than 300 different units to measure various physical quantities. Frightfully complicated—yes, but not when it is *our* frame of reference, as ingrained into brain automaticity as is counting or telling time. Given this degree of attachment, it's hard to imagine, "A gram of prevention" becoming worth "a kilo of cure" in one's lifetime.

On the subject of what America does differently than most of the world, there are a few more aspects of ordinary life we might consider:

* * *

In the Miami airport, before boarding a charter flight for Cuba in the spring of 2015, we all had to fill out a form for the Cuban government that instructed the order for birth date as *day/month/year*. An American born on January 7, 1962, would customarily write 1/7/62, but outside of the United States, it's usually written 7/1/62. Despite our guide's warning, one member of the group went on autopilot and wrote 1/7/62. Although she neatly crossed it out and wrote in the requested birth date order, she was charged $100 for the mental blip and a new blank form. No excuses, no discussion. Although we experienced two weeks of uniformly welcoming generosity from the Cuban people, I suspected this particular act of punitive policy to be a bit of embargo revenge because who else but an American would write month/day/year?

*   *   *

On the subject of airports, a colleague showed up to teach classes on Monday morning, though I was sure she'd said on Friday she was off to Bali or some such exotic and faraway place. With great and sheepish embarrassment, she told me she had misread the itinerary and arrived at the international terminal for what she thought was an 11:00 p.m. flight that had already left at 11:00 that morning. Why aren't we using the twenty-four-hour clock—at least for public transportation—like most of the rest of the world? It *is* used in American hospitals and in the military because lives depend on everyone being synchronized as to when the patient gets a dose of meds or at what time the squadron moves into strategic position. But why aren't the rest of us using it in time-sensitive contexts? Well, because we just don't think of afternoon/evening as 13:00 to 24:00; we have to stop and count on our fingers, and even then are never fully convinced that 19:00 hours really is 7:00 p.m.

*   *   *

Here is another sneaky pitfall with numbers that awaits the innocent American in Foreigndom. You are quite certain that the only way to write your bank balance is $3,400 (envying your brother's at $3,400,000); and that the exchange rate for the euro is now—hallelujah!—1.12 (I know, I know, not good for the export economy, but the travel group going to Barcelona this fall is ecstatic.) I admit to shock in discovering that most parts of the world put commas in numbers where we put periods, and periods where we put commas. It looks like this: Your bank balance is $3.400 (your brother's is $3.400.000—but Mom always liked him best); the exchange rate for the euro is 1,12; and clock time is even written 7,30. I know, it just seems *wrong*, but that just shows how attached we are to our particular meaning of a dot and a squiggle when used with numbers.

* * *

Another oddity that sets the United States apart is that our currency bills are all green and the same size. Though we think this is perfectly normal, workable, and logical, in most countries, bills are different colors and often varying sizes according to denomination. Have you ever had to say to a clerk, "But I gave you a twenty and you only gave me change for a ten"? Colorful bills in varying sizes can be pretty to look at, but it really is more about practicality than esthetics. In our twilight years with eyesight failing, will we struggle to tell the difference between a $5 and a $1?

* * *

Then there is the matter of wielding knife and fork at the dinner table. Watch carefully in slow motion the right-handed version in America: Using the right hand, we transport food from plate to mouth with the fork *tines up*. Then we switch that fork over to the left hand (*tines down* to stab with), take the knife into the right hand and cut our steak. Then we set the knife down, and transfer the fork back to the right hand (*tines up*) to make its way to the mouth. Quite a production! Most foreign knife-fork wielders look on this as inefficient, clumsy (read: "inelegant"), and might even be likened to the way toddlers handle the tool before they've learned to eat properly.

I remember sitting in a café in Antwerp with my Belgian cousin, marveling at how she cut the meat, retained the fork (*tines down*) in her left hand, deftly used the knife with the right hand to assemble a neat packet of meat and accompaniments onto the *back* of her fork, and flawlessly guided it into her mouth. It's called Continental or European style and is obviously more economical and practical; that is, *if* you can master the successful docking of fork plus contents in mouth. I daresay it is also more graceful and am glad to see it is gaining in popularity, although many Americans still regard this style of eating as a lack of good table manners, somewhere between questionable and uncouth.

* * *

As any world traveler has experienced, the countries that use 220 volts vastly outnumber the United States and others that use 120. I made my first trip to Italy just about the time the travel industry was putting dual-voltage personal appliances on the market. Armed with my first such gadget, I still packed my voltage converter *just in case.* My hotel in Siena was a former convent staffed by nuns with the stern and intimidating Mother Superior herself doing front desk duty.

On our first morning, I recall my long mental debate over what to do about the hairdryer, the converter, and the 220 wall socket. I finally decided that the best strategy was to plug the dual-voltage appliance into the converter *just to make sure* it got enough electricity. This well-thought-out act blew the electricity on the whole second floor. (You see, there is a reason I am a linguist and not a scientist or an engineer.) I slunk downstairs to the front desk and confessed in jumbled Italian. Mother Superior was furious with me (was that steam coming out of her wimple?) and, suffice to say, it took a lot of penance to get back in good standing as a tourist at the "convent."

* * *

In my experience of traveling to twenty or so countries on several continents, I will assert that *no one* does bathrooms like we do in America. For us, a bathroom is a sacred place and must be built, outfitted, and appointed as such. I go to a restaurant with friends and one comes back to the table and says, "Oh, you've just *got* to see their bathroom!" Design and decor are treated like curated art installations, and plumbing has developed as one of America's finest arts. The toilet always flushes, and there's always water in the shower—hot on demand and with enough power to rinse the shampoo out of the thickest head of hair.

I used to have a "Lady Godiva"-length mane, and hair washing was always a top concern on my travels. On family visits to Europe, I was stymied by trickling showers and tiny water heaters that put out about enough to wash a teacup in the sink. Electricity and gas were hugely expensive, and people were very frugal with resources and supplies of just about everything. This will be hard to believe, but my Dutch grandmother, even when she came to live in the United States after WWII, only had her hair washed every five to six weeks. In between visits to the salon, she used powders that she combed through to absorb the oil. She burned candles in the evening to save on electricity. Even in the land of plenty, she adhered to a culture of economization. While visiting a friend in Spain, I realized from the start there was no hope of washing my hair in her trickle of a shower with a miniature on-demand water heater of lukewarm output, so I parted with many euros as a regular customer at the nearby salon.

During a study/travel program to Cuernavaca, Mexico, I stayed with a family that was proud to offer me the apartment they had added to their suburban home. The "shower" consisted of a lead pipe (no shower head) emerging from a hole three inches below the ceiling, with a nice strong jet of water that was aimed uselessly and irremediably at the side wall six inches above my right shoulder. One of my fellow travelers to Cuba swore she would pack a toilet seat into her luggage if she ever returned to the island. Bathroom facilities have been the source of some of my greatest travel frustrations, and I'm not alone because hilarious illustrated books, websites, and even a wall calendar have been created by traumatized Americans subjected to interesting but inefficient foreign facilities.

* * *

How differently we all experience the world. Enjoying barbecues late into our balmy summer evenings, I'm reminded that friends in Uruguay and cousins in South Africa are stoking furnaces and wearing woolens through their winter. I look up at the Big Dipper and, though it's one of only three constellations I can reliably identify in our Northern Hemisphere sky, the whole starry expanse looks familiar to me. My mind reaches into the future for the next time I'll be far enough south to search unfamiliar heavens for *their* stellar icon, the Southern Cross.

But for now, I'm trying to embrace the metric system before

my paella cooking class in Barcelona by measuring out 600 grams of rice, 300 grams of prawns, a liter of broth, 100 milliliters of white wine...and it will all be ready to serve between 21,15 and 22,00—the window of time that much of the rest of the world regards as the most civilized hour to dine.

Vive la différence!

Minding the Metaphor, Part I

W e were talking about *metaphor* while keeping an eye on the tango dancers circling the floor. He said that whenever he wanted to express an idea in metaphor, his mind was a *haze* and nothing came up. Then as we both admired a particularly graceful dancer, he said, "She's a *doll*, but when I dance with her, I have *two left feet*." Sure, these are simple ones, but he proved to be quite adept at metaphors after all.

Whether we can define the term or not, we likely demonstrate some mastery of its use all the time. I want to understand metaphor at a deeper level, and what better way than to write about it?! Best to start with something we all have experience with and have a lot to say about, so let's take *life*. We can describe it with adjectives: Life is *hard/exciting/challenging/fun*. But if we want to spice it up, communicate more impact, and fire the imagination and the senses, we could opt for a metaphor: Life is *a bowl of cherries/a rocky road/a rat race/a bed of roses/a beach/"but a dream, sweetheart."*

Of course, metaphors can be original instead of the familiar old *workhorses* that pop to mind. A friend recently said, "My life is one barrel ride over Niagara Falls after another." In a flash (then and now), my imagination creates the roar of the falls, the cold spray in my face, and the horrifying sight of my friend's barrel launching into free fall. My senses are fully engaged, and my heart rate probably spikes as well. And that is precisely why we express ourselves in metaphor: to create image and impact by appealing to the imagination through the five senses.

You're working on a project; it's easy or hard, rewarding or dull, difficult or smooth. You report to friends that this latest challenge is *a bear/Mount Everest/a walk in the park/the icing on the cake.* What you are doing is describing what *is* (A: your project) with what it *is not* (B: a bear). But B works so well as a descriptor because of the image it creates. When clouds *sail* across the autumn sky or tornados *barrel* through the Midwest, the brain has something far more interesting to work with than "move fast."

There is movement in most metaphors, if not overt as in, "Their marriage was a *roller coaster*," then suggested: "Monday morning, and it's back to the *salt mines.*" I get a motion picture of hard labor with bent backs and sweaty arms wielding heavy metal mallets. If there's *an elephant in the room*, its tail swishes while everyone in the overstuffed chairs nervously averts eyes to floor and ceiling, pretending not to see, hear, and smell what's really going on. Dad on a strict diet says his beloved afternoon ice cream bar is *forbidden fruit*, and the metaphor itself intimates the movement of that hand reaching into the tree to pick that of which he should not partake. When the government's response to an intractable social problem is temporary and inadequate, we can "see" that *Band-Aid* being slapped over a wound that begs for deeper treatment. All those loans secured by plastic add up to *a house of cards* and we already picture the impending collapse from a puff of air or the placement of one more card.

Metaphors from literature, history, visual media, and song weave their way into the woof and warp of culture and become such familiar fabric that we might even forget where they came from. Here is a six-point quiz to identify the source of these famous metaphors:

1. "The fog comes / on little cat feet. / It sits looking / over harbor and city / on silent haunches / and then moves on."
2. "Out, out, brief candle! Life's but a walking shadow, a poor player that struts and frets his hour upon the stage and is

heard no more. It is a tale told by an idiot, full of sound and fury, signifying nothing."

3. She finally met her *Waterloo*.

4. "He's a boil on the butt of humanity." (Double points if you get this one.)

5. "My Mama always said *life* was *like a box of chocolates*. You never know what you're gonna get."

6. "When the moon hits your eye like a big pizza pie, that's *amore*."

End of quiz (see answers*), but hmmm...if Mama said life was *like* a box of chocolates, and if the moon hits your eye *like* a big pizza pie, it's a *simile* and not a *metaphor*, right? With all due respect to our middle school teachers, it turns out that *metaphor* is an umbrella term, and *simile* is one of the several literary devices in its shelter. *Simile*, in other words, is the type of metaphor that uses the words "like" or "as."

Jane Hirshfield, renowned poet, essayist, and translator created an engaging animated TED-Ed Original called, "The Art of Metaphor." In it, she states, "A simile is a metaphor that makes you *think* it's making a comparison." The *Oxford Companion to the English Language* defines *metaphor* as, "All figures of speech that achieve their effect through association, comparison, and resemblance. Figures like antithesis, hyperbole, metonymy, simile are all species of metaphor." Okay, but we are not going to touch those first three with a metaphoric ten-foot pole between these covers of *Wordstruck!*

Back to that "pie in the eye": a perfect note to end on because it's a double metaphor (or metaphor plus simile if Sister Josita of freshman English insists). It is action-packed, though question-ably romantic: "Love is the *moon* hitting your eye like a big *pizza pie*." Ah, Love! What fertile *field* for metaphor!

On the very next page, I promise you metaphors of love never to be forgotten; metaphors for the soul from my poet/Scorpio friend Nancy Harris McLelland; a true confession of my life as the Golden Gate Bridge; and some rib-tickling *mixed metaphors*. It won't be long, I can already see the *light at the end of the rainbow*.

*Answers to the quiz:

1. Carl Sandburg's poem, "Fog."
2. Shakespeare of course, but whence? Ah, therein lies the rub! (Macbeth: Act 5, Scene 5)
3. Napoleon Bonaparte was finally defeated at the battle of Waterloo, Belgium in 1815; also the 1974 megahit from ABBA.
4. One of many memorable lines uttered by character Ouiser Boudreaux played by Shirley MacLaine in *Steel Magnolias.*
5. Forrest on the park bench at the beginning of the movie *Forrest Gump.*
6. The hit song from 1953, "That's Amore," sung by Dean Martin, composed by Harry Warren and Jack Brooks; theme song of the 1987 movie *Moonstruck.*

Minding the Metaphor, Part II

W e are back in the land of metaphoric make-believe where nothing is *really* as stated, but where, somehow, the linguistic act of comparison creates a more palpable reality through word and image. Just hearing the metaphors, "A light at the end of the tunnel," or "A pot of gold at the end of the rainbow," might deliver a dose of optimism with the promise of cheer and the hope of good fortune. Before we assume we're all on the same metaphoric *page*, let's consider how one person's metaphor can be another person's mystery.

A metaphor will often be a thing that represents or symbolizes an abstraction. Maybe in your family, some object, person, or activity morphed in meaning over time to become a metaphor, and if so, maybe no one outside your genetic nucleus was in on the secret. I'll let you in on two from the Janssen's: When we say "*V* Street," we don't necessarily mean the physical street we kids grew up on. We mean idyllic childhood years of playing Robinson Crusoe in the orchard (in the blazing summer sun of Bakersfield, California, a "loaf" of mud would bake solid in two hours); riding bikes with our kiddy pals; plying the sidewalks on metal skates; and watching Ed Sullivan's "really big shoe" on Sunday nights.[‡]

My second example is an abrupt pop of that bucolic bubble. Everyone who had a childhood knows or can imagine what a *spanking stick* is. Mom's was the flat, back slat of a kitchen chair, six inches wide and two feet long as I recall (but probably more like 3" x14" in reality). The sides were curvy, so she could grip it

---

[‡]   He pronounced "show" with his lips pursed, and so always famously introduced every show, "It's a really big shoe tonight.

tight and wield it fast and hard. That stick was such a presence in our childhood years that it became a metaphor for everything we kids shouldn't have done/said, or failed to do/say (similar to the word *confessional* if you grew up Catholic). Just hearing Mom intone "spanking stick", as in, "Don't make me get my..."or "Stay where you are, I'm coming back with my..." (it lived on top of the refrigerator, ever within her reach) conjured up a whirlwind of distressing images but always meant one thing: *You're in trouble.*[§]

It's also worth mentioning that one culture's metaphors likely will not be easily grasped by another. This is so obvious it needs no illustration, but it's fun to think about a foreigner's confusion if he's told by his American friend that learning English is not a "walk in the park," or if another friend offers to "show him the ropes." I was delighted to hear from Barbara, a reader of my newspaper column, who told me that in Norway, the word "Texas" has become a slang metaphor for something *really out there/completely crazy.*

Sure enough, there's a photo online of an enormous swordfish leaping from the waters off the coast of Norway with the caption, *Det var helt Texas.* Best translation: "It was totally bonkers." I wonder if that new metaphor makes Texans polish their star with pride or snort into their ten-gallon hat[¶] with disdain.

[§] It never occurred to me to engage in defensive maneuvers, but my little brother was smarter, more agile, and less fearful than I. One day, as the legendary stick was slicing through the air toward his (standing) backside, he deftly dodged sideways and instead, it crashed down upon a nearby chair with enough force to split it lengthwise down the middle. Now Mom had two sticks, and there were other generations of spanking sticks after that, but none was ever as spring loaded and atomic powered as the original.

[¶] There are two possible origins for the name of this famous cowboy hat, but both originated with Spanish, and the hat itself was imported from south of the border. The first explanation offers that the Spanish phrase *tan galán,* was applied to a sombrero that was "so fine", easily anglicized by American cowboys to "ten gallon." The second and more likely comes from the Spanish word "galón" which was a thin strip of braided trim around the crown of a hat. On the preferred high-crowned *vaquero*-cowboy style, not just one galón, but ten might adorn it.

In the richly metaphoric realm of love, here are some unforgettable ones: "Happiness is the china shop; love is the bull" (H.L. Mencken, *A Little Book in C Major*, 1916); "They say love is a two-way street. But I don't believe it, because the one I've been on for the last two years was a dirt road" (Terry McMillan, *Waiting to Exhale*, 1992); "Love is an exploding cigar we willingly smoke" (Lynda Barry, cartoonist); "Love must be as much a light as a flame" (Henry David Thoreau, letter, 1852). My poet/ Scorpio friend Nancy Harris McLelland wrote: "I would like a love IV: a slow and steady flow of affection." Nancy writes and speaks in metaphors that fill me with wonder, inspiration, amusement, sometimes longing, even sorrow. Here is a gem I found on her website, Adobe House Artists: "I could no longer swallow my resentments whole. The heartburn was overwhelming"; and another: "I feel like a Red Cross volunteer, likely to get shot by either side."

Long ago, Nancy told of a paradigm shift she had at her ironing board: "I was always bothered by my ironing basket filled with ironing, until the morning I changed my *POV* and told myself, 'That's the way an ironing basket is *supposed* to look!'" In addition to appreciating her change in *point of view* toward the task, I took on the image of that ever-full basket as a metaphor for how we knock off life's chores only to have more pile on, and stress ourselves to breaking point with the misguided belief that the goal of life is to keep the basket empty.

Not unlike Nancy's ironing basket, my most enduring and bracing metaphor for life as I live it is the job of painting the Golden Gate Bridge, San Francisco's most iconic symbol. The GG Bridge Highway and Transportation District confirms that the structure is painted continuously: International Orange fifty-two weeks a year. That quite perfectly describes my eternal project of dealing with the clutter in my life. I'm immune to self-reminders that "flat surfaces are not storage areas" and that I don't need to clip more recipes, save those articles, or take notes on every available scrap of paper about book titles, good movies, interesting words, and secrets to enlightenment. In order to manage, I keep "painting the Golden Gate Bridge" year after year. Once the full-house declutter and reorganization project is complete, I gleefully pop a champagne cork...and then begin again, continually reminding myself to stop grousing and celebrate that there is still a bridge to paint and that I'm still able to wield that brush every day.

In his article, "Why Metaphors Beat the Snot out of Facts When It Comes to Motivating Action" (a title that practically says it all), Douglas Van Praet asserts metaphors motivate us to buy because they "evoke feelings that bypass critical thinking." When you see that sweet family and their little house safely nestled in the "Good Hands" of Allstate, you just get a warm feeling that everything is going to be alright. Tropicana's irresistible orange juice metaphor, "Your daily ray of sunshine," speaks of warmth, health, and vibrancy. "Show 'em you're a tiger" is a powerful promise that keeps the kids clamoring for Frosted Flakes. If you run out and buy yourself a new Lexus, you will "Unleash the Beast!" and become powerfully unstoppable.

Wishful thinking and belief in all that hype aside, now we're going to top off the tank with a few mixed metaphors, so "button your seatbelts" (Rush Limbaugh) because "the dirty laundry is coming home to roost" (Ray Romano): "A leopard can't change his stripes" (Al Gore); "Can you read the handwriting in the wind?" (Major Frank Burns, MASH unit); "These hateful few who have no conscience, who kill at the whim of a hat." (George W. Bush); "She's a sharp cookie" (oops, Yours Truly).

Amid this inviting potential for enlivened thought, enriched expression, and ignited imagination, I say *embrace* the metaphor! Be it slang, cliché, commercial, mismatched, or provocatively original as Nancy Harris McLelland's, metaphor is a *window* into the mind and soul, and into the milieu in which we perceive, think, and speak.

Let's Play the Dictionary Game

I love this game! And that says a lot because I don't play cards, get mostly bored with board games and, a few pages ago, you learned of my abysmal performance at Scrabble with Mom. I only just acted out my first *ever* charade last Thanksgiving, and back when Pictionary was all the rage, I failed due to insurmountable artistic challenges. But *Dictionary* (also called *Fictionary*) is a game I can sink my teeth into and wrap my mind around. Lest you think it's played by a table of stuffed shirts with coke-bottle eyeglasses beneath haughtily raised eyebrows, let me say that playing this game with family and friends has provided some of my life's greatest moments of suspense and hilarity, to say nothing of gloating victory and ignominious defeat.

Before I describe the simple rules and play a round with you, I must digress a moment about dictionaries. Are they becoming dinosaurs? I occasionally look up words online if I'm already on the computer because it's so convenient, but it feels very cold and unsatisfying. I may get what I need at the moment, but it's nothing compared to the visual, tactile, and intellectual stimulation of opening a beloved dictionary. It's like eating a piece of stale bread versus glorying in a whole pan of perfect Saucy's pizza. (But unless you live in Ukiah, CA, you'll have to travel a ways to experience one. This is what happens while writing when hungry.) Frequent use of a behemoth dictionary also affords fitness advantages, especially in the prevention of osteoporosis. My *American Heritage* weighs in at over five pounds, and getting it down from the bookshelf must surely qualify as a weight-bearing exercise.

Okay, let's get down to details so we can have some fun. To play the Dictionary game, you will need five to ten players, paper, and pencils or pens of the same color ink, and a good-sized dictionary that all players will agree to use as the reference. Do not under any circumstance use your Scrabble dictionary for, as I alluded to in "The Tower of Scrabble Babble," it comes from a different lexical solar system and contains words only known to my mother and impossibly distant or long-extinguished ancient civilizations.

When it is your turn, the challenge is to choose a word from the dictionary, from your vast vocabulary, or from your secret list, that you hope none of the other players will know the meaning of. You say the word aloud and spell it for your opponents. Each player (including you) has a small piece of paper. *You* write the correct definition on your paper in erudite, zany, minimalist, or primitive language—you decide—but it has to be the correct one. The other players will each invent a definition (even if some know the meaning of your word, they will still invent) and write it on their paper in the most believable fashion possible. You collect all the papers, shuffle them, number them, and in no particular order, read them aloud as impartially as possible.

This is usually when the hilarity starts and sometimes progresses into pig-snorts and the loss of control over bodily functions. Each player (you excluded) will vote on the definition they believe to be the true one. Two points are scored by each person who chooses the correct meaning; players get one point every time someone votes for their phony definition. You can only score during your turn if you stump all the players and none of them votes for the correct definition. The turn to present a new word now passes to the next player.

Here are some tips on choosing great words to play in the Dictionary game. The most challenging and entertaining ones have a meaning that is comical, strange, or unbelievable. Steer clear of chemical compounds or arcane botanical references because, though they are weird words, they are no fun. No foreign words allowed. Try to design your definition to fit the part of speech: noun, verb, adjective, and so on. Best to avoid words with multiple and divergent meanings like "conjugate," which has several definitions, including a) to inflect a verb as in the Spanish *hablo, hablas, habla* (I speak, you speak, he/she speaks), or b) to have sex.

Okay, let the play begin. It's my turn, and my word is "orotund." There are seven of us: me, Ross, Pattie, Candie, Ricardo, Tom, and Barbara. I write down the true definition while the other five players invent phony ones. Now I've collected, shuffled, and numbered the papers. Making sure no one can see the author's handwriting, I read each definition aloud a couple of times:

"Orotund":

1. A kind of permafrost that gives off a warm glow
2. Bullion formed in a round shape during the Spanish conquest of the Americas
3. Referring to anything pear-shaped; wider and heavier on the bottom than at the top
4. The technical name for airport bathrooms with different entry and exit doors
5. Said of a pompous person who loves the sound of his or her own voice
6. The type of tuna most commonly used in commercial canning
7. A word that describes mountains that are large and round

After thirty seconds, the laughter and derision dies down. Tension is running high.

For the sake of my illustration, the number in front of the name below indicates which false definition each player wrote, and after the name you see which definition each voted for.

The votes have been cast thusly:

1. Ross: voted for #2
2. Pattie: voted for #7
3. Candie: voted for #5
4. Ricardo: voted for #3
5. Susanna: no vote; my word
6. Tom: voted for #5
7. Barbara: voted for #6

Here's the scoring:

1. Ross: 0—No one voted for his definition #1
2. Pattie: 1—Ross voted for her definition #2
3. Candie: 1 + 2—Ricardo voted for her definition #3; she voted for the correct definition #5
4. Ricardo: 0—No one voted for his definition #4
5. Susanna: 0—Both Candie and Tom voted for my correct definition #5
6. Tom: 1 + 2—Barbara voted for his definition #6; he voted for correct definition #5
7. Barbara: 1—Pattie voted for her definition #7

The play goes on at least until all seven of us have presented one word, and it can continue for more rounds after that.

So there you have it, and the evening has been provocative and delightful. I can't claim the Dictionary game will increase your vocabulary, make you a more persuasive speaker/writer, or win you a contestant slot on *Jeopardy*, but your brain neurons will be pushing out miles of dendrites, and your gray matter might just be more vibrant and lit up by the end of the game, even if you come in last. I cast my vote for activities where people are actually sitting in the same room looking at each other and not at the screen of their electronic devices. This game is free and loaded with benefits for body and mind. All you need to do is haul that dictionary down off the bookshelf (anti-osteoporosis), open a bottle of red wine (cardiovascular health), assemble the players (greater longevity through social contact), and try to fool every one of them (brain strengthened through firing neurons and dendrite growth). And in the course of play, you just might engage in laughter, which, as we all know, is one of life's best elixirs for mind, body, and spirit.

I keep a top-secret list of words stored up for my next round of Dictionary play. Are you game? I'll bring the wine!

Pants on Fire

B ig and fat or teeny and white, researchers say that a lie comes at us as often as two hundred times a day. Seems impossible until we consider a few possible sources: online dating profiles (reports say 90% contain a lie), job resumes (estimates at 40%), family and friends (average 75%), product hype to make our wrinkles disappear and grow back our hair (this author estimates 99.9%), and presidential candidate debates (your turn).

According to a study by the University of Massachusetts, in ten minutes of conversation, 60% of adults lied an average of three times. I'm sure all of *us* are among the perfectly honest 40%, right? Actually, the 60% who lied thought they were, too, and didn't believe the outcome until they listened to their conversation played back. It goes without saying that the lies, in the great majority, are not damaging. They are the fibs we tell to come off as smarter, witty, more "with it", and worthy. We want to fit in, be liked, gracefully back out of a social obligation, or not hurt someone's feelings.

Lying is a skill that most of us discovered around age four, honed through childhood, and practiced avidly in the teen years. As adults, our patterns are pretty well set. When my grandmother left post-WW II Europe to come to America, her new life included major plot alterations of the one she'd left behind. They became such a part of her new identity that she probably died believing her father *had* been a surgeon and that she *did* study music at the Sorbonne.

The Italians have that wonderful expression to articulate their prime cultural commandment: *fare la bella figura*, literally, "to make the beautiful figure," meaning to create the best possible impression in every situation while looking and sounding great throughout. It comes down to impeccable fashion sense, good manners, and a flair for producing just the right words and actions to fit the moment. One can't help but wonder how many *piccole bugie bianche* (little white lies) it takes to keep all that glued together.

It would be fun to go on in an anecdotal vein, especially since I was on the verge of confessing a *bugia* or two of my own, but I'll save them for later and turn now to the "lexicon of lying," the real motive for this piece. I became interested in the subject years ago when my ex was a detective for the state police, and I used to read his training manuals on lie detection. Everyone knows at least a few of the "what-to-look-fors" in terms of gestures and body movements that might indicate a person is lying: no eye contact, touching the mouth or throat, shuffling feet, excessive fidgeting, and so on. However, what follows is the "Dirty (Baker's) Dozen" of *verbal* clues that might indicate someone is lying:

1. Say you've just asked, "Did you eat the cookies I made for the potluck?? **Stalling tactics** include "Huh?" or "What?" to get you to repeat the question, or "Well...", all three designed to buy time to figure out how to construct a believable, but less-than-straightforward, answer.

2. **Repetition of the question** is another way of buying time. Your question, "Did you go to Taylor's Tavern after work today?" is repeated right back at you, "Did I go to Taylor's Tavern after work today?"

3. Another form of **repetition** is all the words of your question included in the answer: "No, I *did not* go to Taylor's Tavern after work today."

4. **Assertions of truth** like "To be perfectly honest," "To tell the truth," "You listen to me," and "I swear to..."

5. A very common red flag is not using **contractions**. Notice "did not" instead of "didn't" in #3. This is also a way of **asserting truth** or showing indignation.

6. **Retort question**: Teacher: "Did you lift that term paper from an online source?" Response: "What do you mean?" The tone can be aggressive, innocent, or confused. Speaker is hoping to throw you off and, again, stall for time.

7. Use of **nonspecific words and generalizations**. You texted: "What happened to our lunch date today??" Texted reply: "We got hung up in a bunch of crazy stuff." Neither "hung up" nor "a bunch of crazy stuff" tells you anything about what actually happened.

8. In that same texted reply, notice the subject "We." A liar will unconsciously try to **create distance** by avoiding the words *I/me/* and using the plurals *we/us/*, as well as *the* instead of *my*. Saying *that* instead of *this* also creates distance: "I have no idea how *that* jewelry got into *the* purse."

9. **Very short answer with no detail**: Jiltee asks, "Why don't you ever call me anymore?" Jilter's reply: "It's complicated."

10. Or the opposite: **Long rambling blah-blah-blah** that doesn't answer the question. Confession #1 in the way of illustration: I told my parents I was going to see an old movie with my boyfriend (*Call Me Bwana* starring Bob Hope), when we were really going to a party. The next morning, in answer to, "How was the movie?" I blabbed on for a good ten minutes about how funny Bob Hope was and how cool it would be to go on an African safari someday.

11. Statements made in **monotone**. (example coming right up)

12. **Overemphasis** of words. (ditto)

13. The speaker **abruptly ends** the communication. (ditto)

To illustrate, it would be most effective if I could embed a video into this page, but you will have to use memory and imagination, or just google "Bill Clinton Lied about Monica Lewinsky." The intent is not to rehash the incident or to bash William Jefferson, but rather to study this classic and powerful example of lying from January of 1998. Watch for the clues:

"But I want to say one thing to the American people. I want you to listen to me. I'm going to say this again: I—did not—have—sexual—relations—with—that—woman, Miss Lewinsky. I never told anybody to lie, not a single time, never. These allegations are false, and I need to go back to work for the American people." (He stands up and leaves the press conference.)

Here it is again cued to the list of verbal clues:

"I want you to listen to me (4). I'm going to say this again (12): I—did not (5)—have—sexual—relations—with—that (8)—woman (11, 12), Miss Lewinsky. I never told anybody to lie, not a single time, never (4, 12). These allegations are false (4), and I need to go back to work for the American people." (13)

* * *

The Pulitzer Prize-winning fact check project, PolitiFact, bestowed on Donald Trump its infamous "Liar of the Year" award for 2015. The fact-checkers determined that 76 percent of his official statements fell into one of the categories: *Mostly False, False,* or *Pants on Fire.* In June of 2016, Politifact revealed that only 23% of his claims made during the first half of the campaign year were *True, Mostly True* or *Half True*; 58% were *False* or *Mostly False*; and a whopping 18% were *Pants on Fire!* According to the fact-checking project, none of Hillary Clinton's pants have gone up in flames, though they have identified a list of *false* claims.

Maybe you'll agree that most people are well intentioned and basically honest, but it can be useful to know what to listen for when we suspect someone might be lying. I'll optimistically wager that the researchers' finding of two hundred lies per day will decrease appreciably in a non-election year.

* * *

In conclusion, Confession #2: Susie Janssen, age six, repeatedly and righteously asserted it was not she who stuck a bobby pin in the bathroom wall socket of the big house on *V* Street. She experienced "pants on fire" for a good twenty-four hours after that spanking and actually had something worth confessing to the priest before Sunday Mass.

How Are You Fixed for Time and Money?

I got to thinking about how we take for absolute truth values unique to our culture, going so far as to assume all peoples on earth believe, think, and react as we do around essential aspects of their lives. *Culture* can be defined in simple terms as everything people learn to think and do from those who raise them and the environment they live in. There is a wonderful and very illustrative analogy, the iceberg model, to help us think about culture. The part of the iceberg we can see above water is massively obvious and identifiable, but that's only a fraction of the whole. What's below the surface is huge and hard to detect or anticipate. The protruding iceberg of culture includes things like foods, music, traditional dress, and holiday customs. Below the surface lurk deep familial and social conditionings such as gender roles, attitudes toward social status and the treatment of women, romance and relationships, religion and spirituality, and basically everything that is so ingrained that we might say, "That's just the way it is."

Let's consider cultural conditioning around *time* and *money* because most of us perceive these as dominant, if not controlling, factors in our lives. Our attitudes about them are deeply and subconsciously ingrained into our thoughts, feelings, language, and actions. This conditioning is created and reinforced from birth to death by parents, schooling, government, TV and movies, advertising, and the lyrics of popular songs. Our basic cultural assumption about them both is that there is never enough of either. To one degree or another, we struggle throughout life with issues of time and money, continually trying to do exactly what Einstein told us would be at best utterly impossible, and at worst, the road to insanity: solve a problem with the same thinking that created it in the first place (leading one to doing the same thing over and over again and expecting different results). We strive to create abundance from a deep sense of scarcity, and from that launching pad, the rocket always goes down in flames.

This scarcity of time and money is a slippery slope, almost like a love-hate relationship. Our perception of time is a cultural value, not an absolute. We actually promote, admire, and highly prize its scarcity in others, yet spend endless energy trying to find more time for ourselves, while boosting our personal sense of worth by staying busy and advertising how we haven't even time to take a breath. In America, we equate being busy and having no time with being important and even *worthy*. Those who are so busy that their calendar is jammed and they haven't a moment to themselves will be thought of as successful and valuable, hence the saying, "If you want something done, ask a busy person." On the other hand, we may cast a suspicious eye or be prone to a negative value judgment toward the person who walks the office halls with a relaxed gait and stops for casual conversation, even if he always does get the job done.

We are totally accepting and sympathetic, even admiring, when acquaintances comment about the scarcity of money, be it their personal funds, an aging parent's bank account, or government spending. But when a colleague said in a faculty meeting, "I don't really need this raise because I feel I have enough money," eyebrows shot up, emails started flying, and her sanity came into question. If you have bought into and live by the law of scarcity, we totally "get" you and resonate with your dilemmas. However, if you are floating on some cloud of temporal or fiscal abundance, you are suspect, and we might wonder what you're sprinkling on your breakfast cereal.

Let's look at the language we commonly employ to speak about our two favorite purgatories of time and money. What about the verbs we use in relation to *money*? We earn, make, spend, save, and hoard money. We lose it, but rarely find it. We bleed money, but far less often transfuse it.

When it comes to *time*, the terms take a turn toward the violent. Yes, we can spend it, borrow it, and save it, but too often time runs out, or is against us. It flies by, but only stands still for an emotionally overwhelming moment. We buy it, waste it, steal it, cheat it, and kill it. We long to save time in a bottle, but it is always running through our hands. We can feel in our viscera how Ben Franklin's claim that, "Nothing is certain but death and taxes," plays on our fear of having the time and money we so long to control snatched from our grasp by an invisible hand of fate.

It's said that we get exactly as much in life as we *think* we deserve. It is also said that whatever we focus our attention on, we get more of. Our attention might be totally glued on money because there's not enough coming in. Does that mean we'll get more of it? Not until we stop fighting *what is*, and practice shifting our cultural default from scarcity to abundance; from, "There's not enough and I'm running out," all the way over to, "There's an unlimited supply and I am able to tap into it."

It's true we lead busy lives in the twenty-first-century, especially with all our "time-saving" devices. Time, however, is not an absolute. That's why it is known to both "drag" and "fly." What might happen if were to befriend time and invite it over to our side? What if we started each day *knowing* there would be ample time for work, rest, and play? It would definitely take some practice and cultural retooling, but could result in us getting more of what we *say* we really want and need.

That could be taken by some as impossibility or cultural heresy.

It's a provocative conundrum to live in a culture that simultaneously admires and decries an insufficiency of time and money. But there's always choice, and we can step outside of considerations of fate, one's lot in life, who does and doesn't get a hit of g.l.a.d. (good luck angel dust), and "that's just the way it is," to actively cultivate a consciousness of abundance. Culture is created, and so is both the abundance and the scarcity of time and money.

CHAPTER TWO

Whence these Words?

The Herd Mentality

Why just a "flock" of flamingoes when you can visually create a "flamboyance" of them? Why a "herd" when you can describe what's coming at you as a "crash of rhinos" (with a "tower of giraffes" in the background.) *Terms of Venery*: Their origin is captivating and, as you will see, the possibilities for continued creation are endless.

Shakespeare, the Legacy in His Lines Part I

The Bard forever changed the English language with creative word mashups, and what were to become the proverbs and expressions that seem to have been with us for all time.

Shakespeare, the Legacy in His Lines Part II

Here we take a look at Shakespearean idioms and insults as we attempt to convey and grasp his legacy and genius. There's a delightful surprise at the end that I think the Bard himself would have endorsed.

On the Trail of Word Origins, Part I

Words feel richer on the tongue and to the ear when we know their origins. Here we look into the etymology of words derived from place names (*denim, jeans, dollar*), people's names (*derrick, raglan, crapper*), and some very violent and bloody acts (*assassin, berserk, amok*).

On the Trail of Word Origins, Part II

More etymology, this time of innocent words gone bad (*idiot*); words so close to, yet unrecognizable from, their foreign source (*alligator*); words that are delightfully much more than meets the eye (*muscle*); and words we forget are really acronyms.

On the Trail of Word Origins, Part III

This final chapter on the endless subject of etymology scoops up words born from misconception (*lunatic, hysteria*), and words that are exactly what they say they are but with great stories to tell (*toady, infantry, whipping boy, white elephant*).

The Familiarity of Foreign

English is a sponge for foreign words and the circumstance of their acquisition is the stuff of history and comedy. Here you'll discover a sampling of words lifted from other languages, but now so easy on the American tongue and ear.

The Scholar's Ink and the Martyr's Blood

We barely acknowledge the Arabic influence in the English language, but it is significant and so enriching to understand and be able to identify. Hint: there is one simple characteristic that tips us off to a large percentage of the Arabic words in English. Revealed herein!

The Herd Mentality

It was a sleepless night. In addition to the spotlight of a full moon shining through my bedroom window, I was subjected to the successive and sometimes simultaneous operas of a *kennel of dogs*, a *clowder of cats*, and a *chorus of frogs*. Sunrise came and with it, the cacophony of a *scold of jays*. I looked out the window and was horrified to witness a *murder of crows* in my own backyard! Well, there goes the neighborhood. Even the *exaltation of larks* that followed couldn't lift my spirits. What's next—a *plague of locusts*?

If there's a group of something, we might casually call it a *lot*, a *bunch*, a *pile*, a *mess*, a *crowd*, a *hoard*, or a *ton*. When it comes to animals, if they have hooves, we'll probably call them a *herd*, and if they have wings, a *flock*. Ah, but this is English, so it can never be that simple—or thankfully, that boring. If a collection of graceful white water fowl shows up in my yard, I could shout to the neighbors to come see this *bank, team, bevy, ballet*, or—my favorite—*lamentation, of swans*.

I would bet my bank account that there's no other language on earth that has so many different and specific words for groups of animals. There's drama in an *ambush of tigers*, poetry in a *bouquet of pheasants*, rhapsody in a *flamboyance of flamingoes*, hilarity in a *lounge of lizards*, rhythm in a *rhumba of rattlesnakes*, and endless possibilities for political commentary in a *congress of baboons*. When you come back from your photo safari in Africa, your mesmerized friends will clamor for yet another thousand photos of a *tower of giraffes*, an *implausibility of gnus*, a *bloat of hippos*, a *zeal of zebras*, a *crash of rhinos*, a *memory of elephants*, a *cartload of chimps*, a *congregation of crocodiles*, a *pride of lions*, and a *leap of leopards*.

There's something menacing about a *descent of woodpeckers*, a *sneak of weasels*, and a *shiver of sharks*, yet I'm strangely comforted at the prospect of encountering a *parliament of owls*, a *coterie of prairie dogs*, or a *gaze of raccoons* on future nature walks. These colorful, collective nouns for animals are called *terms of venery*, and originated with the gentleman's sport of hunting in fifteenth-, sixteenth-, and seventeenth-century England and France. Many of them were recorded in the *Book of Saint Albans*, published in 1486, to itemize and describe the sorts of topics and interests a gentleman might allow to occupy his time. There are articles on hawking, hunting, heraldry, and fishing (angling). Interestingly, authorship is attributed (though perhaps only the sections on hawking and hunting) to the Benedictine prioress (Mother Superior) of the Priory of St. Mary of Sopwell, near St. Albans in Hertfordshire where the St. Albans Press, only the third printing press in England, had been established in 1479. Wealthy lords entertained and competed with each other, inventing creative and descriptive collective terms for animals, such as a *clutch of chickens* and a *school of fish*, which then became accepted terms of venery.

What about collective nouns for groups of people? A *bevy of girls* followed by a *gaggle of onlookers* sounds pretty commonplace. Terms for lawyers in the collective might depend on the recent experience of the client, but officially they are: an *argument*, a *disputation*, an *eloquence*, an *escheat*, a *greed*, a *huddle*, or a *quarrel*. Doctors clump together as a *dose*, a *doctrine*, a *scope*, or a *field*. In addition to the predictable *cast of actors*, *den of thieves*, and *team of athletes*, modern terms include the following collective nouns for people: a *tabernacle of bakers*, a *babble of barbers*, a *promise of barmen*, a *shuffling of bureaucrats*, a *goring of butchers*, a *sneer of butlers*, a *shrivel of critics*, a *conjunction of grammarians*, a *herd of harlots*, an *illusion of magicians*, an *unction of undertakers*, and an *ambush of widows*. (We set aside considerations of political correctness for another day.)

One clever contributor to my newspaper column proposed a *mandible of dentists*, and I'll toss off a few inventions of my own: a *couch of psychiatrists*, a *toil of teachers*, and a *wrench of plumbers*. Other readers have offered: a *combo of safecrackers*, a *magnificence of models*, a *sash of seamstresses*, a *brace of orthopedists*; and, returning to the four-legged subjects: a *racket of raccoons*, a *dollop of dalmatians*, and a *mixed bag of labradoodles*.

In closing, I give you my good wishes with a warning attached: I hope you soar with a *convocation of eagles* and find delight in a *charm of hummingbirds*, but be wary when approaching a *business of ferrets*, and stay on the safe side when crossing paths with a *wake of buzzards* or a *prickle of hedgehogs*.

Shakespeare, the Legacy in His Lines, Part I

O n the four hundredth anniversary of the death of William Shakespeare (1564–1616), it seems most fitting and fun to celebrate how English has been deeply enriched and forever changed by the way the Bard of Avon invented, combined, and repurposed words in wholly new and unique ways. Let us begin not with biographical detail, but with a look at how many words are in one's verbal domain, beginning with our own.

Our *receptive vocabulary*, the words we recognize, is somewhere in the vicinity of twelve thousand to twenty thousand words. Yours will be on the high side, I'll wager, because you are reading this book and perhaps have an affinity for words. Our *productive vocabulary*, the words we actually use in speech and writing, comprises a smaller number, hugely variable due to age and reading habits. Homer used a total of nine thousand different words in the *Iliad* and the *Odyssey*. If that seems rather paltry, we must cut him some slack because without Facebook, global warming, the *Huffington Post*, and the millions of distractions that drag our attention hither and yon from moment to moment, life in the late eighth century BC may have required fewer terms than it does today. Further- more, maybe a lot of the words he knew and used in the bathroom, the bedroom, or the kitchen didn't find their way into these ancient classic writings that have survived and thrived as the oldest known works in Western literature.*

---

* Despite the recent surge in popularity of the *Odyssey*, do not name your child or your dog Odysseus as that means trouble—literally so in ancient Greek.

We could also bat about stats on the productive literary vocabulary of John Milton (*Paradise Lost* and dozens of works of poetry and prose), Miguel de Cervantes (*Don Quixote* and thousands more pages of poetry, novels, and short stories), and Sidney Sheldon (eighteen novels, *The Patty Duke Show*, and *I Dream of Jeannie*), but no one holds a candle to the Bard. The number of different words counted in the totality of William Shakespeare's work is over thirty thousand. Statistical estimates as to Shakespeare's total productive vocabulary go as high as sixty thousand words. Again, those are the words he employed to create literature, not necessarily the ones he might have used to woo a maiden or scare up dinner.[†]

We will not attempt to do the Bard literary justice in a few paragraphs but rather to set a simple stage and populate it with words, idioms, and adages from his plays to illustrate the vast expressive impact his works have had on modern English. Shakespeare inducted over two thousand words into the language that had never before been seen in print. He did not invent most of these from whole cloth, but rather by tweaking existing words into another part of speech; for example, from the noun *swagger*, he launched the verb, *to swagger*; and from the verb *to manage*, we credit him with coining the noun, *manager*.

He liberally attached the prefixes *un-*, *in-* or *dis-* to existing words to create theretofore unheard of opposites: *unclog, undress, uncomfortable, uneducated, unreal, inaudible, indistinguishable, inauspicious, dishearten,* and *dislocate*. He was also a wordsmith

---

†   When I finished graduate school, I had an ample literary vocabulary in Spanish and could hold my own in a discussion about *Don Quijote* or the poetry of Pablo Neruda, but I was a babe in the woods and completely out of my lexical element when it came to being in the kitchen (I'd never even heard the word for "frying pan"), in the bathroom ("flush the toilet" wasn't in textbooks), and as for the bedroom—we won't go there.

with suffixes like *–able, -ful,* and *-less: fashionable, eventful, daunt-less,* and *remorseless.* But perhaps his most *zany* (another of his words) inventions are the many compounds in which he married two, sometimes three, simple words into a whole new concept. To name just a few: *bold-faced, hot/cold-blooded, fainthearted, lack-luster, newfangled, fancy-free, bedroom, eyeball, eyesore, fortune-teller, laughingstock, birthplace, moonbeam, puppy dog, shooting star, star-crossed lovers, madcap, outbreak, full circle, primrose path,* and *wild goose chase.*

The popular proverbs and expressions that come to us from Shakespeare's plays are legion. A few years back, I watched a local production of *Hamlet,* and this is just a sampling of what I heard from the stage: "Neither a borrower nor a lender be"; "To thine own self be true"; "Though this be madness, yet there is method in't"; "The lady doth protest too much, methinks"; "A little more than kin, and less than kind"; "Brevity is the soul of wit"; "Conscience does make cowards of us all." In the most famous soliloquy of all time, there is much to recognize and perhaps reso-nate with in Hamlet's heartache and existential crisis. Here are the first thirteen of his thirty-five agonized lines:

> To be, or not to be—that is the question:
> Whether 'tis nobler in the mind to suffer
> The slings and arrows of outrageous fortune
> Or to take arms against a sea of troubles
> And by opposing end them. To die, to sleep—
> No more—and by a sleep to say we end
> The heartache, and the thousand natural shocks
> That flesh is heir to. 'Tis a consummation
> Devoutly to be wished. To die, to sleep—
> To sleep—perchance to dream: ay, there's the rub,

For in that sleep of death what dreams may come
When we have shuffled off this mortal coil,
Must give us pause.

Alas! Parting is such sweet sorrow. But let us do take a pause to shake off that dire contemplation and meet again at the turn of a page whence we will continue the staging on a lighter note with Shakespearean proverbs and expressions in popular use today—and a few insults thrown in for good measure.

Shakespeare, the Legacy in His Lines, Part II

Knock, knock. Who's there? The Bard, once again. Yes, that entrance to silly jokes is attributed to Shakespeare in *Macbeth*. Sayings, oft repeated, can become proverbs, but though they express a widely held truth, someone has to be the first to tack together that particular sequence of words. The King James Bible ("in the twinkling of an eye," "the writing on the wall") and William Shakespeare are the two most prolific sources of English expressions and proverbs. Part I of this four-hundredth anniversary celebration of the Bard of Avon ended with some of the many proverbs that have come to us from *Hamlet* ("Neither a borrower nor a lender be") and a cliff-hanger as the tortured protagonist asks himself if he should continue "to suffer the slings and arrows of outrageous fortune" or end his life with a "bare bodkin" (a sharp dagger.) We all know the tragic outcome of that existential debate.

From Shakespeare's numerous other plays come a trove of adages including: "The truth will out"; "What's done is done"; "The better part of valor is discretion"; "A rose by any other name would smell as sweet"; "Parting is such sweet sorrow"; "The world's my oyster"; "All that glitters is not gold." I have a couple of favorites that aren't yet as widely known, but I present them here as candidates for your adoption. From *The Comedy of Errors*, "There's many a man has more hair than wit," and from *The Twelfth Night*, "Many a good hanging prevents a bad marriage."

Here are some favorite Shakespearean idioms that sound like they've been with us forever, rather than a mere four hundred years: "In my mind's eye"; "As luck would have it"; "To break the ice"; "Be-all and end-all"; "Forever and a day"; "In my heart of hearts"; "In a pickle"; "Brave new world"; "Dead as a doornail"; "Seen better days"; "Eaten me out of house and home"; "It was Greek to me"; "Kill with kindness"; "Into thin air"; "Neither rhyme nor reason"; "One fell swoop"; "Play fast and loose"; "Pomp and circumstance"; "Set my teeth on edge"; "Make short shrift"; "Wear my heart upon my sleeve." It's a thrill to recognize and to experience this exquisite bond of words and concepts creating a bridge over four centuries between Shakespeare and English speakers of the modern day.

The immensity of this legacy of words, wit, and wisdom is awe-inspiring to the mortal mind, and ever more so as we deepen our investigation. What intelligence! What creativity! What a sense of pathos and humor! And what a deep well of understanding and compassion for the human condition. It is incredible that such exalted literary, lexical, and humanistic creation flowed from the soul and into the pen of this sixteenth-century man of humble origins with no documented educational background. Hence there are "Anti-Stratfordian" minority theories claiming a different author or multiple authors, but the vast majority of scholars recognize William Shakespeare of Stratford-on-Avon as the single mind and hand of the entire body of work: thirty-seven plays (Comedy, History, and Tragedy) and many works of poetry, including 154 sonnets.

Returning to Shakespeare's use of words, let us recall that his insults are legion and legendary—and a far cry from "Shall I compare thee to a summer's day?" (Sonnet 18). Some insults might seem almost courteous in their subtlety as, "I do desire we may be better strangers" from *As You Like It* (Act 3, Scene 2) and "Go to Hell for an eternal moment or so" from *The Merry Wives of Windsor* (Act 1, Scene 1). More often than not, Shakespeare's insults are double-barreled and fully loaded: "Thou art a boil. A plague sore, an embossed carbuncle in my corrupted blood" from *King Lear* (Act 2, Scene 4); and "You bawling, blasphemous, uncharitable dog" from *The Tempest* (Act 1, Scene 1). Withering, yes, but so pungently creative that if such verbal volleys were fired today, the intended targets might pass several moments in awe of the linguistic acrobatics before they would even think to take offense. If "You lunatic, lean-witted fool" (*Richard II*, Act 2, Scene 1) and the like hold a certain appeal, you can download any number of handy Shakespearean Insult Generators that will guide you to recombine the Bard's own words to your own unique taste and needs.[‡]

* * *

Since 1993, the *Washington Post* has held its weekly "Style Invitational," challenging readers' knowledge of politics, history, and current affairs, but most of all, their cleverness in manipulating words to humorous effect. For example, a favorite contest challenges readers to change one letter of a word and give it a new meaning (e.g., "Reintarnation": coming back to life as a hillbilly; "Foreploy": any misrepresentation about yourself for the purpose of obtaining sex; and "Sarchasm": the gulf between the author of sarcastic wit and the person who doesn't get it).

In one *WP* "Style Invitational," readers were invited to submit instructions for any activity, written in the style of a famous person. Winner Jeff Brechlin gave to readers the "Hokey-Pokey" as it might have been written by William Shakespeare:

[‡]   See References for my favorite ones.

O proud left foot, that ventures quick within
Then soon upon a backward journey lithe.
Anon, once more the gesture, then begin:
Command sinistral pedestal to writhe.
Commence thou then the fervid Hokey-Poke,
A mad gyration, hips in wanton swirl.
To spin! A wilde release from Heaven's yoke.
Blessed dervish! Surely canst go, girl!
The Hoke, the poke – banish now thy doubt.
Verily, I say, 'tis what it's all about.

I think somewhere-on-Avon, the Bard is "shakin' it all about"
with a smile.

On the Trail of Word Origins, Part I

My sources tell me that you enjoy delving into word derivations, or *etymologies*, and since this is one of my fondest pursuits, I have been looking forward to sharing some of my favorites in these pages.

We'll start with a few English words that are derived from place names. Aside from mom and apple pie, is there anything more American than denim jeans or the dollars it takes to buy them? Let's have a look:

Denim: This iconic fabric started out as a coarse cotton originally imported *from* Nîmes (*de* Nîmes), a city in central France that was a prominent manufacturing center before the French Revolution.

Jeans: A similar coarse material was woven in Genoa, a city called Gênes in Old French. It is said that this fabric first came to America as the sails on Columbus's ships.

Dollar: West of Prague in what was then Bohemia, there was a rich silver mine near the town of Joachimsthal. In 1519, a large silver coin was minted there called a *Joachimsthaler, thaler* for short. It was a currency in Denmark and Sweden as well as in the German states, and American colonists used the same word to refer to Spanish coins. In the Continental Congress of July 6, 1785, the word "dollar," derived from *thaler*, was adopted as the name of US currency because it was widely understood, and more importantly, *not* British.

Siamese twins: The first of these twins to be publicly exhibited were born in Siam (now Thailand) in 1814. They eventually moved to the US, married two sisters, and settled down as farmers in North Carolina. Chang and his wife had six children; Eng's wife bore him five. Chang and Eng lived their sixty years of life joined at the waist—a challenge for the imagination.

Canter: This describes the easy pace at which Pilgrims rode their horses to Canterbury, England in the Middle Ages to pay homage at the shrine of St. Thomas à Becket.

* * *

Words constantly come into being derived from the name of a person or group of people. Here are some notable ones:

Derrick: From the last name of a seventeenth-century English hangman in the Tyburn gallows of London. Since his job was to execute people by hauling them up by means of a rope on a stationary arm, a crane came to be known as a *derrick*.

Clerk: In the Middle Ages, when only the clergymen knew how to read and write, any person with this ability was assumed to be a cleric, shortened to *clerk*, and extended to anyone who performed these literate duties.

Boycott: Irish Captain Charles C. Boycott demanded unreasonably high rents from his tenants who finally revolted and refused to pay. His neighbors shunned him, his own servants deserted him, and no one would sell him food. The Irish Land League Organization adopted similar disciplinary measures along with the phrase "Let's boycott him," meaning let's give him what Mr. Boycott deservedly got.

Hocus-Pocus: This is a good example of a word whose origin is uncertain. It's possibly a variation on the name of a wizard in Scandinavian mythology, Ochus Bochus. But, provocatively, some sources claim it's a corruption of the Latin *Hoc est corpus*, the phrase said in the Catholic Mass at the moment the bread becomes the body of Christ. Scholars of etymology love to argue this stuff.

Raglan: This is a type of sleeve that starts at the collar, with no shoulder seam. It was a favored style of Lord Raglan, British Field Marshal, who lost his right arm in the 1815 defeat of Napoleon at Waterloo. Do you think it ever crossed his mind that losing his arm in battle would affix his name to a style that has lasted two centuries?

Crapper: Oh, we do wish this colorful etymological legend were true, but I include it because it's not. Yes, there was a Londoner named Thomas Crapper (1837-1910) who worked as a plumber and may have contributed to the development of the modern toilet (although Arab peoples had been flushing for around five hundred years by then), but his unfortunate name was purely coincidence. In Middle English, *crappe* meant "residue," "rubbish" or, in agriculture, grain left on the barn floor that was trodden underfoot. As writer and word master Willard Espy concludes: "Though 'to crap' may have antedated Mr. Crapper, he undoubtedly nailed the word to the mast," or, I might humbly offer, to the outhouse door.

Tantalize: As punishment for offering humans the food and drink of the gods from Mt. Olympus, Tantalus, son of Zeus, was condemned to spend eternity in the nether world, standing up to his chin in water that receded when he tried to drink it, and with clusters of grapes over his head that remained forever out of his reach. In the world of mythology, there are seldom second chances. It seems the human foibles committed by gods, goddesses, and their offspring receive the harshest, swiftest, and most irrevocable punishment.

Mosey: Whenever the dictionary says "origin uncertain," I'm sure there will be something fun to dig for. *Vamoose* was early cowboy slang in the nineteenth century, corrupted from the Spanish *Vamos* (let's go). One of my favorite etymology sources, professor emeritus Jordan Almond, suggests that "mosey" derives from "vamoose," but I opt for Willard Espy's theory. He maintains that Jewish vendors in olden days were so weighted by their wares that they made slow progress along the road. Because many of them were named "Moses," well, that should illuminate his conclusion.

* * *

This next category of derivations I call "Not a Pretty Sight," and you shall see why:

Amuck/Amok: The phrase "to run amok," first noted in the 1670s, referred to some people of Malaya who, when under the influence of opium or stimulants, would go wild and run through the streets attacking unfortunate passersby with daggers while yelling, "*Amoq! Amoq!*" (Kill! Kill!)

Assassin: In another drug-related murderous etymology, there was a fanatical Mohammedan sect in eleventh-century Persia (now Iran) whose members would murder Christians during the Crusades after getting high on hashish. They were known as *hash-hashin*, "hashish-eaters."

Havoc: A word of early Germanic origin, *Havoc!* was a signal yelled out by the chief to his invading horde that they were now free to pillage and plunder the village at will. To "wreak havoc" in this day is so very tame in comparison.

Vandal/Vandalism: The Germanic tribe known as the Vandals sacked Rome in 455 AD. Although this is not historically verified, some accounts claim they gratuitously mutilated works of art and public monuments, hence the modern meaning.

Amazon: The most popular derivation comes from Greek mythology: a race of female warriors who were so fearlessly determined that they cut or burned off one breast so not to have it interfere with the drawing back of the bowstring in battle—*a* (without) + *mazo* (breast).

Berserk: A *berserker* was a "warrior clothed in bearskin." These were Norse warriors of superhuman strength and ability who fought like wild animals in battle, foaming at the mouth and attacking with enormous strength and fearless aggression.

Well, that's it for the blood and gore. We'll take a short break from violent images of berserk assassins running amok with the promise of more etymological excitement to come.

On the Trail of Word Origins, Part II

We ended our first foray into word origins on a violent and bloody note with the derivations of the words "assassin," "havoc," "berserk," "vandal," and "Amazon" (not the .com variety). Today's exploration will be gentler but I hope equally riveting.

The words in this first category started out innocently enough, but you'll soon see where they ended up:

Marooned: In Spanish, *marron* means dark-brown or chestnut colored. In the seventeenth century, a *maron* was a fugitive slave in the jungles of West Indies. From this, our English verb "maroon" came to mean, "to be abandoned on a desolate island or coast."

Fiasco: No one disputes that *un fiasco* in Italian is simply a glass flask, but how this word came to mean "a failure or a disastrous outcome" remains in debate. Some say that the famed Venetian glass blowers would toss aside defective art pieces to later be made into simple flasks. Another more colorful theory relies on the Italian expression *fare il fiasco*, meaning "to play a game so that the one who loses will buy the *fiasco*," that is, pay for the bottle of wine. Imagine what a "fiasco" the cost if you lost three times in a row!

Cheat: From the legal term *escheat* whereby under English feudal law if the tenant died without legal heirs, his land would become property of the lord. This was not looked on as fair play by the tenant's family, hence a shortening of the word into a verb meaning "to swindle or defraud."

Idiot: Innocently enough, the Greek word *idiotes* referred to one who did not hold a public office or was lacking in professional skill. In the twelfth century, it was "an uneducated or ignorant person" and by the fourteenth century meant, "one so mentally deficient as to be incapable of ordinary reasoning." And that's evolution for you!

Villain: Going back again to feudal times, it was simply a peasant or farmer who worked at a villa (the manor house). Etymology wizard Willard Espy suggests that "the notion of wickedness grew out of the assumption on the part of the lord that all servants were knaves."

Alimony: From the Latin for "food or nourishment," in the mid-seventeenth century, the word came to mean "allowance to a wife from a husband's estate." As an aside, the variation *palimony* (pal + alimony), "financial support after the termination of a live-in relationship out of wedlock," is said to have been coined by the divorce attorney during an unsuccessful lawsuit in 1977 against movie actor Lee Marvin by his long-term companion, Michelle Triola.

* * *

Here are several fascinating words, so close to their foreign source, and yet...

Gargoyle: This derives from Old French meaning "throat" (hence, our verb *to gargle*.) These fantastical stone figures at the corners of the roof were downspouts to channel off the water, which then spurted out the mouth of the sculptures. Usually grotesque in appearance, they did double duty by frightening away evil spirits.

Alphabet: A combination of the first two letters of the Greek alphabet: *alpha* and *beta*.

Point Blank: To fire a weapon "point blank" is literally to aim at the white spot in the center of the target, and is from French *point* (aim) and *blanc* (white). It has come to mean to fire at close range for maximum impact, whether with firearms or words.

Tycoon: From Japanese in the nineteenth century, *tai* (great) and *kun* (lord), this came to mean "a wealthy and powerful businessman" after WW I.

Alligator: From Spanish *el lagarto*, "the lizard." To American ears, it sounded like one word and was scooped into our language as such.

Arena: From Spanish *arena*, simply meaning "sand."

Dandelion: The French *dent de lion*, "tooth of lion" (describing the pointed leaves of the flower) got anglicized into our dandy word for this edible (but not if you have dogs in the yard) flower.

* * *

And now, three words that are delightfully much more than meet the eye:

Inaugurate: This is what we do to bring in every new president and initiate other grandiose projects, right? The Latin verb *inaugurare* means "to take omens from the flight of birds." Before any ancient Roman was installed into office, there was the requisite interpreting of signs and omens by an *augur*, a "soothsayer." Do you think our political polls and pundits (from Hindi *pandit*, "a learned man") predict the future of our government and its elected officials with greater accuracy than the reading of tea leaves, animal entrails, or birds in flight?

Muscle: The Latin word *musculus* means "little mouse" and gives us our word because the shape and movement of some muscles was thought to resemble a little mouse moving to and fro. Try flexing your biceps in the mirror.

Pupil: From Latin *pupilla*, "little girl doll," for the tiny image seen of oneself reflected in another's eyes. As Plato wrote: "Self-knowledge can be obtained only by looking into the mind and virtue of the soul, which is the diviner part of a man, as we see our own image in another's eye."

* * *

Let's consider acronyms that are so common we may forget to wonder when and how they came into everyday use:

GI: The US Army stamped *GI* on all goods, supplies, uniforms, and so on used by soldiers to identify these as "Government Issue." With this ubiquitous monogram on every cap and canteen, it's no wonder the enlistees themselves soon became known as GIs.

Jeep: In the early 1940s, this was American military slang for the sturdy car that had *GP* painted on the side, to identify it as a "general purpose" vehicle.

OK: This comes off as downright silly, but here goes: In Boston and New York of the late 1830s, it was all the rage to misspell and abbreviate colloquial sayings, for example: *K.Y.* for "know yuse" (no use) and *N.C.* for "nuff ced." *Oll Korrect*, the humorous form of "all correct", shortened to OK during the re-election campaign of President Van Buren (1840) who was nicknamed "Old Kinderhook" after his place of birth. *OK* captured imaginations and tongues across the nation and, thankfully, is the only survivor of this fad.

Here's a research assignment for you lovers of the lexicon and enthusiasts of etymological trivia:

Your mission, should you choose to accept it, is to investigate how and when the term *snafu* came to be. You may have heard this one before and thought it was a joke. But no, it's the real deal and if I printed it, this chapter might self-destruct. Have fun with that!

On the Trail of Word Origins, Part III

How rich the flavor of the word on our tongue when it evokes not only meaning but something of its birthing and history.

We begin with two interesting words born mostly from misconception:

Lunatic: The other night with the full moon shining in my east window, I was feeling a little bit crazy under the spell of *la luna*. Ancient Romans blamed madness on the moon, and *lunacy* is sometimes still attributed to lunar cycles.§

Hysteria: From Latin and Greek meaning "of the womb" (womb: *hystera*), it was a neurotic condition in women believed to be induced by uterine dysfunction. There you have it. It's etymology and we're stuck with it.

* * *

This next group has origins that are quite literal, yet not totally obvious. The first few are deeply medieval and you can almost hear the clanging chaos of battle and smell the smoke from fireplaces in great stone halls.

Freelance: Coined by Sir Walter Scott in his historical novel *Ivanhoe* (1820), it refers to a medieval mercenary soldier without loyalty to a particular leader or kingdom. He and his "free lance" were hired to fight where needed. This makes me think of Richard Boone as Paladin in the '50s-'60s TV western, *Have Gun, Will Travel*.

Infantry: While not referencing "infants" as we know the

---

§　The Italian *lunatico* and the French *lunatique* both mean "moody."

word in modern English, this part of the army was made up of the knights' page boys, youths who assisted the master and were in training to become knights themselves, that is, if they survived the front lines of battle.

Mantelpiece: A ledge over the fireplace, this was originally where you hung your *mantel* or loose, sleeveless cloak to dry and then returned it to your shoulders the next morning, singed and smoky, but totally serviceable.

Whipping Boy: The king's son, being of royal blood, was exempt from whippings, so it was the custom to keep handy in the court another boy of lower status who could take the punishment in the prince's stead. I would have begged, borrowed, stolen, and thrown in my ten-cent-a-week allowance to have had such a one in the wings of my childhood home and on the (ouch!) receiving end of the spanking stick.

Toady: This is a "sponger" or a "flatterer." Originally in the mid-1700s, the magician had an assistant whose job it was to eat the toad during the show. Since toads were considered poisonous, the master could then demonstrate his magical healing powers and "save" the young man from certain death.

Tumbler: (mid-1600s) This drinking glass with a pointed or curved base would literally tumble over if you tried to set it down before you drained the brew. Bottoms up!

Trump: In card games, it is a variation of *triumph*. Another more common use of the word, as in "trumped-up" charges derives from Old French "to deceive" or "to mock," and is definitely tied to the musical instrument, *trumpet*, alluding to charlatans who blew a horn to attract a village audience and then cheat them into buying some worthless product. Best to leave it at that without reference to the 2016 presidential race.

Windfall: (mid-1500s) When all timber was reserved for the exclusive use of the English Royal Navy, land dwellers were only allowed to take the trees that were blown down by wind. With this unexpected stroke of good luck, they would have building materials plus warm hands and a fire to cook by.

Scapegoat: Meaning "one who is blamed for the mistakes or sins of others." According to the Book of Leviticus in the Old Testament (English translation from Hebrew), during the celebration of the *Day of Atonement*, the sins of the people were ceremonially transferred onto the head of a goat, which was "cast" (made to *escape*) into the wilderness, thus releasing the sinners from their guilt and God's punishment.

White Elephant: The story goes that the King of Siam devised the strategy of presenting his enemies with the gift of an albino elephant. Since the animal was sacred, it could not be put to work, and because its upkeep was an enormous expense, the enemy of said king would go bankrupt with its care and feeding. The ultimate in passive-aggressive gift-giving!

Earmark: English farmers would cut a notch in the ear of their cattle and sheep as an identifying mark. This was also a practice used on some criminals. As an aside, during the 2015 disastrous "Valley" fire in Lake County, CA, I heard of horse owners marking their animals' hooves with a permanent marker to identify them if they became displaced—an effective low-tech method; faster and more humane than notching or branding.

Undertaker: Previously called a *grave digger*, now officially known as a *mortician*, this was simply a euphemism for one who "undertook" the onerous (but mostly very profitable) task of preparing and burying the corpse. One of my most colorfully memorable times during travels in Ecuador was hanging out with a ragged but cheerful crew of grave diggers on the early morning shift in a rural cemetery who were passing around the bottle while waiting for the cadaver to arrive. We chatted, they passed me the bottle, and of course I took a gulp because they were offering to share with me what little they had. And with *aguardiente* (firewater) that raw, one didn't worry about germs.

Alarm: This came into English from Old Italian *all'arme!* To arms!

Minutes of a meeting: Rather than from the minutes of the hour, this term derives from the adjective *minute* (tiny) because, before shorthand was invented, the notes were taken in small handwriting to save ink and parchment.

Companion: From the Latin, *com-* (together) and *panis* (bread.) The *companion* is one you share bread with. Here in the wine country of northern California, I'm lucky to have wonderful companions and *comvinions* with whom to break bread and enjoy a glass of great local wine.⁋

Quarantine: (Italian *quaranta*: forty) In the 1500s, the word developed because a widow was allowed to remain for forty days in her husband's house after his death. In the 1600s, it became the term used for holding a ship out of port for forty days if it was suspected of carrying a contagious disease. The use of the number forty by the ancient Jews and in the Bible meant not a specific number of days, but a really long time. So, for example, when it's recorded in the New Testament that Christ fasted in the desert for forty days and forty nights, the number is a metaphor for a long and difficult task over time. However, forty days as applied to widows and disease-infested ships was meant quite literally.

Real estate: Here we must take the Spanish meaning of *real*: "royal," as in *El Camino Real* (The Royal Road/The King's

---

⁋ Every linguist has the right and perhaps the obligation to coin at least one new word a year. It's like botanists looking for an undiscovered plant or biologists in search of a new bacteria.

Highway/Hwy 101) connecting California's twenty-one missions from Misión San Diego de Alcalá in the South to Misión San Francisco de Solano in Sonoma County. A *royal estate* was a land grant, and since all land belonged to the Spanish king, having him reward you with a small patch of dirt or the entire valley of Oaxaca, México (as was granted to Hernán Cortés after he overthrew the Aztec Empire in 1521), was the only way to become a legal land owner. Of course, the concept of "owning" land was a European import to the "New" World. The native peoples, though often territorial, could not grasp it fast enough to clue into what the planting of the banner in the sand and the accompanying proclamation of "I claim all of this for the King of Spain" would mean in their lifetime (not likely to last much longer after that momentous pronouncement) and for all time.

* * *

I haven't yet run out of fascinating word origins, and I accumulate new ones every day that I love to share with fellow word lovers. For now, I shall save them for another volume as we move to other topics in this smorgasbord of words.

The Familiarity of Foreign

We Americans are endlessly creative with other languages. Whether on our own soil or another land, we hear some foreign word or expression that serves the moment well. Then we mimic the sounds, guttering up the vowels from the back of our throats, and twirling the consonants around our American tongues. Then, faster than you can say *voilà* or *chop-chop*, it becomes firmly planted, if not yet in the dictionary, at least into the lexicon of popular usage. All languages tend to absorb the foreign words they're exposed to, but English (the American variety in particular) seems to vacuum them up from all corners of the world, even though it's already over a million words strong. In the acquisition process, pronunciation Americanizes radically, and often spelling does as well.

Picture American soldiers in France during World War II hearing the locals bid each other a breezy, or perhaps hopeful, "See you soon," sounding like *too tah leur* and spelled à tout à l>heure. The GIs got the general gist and at some pregnant moment of linguistic critical mass, one of them cut loose with his own attempt to let the *mademoiselle* know he might drop by the *patisserie* again a bit later. The new word spread throughout the battalion and beyond, and soon everyone back stateside was calling out "toodeloo" as they drove off in their Ford Deluxe Tudor sedans. And if they were really in a hurry, "toodles" would suffice.

If French speakers call out "help!" they will say *m'aidez!* In 1924, the senior radio officer at the airport in London needed to come up with a word that would be easily recalled in an emergency and widely understood. Since most of the air traffic was between London and Paris, he chose *m'aidez* but wisely simplified the spelling while retaining the basic pronunciation. Thus, English acquired the term "mayday" as an international radio code distress signal.

Let's return to the WWII era again, this time in England, and listen in on another conversation. Dodging Nazi fire, the Allied soldiers consoled themselves by talking about a favorite subject, which happily used the same word in both versions of English. But something just sounded odd with the Americans talking about "girls" and the English going on about the same thing but calling them *gehls*, roughly halfway between "gales" and "gulls." The word *gal* had been used in some parts of Britain since the late eighteenth century as slang for "girl," and had already made its way into American English. The song, (*The bells are ringing...*) "For Me and My Gal," was written in 1917, but a Hollywood movie of the same name came out in 1942 starring Judy Garland and Gene Kelly, leaving no doubt that "gals" was as firmly established in Americana as hot dogs and apple pie.

You'd have to be from another era to express your consternation, disagreement, or ridicule by saying (take your pick), "That's just *balderdash / rubbish / claptrap / blather / poppycock*!" In the twenty-first century, they all sound so quaint! These days, you might still call it "garbage," but in casual speech, many would say, "That's *bullshit / BS / bull / a crock*," all referring to excrement—its source, the container, or the stuff itself. Of those erstwhile terms, the cutest-sounding is *poppycock,* and given my 50 percent Dutch heritage, I think I'll adopt that one because it combines my father's native tongue and the same substance preferred in today's disparaging remark, though somehow less brown and stinky. It's the Dutch word *pappekak* —*pappe* (soft food) and *kak* (dung)—meaning soft (edible?) shit. Being aware of that derivation *does* detract from its seeming innocence, but only *you* will know the depth of your disgust at the neighbor's explanation of those tire tracks on your front lawn when you adjust your monocle and firmly announce, "That's poppycock!"

In the spring, we clean up the patio, fit the canvas umbrella into its concrete doughnut, start making piña coladas, fire up the grill, and invite friends over to dine *al fresco*. That's an Italian term for an American tradition, and in Italy, not just eating and drinking but most of life takes place out of doors in the open air (in *bella figura*, of course). I was brimming with confidence as we approached *un ristorante* just off the Piazza del Campo in Siena. I had mastered a few present-tense verbs and had learned some basic vocabulary at the Dante Alighieri language school just up the *strada*. I mashed up one verb, one noun, and that seductive Italian term from our English repertoire: "C'è una tavola *al fresco?*" The waiter looked wearily amused, as if he'd just been asked if there were a leaning tower in town, or if the Coliseum was within walking distance. While leading us to a lovely outdoor table, he combined words and mime until I finally got that it sounded like I was asking if there was a table for us "in prison." *Al fresco* to Italians is colloquial speech for to be "in the cooler"; in "jail."

Who would have thought! But it made me think twice before again assuming that a word or phrase must mean the exact same thing just because we've absorbed it intact or mostly unchanged into our English language. I don't think I'll be trying out, "Oh, poppycock!" on my Dutch aunties any time soon.

The Scholar's Ink and the Martyr's Blood

There's something different about Spain. Hard to pinpoint, but it's just not quite like most of the rest of Western Europe. Yes, it's geographically unique—on a huge peninsula jutting away from the Mediterranean and into the North Atlantic, so close to kissing North Africa that even those 8.9 miles seem to disappear on a clear day. But there's more: After the fall of the Roman Empire, the rest of Europe lived the chaotic and violent Dark Ages until the tenth century, followed by the turbulent Middle Ages lasting until the fifteenth century while, despite the Crusades and local wars, the Iberian Peninsula (Spain and Portugal of today) enjoyed the early flowering of philosophy, sciences, literature, education, and the arts.

By the time of his death in 632 A.D., the prophet Muhammed had united Arabia into a single Muslim regime. The second massive expansion of the Arab empire from 632 to 661 scooped in everything as far as Central Asia in the east, the Caucasus in the north, and North Africa from Egypt to present-day Tunisia in the west, forming the largest land empire in history up until that point. It is the third Arab campaign from 661 to 750 that occasions this lexical investigation because it is the reason why a few hundred Arabic words have found their way into the English language. It was during this expansion that the Arabs conquered the Iberian Peninsula in 711, and although the peninsular lords (too early in history to call them Spaniards or Portuguese) immediately initiated the *Reconquista* (Reconquest) to take back their lands, the Arabs were not finally vanquished until 1492.

In that year, King Fernando and Queen Isabel were already

up to their royal earlobes with getting Columbus and his three ships launched for a New World; solidifying the union of the five principal kingdoms of Iberia and their jealous rulers into a single country; and ramping up the infamous Spanish Inquisition targeting Muslims and Jews, with tragic consequences ricocheting into the present day. Nevertheless, they laid relentless siege to the last Moorish kingdom, and Granada fell to the Christians in that unbelievably eventful year.

Before we examine some of the Arabic words found in the English language, a few clarifying notes:

- The Arab occupation of the Iberian Peninsula is usually referred to as the Moorish occupation and the invaders as Moors because they advanced toward the peninsula from the Moroccan coast. While many of them were Berber Northwest Africans, the bulk of the armies hailed from other parts of Arabia.
- Although the Reconquest was a series of military campaigns in which Christian armies pushed back the Arabs over centuries, it's essential to realize that Arabs, Christians, and Jews mostly coexisted peacefully and intermarried, sharing culture and knowledge over the same pot of stew during those 781 years.
- Ultimately, the Moorish occupation had a profound cultural and scientific influence on all of Western Europe because of advancements in arts and sciences on the Iberian Peninsula.

Most Arabic-derived words in English have entered via Spanish, and many of those via Mexico after its colonization by Spain. While English includes some three hundred such words, Spanish has around four thousand, comprising 8 percent of the

Spanish dictionary and making Arabic the second-largest lexical source after Latin. You will immediately see what these words have in common: "albatross" (*al-ghattās*: the diver); "algebra" (*al-jabr*: restoring of broken parts; method of equation solving that first appeared in a ninth-century book by mathematician Mohammed Ibn Musa al-Khwarizmi); "algorithm" (from a corruption of the mathematician's name, "al-Khwarizmi"); and "alchemy" (al-kimiya.) In Spanish, there are hundreds of three- and four-syllable words that start with *al-*. The peninsular speakers of Celtic, Latin, Hebrew, and so on simply mimicked the Arabic sounds to create new words, not aware that "the" (*al-*) was part of their creation. So, if we analyze multilingually for a moment, "the artichoke," or in Spanish, *la alcachofa* (from Arabic *al-kharshuf*) is like saying "the theartichoke." This is a common phenomenon when a foreign word is adopted into a language. Witness the creation of our word "alligator" from the Spanish *el lagarto* (the lizard), and "lariat" from *la reata* (the noose).

In that era of Muslim history, learning and scholarship were revered and promoted, even mandated. Muhammed taught that "the scholar's ink is holier than the martyr's blood," and that "seeking knowledge is required of every Muslim." Under Arab tutelage, mathematics and sciences flourished in Iberia. From them, English has "zenith," "nadir," and "chemistry." From the Arabic-derived *"cipher,"* comes not only our word "zero" but the actual concept of this digit that originated earlier in the Orient and reached Europe via Moorish Spain.

English has absorbed many Arabic words for foods, products, animals, and plants: *apricot, alfalfa, jasmine, julep (julāb:* rose *water), lemon, orange, lime, spinach, sugar, candy (qandī:* sugared*), coffee, syrup, sherbet, safflower, saffron, tamarind, tarragon, tuna, ambergris, alkali, cotton, benzene, borax, gazelle, gerbil,* and *giraffe*—several of which were brought to Sicily from Cairo in the 1400s. For the home and furnishings, we have *alcove, adobe, mattress,* and *sofa*. In fashion, witness *gauze (qazz:* silk*), sequin (sikki:* coins*), crimson,* and *carmine*. Here are some words one might easily relate to Arabic: *henna, hummus, hookah, hashish, harem, lute, mecca, monsoon, mummy, safari,* and *typhoon*. But with *ghoul, loco, serendipity,* and *Swahili,* who would ever guess?

In his excellent article, "What Did the Moors Do for Us?" Nick Snelling describes Córdoba, Spain in the tenth century as, "One of the most important cities in the world, rivaling Baghdad and Constantinople. It boasted a population of 500,000 and had street lighting, 50 hospitals (with running water!), 300 public baths, 500 mosques, and 70 libraries. All of this at a time when London had a largely illiterate population of around 20,000, and had forgotten the technical advances of the Romans some 600 years beforehand."

It may be difficult to envision such a flowering of science and humanistic culture from the perspective of this age of ISIS and Boko Haram, but perhaps even the imagining opens a door to greater hope for peace and understanding. May it be so.

CHAPTER THREE

Grammar Grievances, Malaprop Muddles, and Pronunciation Pickles

Inconstant Consonants and Sudden Vowel Movements

If you're not already in awe of those who have learned English as a second language and can pronounce it at least passably well, you might be after reading this. I thank my linguistic stars that English is my native language.

Grammurder in the First Degree, Part I

Fun grammar: Is that an oxymoron like "pretty ugly", "jumbo shrimp" or "act naturally"? You'll be the judge, but even grammar is palatable with humor and a light heart.

Grammurder in the Second Degree, Part II

There are two possible rewards from reading this chapter. One is the resolution of any remaining doubts about *him and me* vs. *he and I*. The other is the revelation of what Sir Francis Drake was really doing out there on the high seas, at least according to a certain seventh grader.

The Law of Schwa

You know the vowels in English: A, E, I, O, U...and Schwa?? Yes, it's the most common of all vowel sounds, contributing to challenges for us native speakers, and untold headaches for English learners trying to spell and pronounce accurately.

The Abdominal Snowman on the Cal-Can Highway

What planet are you on if you "plummet to the top", where Spaniards dance the "flamingo", where our opinions are "diabolically" opposed, and where we all mope around and "commensurate" about this sad state of affairs? Why the planet of Malaprop, of course!

Into the Prepositional Fray

This piece is dedicated to my Chilean friend Mónica who, for all her enthusiastic diligence in learning American slang, never quite mastered the unsubtle differences between *screw up, screw over*, and *screw off*.

Inconstant Consonants and Sudden Vowel Movements

Is it possible to get through school without being subjected to a spelling bee? Not if you attended American (or British) K-12. But what if you grew up in Mexico, Munich, or Moscow? There wouldn't be much point in staging one in Spanish, German, or Russian because, unlike English, these and most languages are phonetic: you see it, you say it. Thus, if it's a word you've never encountered, you hear it and you'll know how to spell it with minimal margin for error.

Do you see that word *it's* in the previous sentence? That's what flunked me at round one in my fourth-grade spelling bee. I can still hear the nun's voice as she gave me my word; I can still hear myself thinking, "Oh, three letters—that's so easy." Sister Mary Spelling Bee then gave me the sample sentence: "The cow rubbed its horns," and I gave back, "i-t-apostrophe-s." Ouch! I was out of the running and back sitting red faced at my little wooden desk. It was so belatedly obvious to me! Am I the only one who still mentally slaps my forehead in shame a half a century after the regrettable event?

There are legions of world languages considered harder to learn than English: Greek, Hebrew, Arabic, Russian, Polish, Vietnamese, and Japanese, to name just a few. But I am in grateful certainty that I would *not* want to be learning English as a second language for all the tea in China or half the kimonos in Japan. Compared to other languages, there *are* some aspects of our tongue that make it relatively "easy" to learn, and if you've ever been a foreign language student, you'll appreciate these four:

1. There aren't two ways of addressing a person (formal and informal). Good old *you* suffices for anyone, and it's even the same for the plural, giving rise out of necessity to the charmless, "you guys."

2. English verb conjugations are stunningly simple: I *honk*, you *honk*, he/she/it *honks*, we *honk*, you guys *honk*, they *honk*. In the past tense, it's even easier: *everybody,* including I, you, he, she, it, we, y'all, and they, *honked.* Most verbs just throw *–ed* on the end to make the past: *opened, cooked, winked, dressed.* There are those pesky irregulars like *went, saw, met, brought, lost,* and so on, but the *–ed* is so dominant that children in the learning stage will almost always pattern with it: "he hitted me first"; "it goed away"; "they bringed it"; "I losed it."

3. Nouns in English aren't masculine or feminine and our adjectives don't have to adjust to what and how many they are describing. The adjectives *long* and *delicious* can apply to a nap as well as, unchanged, a Cuban cigar, a handful of red vines, or Sunday suppers at Grandma's.

4. English has no subjunctive except for a few vestiges like, "If I *were* you." We won't even go into what subjunctive is (or the sound of fingernails scraping on chalkboard when you hear, "If I *was* you..."), but suffice to say it causes volumes of grief for English-speaking learners of most foreign languages.

There are now more second language speakers of English in the world than there are native speakers*, and that is cause for awe when we consider these five factors that make our language truly daunting to learn:

---

* In his delightful book, *The Mother Tongue,* Bill Bryson informs, "There are more students of English in China than there are people in the Unites States."

1. The way we use prepositions to change the meaning of a verb, for example *carry over, carry through, carry forward, carry off, carry on, carry out.* My Chilean friend Mónica (see "Into the Prepositional Fray"), never did internalize *screw off* vs. *screw over*, and continued to *screw up* her prepositions throughout grad school.

2. Our neat little tricks with contractions: "You're coming, *aren't* you?"; "They left, *didn't* they?"; "He *couldn't* have known."; "It *isn't* the end." Listening to the speech of English learners, you'll notice they rarely master this major feature of English, but that doesn't mean they can't get their point across.

3. That crazy way we have of using *do/does/did* to ask and answer questions ("*Did* you see that?"; "No, I *didn't*."), when every other language in the world, except Celtic, says something more direct along the lines of, "Saw you that?"

4. Inconsistent pronunciation that must feel like a game of roulette to non-native speakers. To illustrate, here are several words containing the combination *-ough-.* Dictate this sentence to an English learner, and they'll run screaming from the room: "Though I thought it through, the bough I bought and wrought was too rough and made me cough." And what about those words in which a shift in the stressed syllable changes the meaning (usually noun to verb): *próduce/prodúce; áddict/addíct; cónflict/conflíct; ínsult/insúlt; présent/presént; récord/recórd; óbject/objéct, dígest/digést?* Then we have words that switch from one syllable (verb) to two syllables (adjective) to further flummox English learners: blessed/**bles**-sed; supposed/sup-**pos**ed.

5. Downright impossible spelling. Why is English so hard to spell? Mainly because it's a mash-up of Germanic (Anglo-Saxon) and Latin (Old French). In 1066, when William

the Conqueror of Normandy crossed the channel, charged into England, and defeated the Anglo-Saxon King Harrold, English was already a complex tongue created by Celts, Angles, Saxons, Jutes, Frisians, and Vikings. With the Normans now ruling England, Old French was added to the pot to make an even richer—but very inconsistent—linguistic stew. Willy tried to be a sporting chap and learn the local Anglo-Saxon language but gave it up as indecipherable and unpronounceable. Thus, all government and church affairs were conducted in French. Angles and Normans intermarried, of course, but English remained the language of the common folk, though increasingly altered by French influence. In modern times, we have word pairs that illustrate this cultural-linguistic divide, the Latin-based words from Old French usually being less common and sounding more "cultured" than the Germanic: *brotherhood* (G)/*fraternity* (Fr); *weakness* (G)/*debility* (Fr); *begin* (G)/*commence* (Fr); *brainy* (G)/*cerebral* (Fr).

The English alphabet has forty sounds but five hundred different ways to spell them. It was George Bernard Shaw who jokingly suggested that *fish* could be spelled *ghoti*:

gh = /f/ as in *enough*
o = /i/ as in *women*
ti = /sh/ as in *nation*.

Perfectly logical when the language is English, though orthographically a nightmare. Imagine yourself as a student of a language that seduces with repetitive sounds but crucifies with indefensible spellings.

Vowels are the worst offenders, and here are a dozen lessons to entertain us native speakers and horrify our English learner friends:

1. I *zoo*m to the fl*u*me with my gr*oo*m to exh*u*me the rh*eu*m in the t*o*mb. Va-v*oo*m!

2. If it's tr*ue* H*ugh* strew the sh*oe* at the y*ew*, near the sl*ough* with a v*iew* of the l*oo*, we'll s*ue* y*ou* t*oo*!

3. The r*eig*n in Sp*ai*n was on the w*a*ne with El*ai*ne, who was so v*ai*n, and J*ay*ne, who was ins*a*ne but sure could f*eig*n a br*ai*n and entert*ai*n in a pl*ai*n but g*ai*nly v*ei*n! Arr*ai*gn the tw*ai*n!

4. On all this *ea*rth the "s*u*rf and t*u*rf" grilled by his s*e*rf was worth the d*ea*rth of g*i*rth.

5. The n*e*rd in the h*e*rd st*i*rred the c*u*rd while he p*u*rred and l*u*red a b*i*rd he h*ea*rd say the word *abs*u*rd!*

6. *I* s*igh* "h*i*" to my g*ui*de for, *a*ye, it's q*ui*te a l*ie* that the g*uy* made me *cry* from mine *eye.*

7. *A*h! I'm in *a*we that I s*a*w a fl*a*w in P*a* after a p*au*se.

8. The m*oo*se signed a tr*u*ce with a b*oo*st from the j*ui*ce drunk with Z*eu*s and Toul*ou*se.

9. The town cr*ie*r was a l*ia*r who sang in the ch*oi*r. As a fl*y*er he went h*igh*er but landed in a p*y*re.

10. It was n*o*t for n*au*ght I s*ou*ght and b*ou*ght the pl*o*t.

11. Will J*oe* know he must g*o* l*o*w to throw a f*au*x cr*o*w at that b*eau*, his f*oe*, who won't s*ew* or m*ow*?

12. In the end, we *a*te the b*ai*t at *eig*ht after a great w*ai*t and g*ai*ned a h*ei*nous fr*eig*ht of w*ei*ght out of h*a*te that the tortures of English spelling will never ab*a*te!

By now, I've probably driven even native English speaking readers around the bend.[†] En*ou*gh of this st*u*ff!

[†] In my younger life, I made the mistake of trying to pronounce the following words before I had the benefit of hearing them spoken: anemone, heinous, halcyon, ubiquitous, massacre, Worcestershire, Yosemite, apocryphal, egregious, and more recently, equanimous. (Even spell check doesn't like that last word.)

Grammurder in the First Degree

When a friend showed me a cartoon that gave me a wonderful belly laugh, I took it as a sign that it was time to write about grammar. Picture this in cartoon style: Very large family dog sniffs at a sheet of binder paper on the floor. He sits down dejectedly and says, "Grammar errors, spelling mistakes—I cannot eat this homework!" I hope it's not just decades of teaching that cause me to find that funny. Yes, the time has come to explore grammar errors. You didn't think grammar could be glamorous[‡] and exciting? Just hang in for another paragraph.

Over 80 percent of Americans regularly make one or more common errors in the language. "Oh, but not me!" Right? Oops, that was the first mistake and perhaps it will be the last, but the odds are against English speakers, you and I included. Uh-oh. That was number two. Neither of these errors are considered egregious, and they will go unnoticed by the majority of people as will error #3 at the beginning of this sentence. We'll return to analyze all three in a bit, but first, more fun with grammar!

It used to be considered incorrect English to drop a preposition at the end of the sentence. We were instructed to say and write, "I don't know about what you are talking" instead of "I don't know what you are talking about" (and if you are under thirty, maybe you don't); "For whom did you buy the chocolates?" and not "Who did you buy the chocolates for?" With a sigh of relief, we note that the Grammar Powers That Be in America (the GPTBiA: self-coined with tongue-in-cheek because I can't figure

---

‡　The word "glamour" evolved from "grammar" because learning was associated with magic and enchantment.

out *who* adjudicates these things) capitulated a while back, and we can now say with impunity, "What did you do that for?" It's hard to imagine asking your neighbor, who has just cleaned up the very large family dog's messes and thrown them into your yard, "For what did you do that?" I'm glad Ernest Hemingway borrowed a phrase from a poem by John Donne and titled his masterpiece *For Whom the Bell Tolls*, but I'm relieved not to feel pedantic pressure to say, "To whom do I need to speak of these charges to my account about which I have no knowledge?" The old preposition rule is famously parodied in the phrase, "This is the type of arrant pedantry up with which I will not put," apocryphally attributed to Winston Churchill.

Thankfully, we are cleared to dangle our prepositions at the end of the sentence, but the GPTBiA are holding firm on *who* vs. *whom* to general dismay across the nation. In reference to the subject of the sentence, we should use *who*: "I told you *who* is coming to my party." *Who* is the subject (doer) of the verb *is coming*. In reference to an object in a sentence, it's *whom*: "I already told you whom I invited." *Whom* is the object (receiver) of the verb *invited*. Hemingway had to write about *For **Whom** the Bell Tolls* because *whom* is the object of the preposition *for*. And depending on to whom you are applying for a job, misuse *who/whom*, and that bell might be tolling for thee. But that's unlikely, and I wouldn't worry excessively over *who* vs. *whom* unless you are aspiring to teach English at a university, address the United Nations, or become a copy editor. It seems that rather than dismay at our confusion over *who* and *whom*, most Americans have given up on analyzing the distinction and instead adopted the attitude of "*Who/Whom* gives a hoot?", also articulated as, *Whatever!*

Now we shall revisit those three errors from the second paragraph:

1. "Oh, but not *me*!" should be, "Oh, but not *I*!" because *I* is the subject, as in, "I don't make errors." That said, I'm sure the first thing to come into my mind and out of my mouth will be, "Oh, but not *me*." I know it's incorrect, but I'll say it for the same reason I don't answer the phone thusly:

Caller: "Hello, may I speak with Susanna Janssen?" (!@#$% marketing calls.)

SJ (option 1): "This is she." (OK, maybe.)

SJ (option 2): "It is I." (Never...unless I was acting in a play set in the time before telephones.)

2. "The odds are against English speakers, you and I included," should be "...you and *me* included." Let's split the pronouns *you* and *I* and try it both ways: "The odds are against *you*"—that sounds fine, but we would never say, "The odds are against *I*." Unlike the need for *I* as the subject in error #1, now we are dealing with an object and must use *me*.

If this makes your eyes cross, hang tight, for it will be clarified in just a moment.

3. "Neither of these errors *are* considered egregious." We'll have to change *are* to *is*. Errors *are* considered egregious, but "Neither *is* considered egregious." *Neither* cannot be plural, only singular.

I'll bet you can hardly wait to check out more grammar errors, so on to some really glaring ones, the kind you'll probably find easy as you cringe at the sound of fingernails scraping on chalkboard. Identify the problems:

1. "I could of went there."
2. "Me and him went with Noah and her."
3. "She came shopping with him and I."
4. "I seen cousins I didn't seen for years." (It hurts my ears as much as it hurts your eyes, but it was uttered by a high

school graduate with a decent GPA and that's the only reason I include it.)

5. "Her and me don't talk no more." (Said by a famous TV personality being interviewed on a talk show.)
6. "We're hoping you can come with him and me."

The most common errors we hear or read revolve around confusion of subject pronouns (*I, she, he, we, they*) vs. object pronouns (*me, her, him, us, them*). The pronouns *you* and *it* are the same for both and so don't cause problems. A *pronoun* is a word that takes the place of a *noun*. If the noun is *Mom*, the pronoun is *she* or *her*, depending on whether "Mom" is a subject (doer of the action: *Mom/She* beats me at Scrabble) or an object (receiver of the action: I have yet to beat *Mom/her*.)

Whew! We'll get to the resolution of 1–6 first thing when you turn the page, *and* there is more investigative intrigue to come in "Grammurder in the Second Degree." But first, it's time to take a short break and very large family dog has done just that. He still will not eat the homework and has gone off to do his business in the neighbor's yard again.

Grammurder in the Second Degree

H ere we go with Part II and another good time with grammar. Part I ended with a cliffhanger: the sound of fingernails scraping down a chalkboard (I know, they've all been replaced by slick whiteboards), and very large family dog standing over a sheet of paper full of grammar errors and spelling *misteaks*, still refusing to eat that homework. We shall now pick up where we left off, fortified with the knowledge that there will most definitely *not* be a Part III.

Let's go for the resolution of 1 through 6 from "Grammurder in the First Degree":

1. "I could **of went** there." We often hear *could of/ should of/ would of* instead of *could have/should have/would have*, perhaps influenced by the colloquially wistful "coulda/ shoulda/woulda." And then there's *went* when it should be *gone*. Let's hear it for, "I **could have gone** there."
2. "**Me** and **him** went with Noah and her" should be, "**He** and **I** went with Noah and her." *He* and *I* are the subjects; *Noah* and *her* are the objects of the preposition *with*. Splitting the pronouns and trying them out separately always resolves the doubt: *Him* went? *Me* went? Oops, no: *He* went; *I* went.[§]
3. "She came shopping with him and **I**." "She came shopping with him and **me**." Self-explanatory, no? But sad to say, if you say that sentence correctly, many people who pride themselves on "proper" grammar will overcorrect and mistakenly tell you it should be, "She came shopping with he and **I**."

§   It is polite to put oneself last in a series. Hence, we say "He and I" rather than "I and he."

Now you can demonstrate to them how that just isn't so by splitting the pronouns right before their eyes and ears: "... shopping with *he*?? ...shopping with *I*?? Sorry, smarty!"

4. "*I seen* cousins *I didn't seen* for years." For the record: "*I saw* cousins *I hadn't seen* for years."

5. "*Her* and *me* don't talk *no more*." *Her* don't talk? *Me* don't talk? Of course not. "*She* and *I* don't talk *anymore*." I don't think the GPTBiA will loosen up on double negatives (*don't...no more*) in our combined lifetimes.

6. Look at this one carefully and split the pronouns: "We're hoping you can come with *him* and *me*." Yes and bravo!—it's correct as is. (I agree, "us" sounds more graceful.)

People often overcompensate because they were corrected so often on *me* and *him* (half the time wrongly, I suspect) that they're afraid to use these object pronouns together and sometimes even altogether. In a restaurant, I overheard a young man order for his date and then start to order his own meal saying: "And for I ...". An acquaintance said of her longtime friend, "I feel the same way about he." Another said, "I saw John and she at the play." And yet another, "This is between he and I." The speakers are trying to be correct with the choice of pronouns but are as far off the mark as with, "Me and him are going to the park." You might see an eyebrow go up when you say, "I'm doing this for him and her" or "Mom bought it for me and them," but the proof of correctness is in the pudding of separation, and it will be obvious every time. Pull the two pronouns apart and try them on separately:

- "I'm doing this for *him*" + "I'm doing this for *her*"="I'm doing this for *him* and *her*." Yay!
- "Mom bought it for *me*" + "Mom bought it for *them*" = "Mom bought it for *me* and *them*. Hooray!

- "*Me* is going to the park" + "*Him* is going to the park" = Oops!
- "I saw John at the play," yes; but, "I saw *she* at the play, no-no!

It all goes back to subject vs. object. "*He* and *I* are going to the park." *Him* and *me* can never be "doers" (subjects), only "receivers" (objects). "She named *him* and *me* in the lawsuit." "The scandal involved *her* and *us*." After a preposition (*by, with, for, to, in, of, about, between, etc.*), there is always an object: "She likes to gossip about *him* and *them*." "This is between *her* and *me*."

Now let's get a bit more sophisticated and identify the problem in these statements:

1. "Each of the yoga postures have several variations."
2. "None of my friends were at the party."
3. "Neither of them have money for a ticket."

All three scare up the same common error: that of using a plural verb with a singular subject. This is very slippery because the plural words *postures/friends/them* trick us into thinking they are the subjects. We examine more closely and see that the real subjects are *Each/None/Neither*, and those words are singular. So we correct these sentences by changing the verbs to singular form:

1. "Each of the yoga postures **has** several variations."
2. "None of my friends **was** at the party." (Even an editor commented, "I know this is right, but it sounds so *wrong*.")
3. "Neither of them **has** money for a ticket."

Bonus quiz! This one is for you to complete:

4. Both of them ___ coming but neither of them ___ dressing up.⁵

---

⁵ 4. Bonus quiz: "Both of them are coming but neither of them is dressing up. (*Both* is plural; *neither* is singular.)

Kudos to you for having come this far! Realizing that grammar errors do not constitute the juiciest of topics, I thought about attaching a five-dollar bill to this page as a reward for the persistent reader. I recall when one of my ingenious colleagues, wondering if anyone ever actually read our yearly *Program Review* reports, slipped into page 15 of hers a one-time offer of five dollars to anyone on the academic committee who actually did. (One committee member claimed the cash.) Better even than a cash prize, I reward you with these recently minted, spliced, and/or mutilated five-dollar words that have *not* yet qualified for inclusion in the "youth friendly" *Merriam-Webster* or any other standard dictionary:

- *Clumbersome*: favorite descriptive adjective of a former college administrator who, mashing up *clumsy* and *cumbersome*, used it with innocence and certainty.
- *Flustrated*: a zany blend of *fluster* and *frustrated*.
- *To conversate*: an unnecessary but increasingly popular invented verb. Thankfully, most people still prefer to *converse*.
- *To pronunciate*, and variation, *to pronounciate*: Is this a fancy way to *pronounce*?

What will be next? *To reservate*? *To cancelate*? *To vacationate*? *To insultate*? It makes me chuckle as I think fondly of my student assistant who complained about having to type on "carbonated" forms. That gaffe would be called a *malapropism*, and in "The Abdominal Snowman on the Cal-Can Highway", we visit them in hilarious depth. A malapropism is defined as the act or habit of ridiculously misusing words, especially by confusing words that are similar in sound. And that definition explains how, according to one middle school student who will remain anonymous, "In

1580, Sir Francis Drake circumcised the world with a very large clipper named The Gold Hand."

Whew! Now that the worst of the grammar errors have been cleaned up, very large family dog has just enthusiastically eaten the homework.

The Law of Schwa

D o you want to be a better speller or at least acquire more evidence of why English spelling is such a minefield and why your spell checker has to work overtime? Let's launch this topic, and you can decide.

How many vowels are in the English alphabet? This is not a trick question so go ahead and shout it out. Yes, right answer! There are five vowels: *a-e-i-o-u*. I agree—that was too easy. Try this one: How many sounds do these five vowels make? Yes, this is a hard one, but if you guessed a number over ten, good for you! Amazingly, our five written vowels produce fifteen to twenty sounds (depending on the dialect and not including vowel combinations). For example, the vowel *a* sounds very different in these three words: *hat, ate, father*.

Here's your next question: What's the most common vowel sound in English? We'd better ponder this one for a moment— Uhhh...Yes, that's it—*uh*! It's the favorite or at least most frequent vowel sound in our language, and we almost never spell it with the letter *u*. Face it, *u* is not a lovable vowel when it sounds like the *uh* in *slug, dung, ugh, underdog, ugly,* and so on. (Sorry, Humbert and Sunny.) We like it better when it sounds like *you*, as in *unity, university, usual,* and *Hugh*.

Now getting back to that ubiquitous sound *uh*; it's called the *schwa* and is shown in pronunciation guides as an upside-down, backward letter *e*: ə. Say the name *Kevin* out loud: *Ke* gets the emphasis, and with the second syllable *–vin* our voice goes soft and low. Do we say "Ke-*vin*" as in the *VIN* number (vehicle identification number) of our car? No, we say, "Ke-*vuhn*" ("Ke-vən").

And whether we spell his name *Kevan, Keven, Kevin, Kevon,* or *Kevun,* it is pronounced the same. Some of our words have different pronunciations between the true vowel sound and the schwa: *today* can sound like *too-day,* but usually leaves the mouth as *tuh-day.* In my neck of the woods, we hear *Mendocino,* as "Men-*doh*-cino," but more frequently by locals as "Men-*duh*-cino," leading to much speculation about what folks are are smoking.

The schwa is one of the reasons why English is a difficult language to spell. Even we native speakers think so, and just imagine how hard it is for foreigners! Friends text to meet for Friday happy hour at a nearby winery and everyone has their favorite spelling of the name: *Ravino, Revino, Rivino, Rovino, Ruvino.* Which is it?—because they all sound the same! Let's go with door number three, but only because we've seen the name in print.

In a radio show, the astronomer Milutin Milankovic was mentioned. I googled him as *Malankovic,* knowing it could just as well be *Melan-, Milan-, Molan-,* or *Mulan-.* You get the idea.

Now it's your turn again. Find the schwa in these common words:

compose
freedom
communication
tropical

Good work! I'll write the schwa sound as *uh* instead of ə for the sake of illustration:

cuhm-*pose*
*free-***duhm**
cuhm-*mu-ni-ca-***shuhn**
*tro-pi-***cuhl**

Now here's a two-part question for you: How long is the word that might contain a schwa, and on which syllable will it appear? Right, the word has to be more than one syllable (one syllable: *beast*; two syllables: *beastly*), and the schwa is always on an *unstressed* syllable. If the syllable carries stress or emphasis (as the *li* in *delicious*), we're going to pronounce that vowel in its unique way, but the unstressed vowels get muttered into the gray slush of schwa more often than not, and in this case, we get *de-li-shuhs*, or even *duh-li-shuhs*.

In English spelling, what you see is often not even close to what you hear. The schwa seems to make pronunciation easier as the mouth gets lazier, but it's curtains if you're trying to win a spelling bee.

There will be more ado about crazy English spelling, but for now, thank you for your *ətenshən* and *particəpashən*.

The Abdominal Snowman on the Cal-Can Highway[**]

admit to being a tad judgmental when it comes to vocabulary errors in English. In truth, I am judgmental about spelling errors, too, although I remind myself every time I write that word "judgmental" that I found only very recently that the *e* of "judge" isn't part of the more accepted spelling of the word. Until then, I thought it was a word my spell check just hadn't learned yet. I also confess I was brought to my lexical knees when corrected while speaking of Dutch and Italian ancestors, calling them my "forebearers." Ever linguistically self-assured, I contradicted smarty-pants when he insisted it was "forebears," then I humored him (thinking, "Hah—*bears*, that's ri-DIC-cu-lous") and let it go, certain that my trusty *American Heritage Dictionary* would vindicate me. But I humbly ate those two letters of crow and never made that mistake again.

It's a given that the more we read, the bigger our vocabulary and the more accurate our spelling. For some people, their grip on the native language is more tenuous than firm, creating occasional confusion and frequent comedy.

Exhibit A: A friend of mine in law enforcement quoted to me from reports written by officers:

[**] A friend and I were tossing around the idea of taking a road trip to Alaska via the Alcan Highway through Alaska and Canada. One of us mispronounced it (our recollection of whom conflicts), perhaps having seen too many dog food commercials on TV. From there, conjuring up an abdominal snowman was only a half hop/skip/jump, and the rest was side-splitting laughter and every malapropism we could splutter in that state of hilarious unravel.

- "We petitioned off the area as soon as we arrived." (**partitioned**)
- "Her husband had died, so the claim was a mute point." (**moot point**)
- "In lieu of the hour, we had to postpone the investigation." (**In view of**)
- "Before the stakeout, we simonized our watches at 9:00 p.m." (**synchronized**)
- "He went off on a tyrant as soon as I started to question him." (**tirade**)
- "She was just trying to nip it in the butt."(**bud**)
- "The whole scene reeked of havoc." (from "**to wreak havoc**")
- "The suspect appeared to be blind and was accompanied by a sight-seeing dog."(**seeing-eye dog**)

During several decades in education, I recorded some memorable mistakes and malapropisms. A former administrator was often "flustrated" by "clumbersome" regulations. Another was preoccupied with paying faculty "stifends" for special projects. One student's greatest desire was to become "fluential" in Spanish. Another's major challenge was in "pronounciating" correctly. The student assistant who hated typing on "carbonated" forms wrote a message informing me she would be out the next week for a "tubal litigation."

A quiz in English on cultural topics in a beginning Spanish class produced the following errors, mostly mix-ups of some of those pesky English homophones, words with different meanings but the same pronunciation:

- "It has a *fare* (fair) trade system for the workers.
- "And they get to work in *there* (their) own language."

- "Gabriel García Márquez is a Colombia *arthur*. "(author)
- "He *one* (won) the Noble *Piece* (Peace) Prize"
- "Francisco Franco was a *dicktater* (dictator) of Spain."

It was around that time I began seriously planning my retirement.

An acquaintance in the retail business lamented that there is such a "stigmata" about buying used clothes. A family member maintained that it was just a "plutonic" relationship. And who needs a comedy writer when you can listen to politicians' pronouncements? To wit: Former US Senator from Nevada, Chic Hetch, is immortalized for opposing the waste repository at Yucca Mountain by refusing to have his state become a "nuclear suppository."

The verbal gaffes of George W. Bush could fill a presidential library:

- "Too many OB-GYNs aren't able to practice their love with women all across this country."
- "...so when the history of this administration is written, at least there's an authoritarian voice saying exactly what happened."
- "Our enemies are innovative and resourceful, and so are we. They never stop thinking about new ways to harm our country and our people, and neither do we."

Dan Quayle was the vice president of the George Bush Sr. administration when he infamously stated, "Republicans understand the importance of bondage between a mother and child." On another occasion he said, "I believe we are on an irreversible trend toward more freedom and democracy - but that could change."

Several years ago, when I became the legal guardian for an elderly friend, I met with her lawyer to discuss her welfare. What he said shocked me into taking notes, and here they are verbatim: "The last time I saw her she was still *livid* and active." "It *vacillates* whether she eats or not." "There's no point sitting around *commensurating* about it." Would you hire this man to draw up a contract or write your will? That is what I mean by a tenuous grasp of the native language.

And now we'll hear from sixteen-year-olds answering questions on the GED (General Education Development test to obtain a high school diploma):

Q. "What guarantees may a mortgage company insist on?"
A. "To buy a house, you have to be well endowed."

Q. "What happens to a boy when he reaches puberty?"
A. "He says good-bye to his boyhood and looks forward to his adultery."

Q. "What is the fibula?"
A. "A small lie."

Q. "Give the meaning of the term 'Caesarean section.'"
A. "A district in Rome."

In a paper attempting to describe the interconnectedness of all things, the high school student wrote, "The universe is a giant orgasm," inadvertently omitting two crucial letters in the middle of the key word: *ni*. The teacher couldn't resist writing at the end of the essay, "Your answer gives new meaning to the Big Bang Theory."

I humbly admit that I make mistakes, too, but proofreading, lots of research, and a crack copy editor, keeps them in check. All that, and I'm never far from my well-worn copy of *Roger's Catharsis*—you know, that dictionary of synonyms that helps you find just the right word.

Into the Prepositional Fray

f just the sight of that *P* word in the title made you think, "Oh, maybe I'll skip this chapter," I assure you this is not another grammar lesson, I promise to be gentle, and I encourage you to read on. If you're not sure what a preposition is, not to worry— you're in friendly and ample company. And by the time you get into and out of this prepositional fray (alive and smiling, I promise), you'll not only be on friendly terms with, but will have great respect for, these little, mostly two- and three-letter words that communication, most especially in English, cannot survive without.

One of my best friends in college, the beautiful and exotic Mónica from Chile, spoke English with the most beguiling lilt and charming accent. English was her third language, and she was dedicated to mastering as much slang and colloquial speech as possible during our years in graduate school. Alas, there were three expressions she never got right no matter how much we coached and corrected her. When the car mechanic didn't actually fix the problem but overcharged her for it anyway, she complained, "I really feel like he screwed me off." When we walked out of Dr. Castillo's Modernism poetry exam, she moaned, "I really screwed that one over." About the unfaithful boyfriend, she reported to us, "It felt good to tell him to *just screw up!*"

Of course, a native speaker would never confuse two or more expressions created with the same basic verb and different prepositions, but can you imagine how this challenges an ESL (English as a Second Language) learner? There are many idiosyncrasies and complications in our language that cause me to admire *anyone* who can learn it even passably well. The point is that what seems so obvious and unmistakable to the nimble native speaker can be a serious minefield to the brave learner of *any* second language. And English is a wickedly rough one to learn.

Sticking with prepositions, let's take the common English verb *to take* and change its meaning by tacking different little words (*prepositions*) on the end. In no particular order, here's an even dozen for you to imagine how you would use in a sentence: *take on, take after, take off, take over, take out, take in, take down, take back, take upon, take to, take up, take up on.* (Will you *take me up on* that?) You had no trouble making up examples for each, and you even noticed that sometimes there's more than one obvious meaning, such as *take off shoes* or *take off in a plane.* If you were a foreigner learning English, do you think you could accurately manage that prepositional dozen, or might you slip up occasionally and, gazing at a photo, tell your friend, "I can see that you take to your mother"? We native speakers should pause to admire the linguistic leaps of meaning we achieve with something as tiny as a change of preposition. And while we are admiring these linguistic leaps, if English is *not* your native language, and you can manage these dozen *takes*, plus the adverbial combinations like *take away, take apart, and take aback*, then I bow at your feet and kiss the linguistic ground you walk on.

I can't speak *in* or speak *for* all the world's languages, but in the Latin-based Romance languages, (Spanish, Italian, French, Portuguese, Rumanian, and over thirty lesser ones and dialects) there are not twelve variations on the single verb *to take*, but twelve totally different verbs. If you have any Romance language bilingual dictionary, look up this verb and then peruse the expressions following the basic definitions of *take*. You'll see that each is elegantly rendered by one or more verbs (e.g.: "take away": *quitar* in Spanish), and not a train wreck of two- to five-letter add-ons.

For a foreign language student, that is infinitely easier to learn and simpler to remember than having to internalize the difference between *tell on* and *tell off*.

Imagine the poor young man after ESL class trying to be cool but struggling to remember if he wants to ask the girl to *hang in, hang out, hang on,* or *hang over* with him. Does he long for her to *fall in, fall out, fall off,* or *fall for* him? Is he hoping she will *give up, give over, give in* or *give out*? In his heart, does he pray things will *work over, work up, work in, work at, work on, work for* or *work out* for them? Does he promise not to *let her down* or *out*? After their first crisis, do they *make for, make up, make over,* or *make out*? And ultimately, will they *break in, break out, break up, break down, break off,* or *break through*?

A preposition is just a handy little word that usually tells us the relationship between what precedes it and what follows it. "The wart *on* his nose" tells us how the wart and the nose are related. "The wind *beneath* your wings" gives a certain understanding of wind to wings, and "The wind *from* your wings" or "The wind *against* your wings" gives different concepts altogether. Dictionaries manage to give definitions for prepositions, but they are the hardest little things to pin down as to meaning. How would you define *out*? Does your definition cover the expressions *get out, pass out, make out, find out, give out,* and *work out*?

Romance languages do have prepositions (a wart on the nose: *una verruga **en** la nariz*), but it's a rare verb that alters meaning with the addition of one. So, instead of doing mental backflips trying to remember if you need to *come to, come in, come off, come for, come on, come out,* or *come by,* you just learn seven verbs, each with its own clear meaning. Trust me; the only reason that doesn't sound easier to you is because you're lucky enough to have those pesky prepositions hardwired into your English-speaking brain so that they come out right every time. You're not caught in even a split-second debate about whether that toy airplane just *cracked down* or *cracked up*.

Imagine sitting in an office meeting and wondering whether you should suggest that a new hiring practice be *carried over, carried through, carried forward, carried off, carried on, carried out,* or *carried away.* And next you're wondering if you will be *passed out, passed up, passed on, passed by,* or *passed over* for a promotion. The verb *get* takes up over two pages in the English-Spanish dictionary, and it is one of the most essential, yet hard to master, verbs in our language. By now, I'll bet at least a half dozen combos of *get + preposition* are rolling off your mental tongue.

The first group trip I ever organized was to Costa Rica in 1996 with eight intrepid eco-tourists and a great local guide whose English was perfect—almost. One night, we were in our minibus creeping through the jungle in search of nocturnal animals. Intense darkness, complete silence, total concentration. Abruptly, the driver stopped the bus and our guide, Beto, hissed at us, "Get down." We looked at each other for a sign of what was going on and what we should do. While we were still hesitating, mentally debating what could be about to happen, he said more insistently, "Get down!" At this, the lawyer in our group was already on the floor of the bus, and the rest of us were in crouch position ready to flatten against the floorboards. I remember my heart pounding at the thought of someone wielding a machine gun or a machete boarding our bus. Finally, after several tense seconds and fearful scenarios rolling through our heads, the driver flipped on the interior lights and Beto stood in the doorway of the bus, pointing outside and saying in total exasperation, "Get down!!" We all *cracked up* laughing in relief and disbelief, helped the lawyer up off the floor, and then *cracked down* on Beto with a lesson in prepositions I'm sure he's never forgotten.

This is Susanna of Lexiconland signing over, off, out, up, and away!

CHAPTER FOUR

Windows on the World

It's All Bubble and Squeak to Me

Once you get the 'ang of Cockney Slang you'll be chewin' the fat in a whole different tongue, intelligible only to you and your mates. If you really get it down, you might try it out on the blokes in London, but don't expect applause.

Lost (But Not Forgotten) in Translation

This is about what happens when well-meaning people try to translate linguistic items into a foreign language they have no credentials to operate in. I'm at a loss what more to say. You simply must read it and weep, then laugh, and know that I couldn't possibly have made this stuff up.

We Don't Have a Word for It, Part I

Sunil Bali writes that there's no word in the Tibetan language for "guilty" and that the closest translation would be "intelligent regret that decides to do things differently." In this chapter we look at terms from other languages that not only speak volumes, but take a good phrase or two to get their meaning across in English.

We Don't Have a Word for It, Part II

I'm back on my home territory with common Spanish words whose English translation must occupy from several words to a whole paragraph to convey the same meaning. One of the first up is the Spanish word for a citizen of the United States, and *we* don't have a word for it. Imagine that!

News from the World of Words

If you love words and language, then you tune in to news items like these: Foreign Accent Syndrome where one awakens from a brain trauma speaking with a foreign accent or, in rare cases, speaking a foreign language; languages "winking out" all over the world; and the uplifting story of a seventh grader who invented an affordable Braille printer.

Speaking of Tongues

This is a personal tale of tacos and of tongues, the ones we speak, and the anatomical organ with which we speak. It ends with a lovely Afro-Cuban myth that plays beautifully between the two meanings.

Pigments of Our Imagination

Color is language. It speaks of mood, emotion, event, and expectation. But be aware of cultural differences for, while Americans are green with envy, the French are green with fear, the Italians are green with rage, and a Spanish-speaker might be green with dirty thoughts.

Between the Sword and the Wall

While we are "between a rock and a hard place", the Spanish speaker is "between the sword and the wall." Here we explore the parallels and deviations of bi-cultural folk wisdom, and usually find ourselves saying the same thing, just with different words and images.

The Language Police

130 language academies in the world hold the reins on 110 different languages in an attempt to keep them pure and regulated. English is not only influencing other languages more than any other in the world, but also absorbing vocabulary from foreign sources like a global sponge, all without any oversight or regulation. Is this anarchy, creativity, linguistic explosivity, or what?

Rum and Revolution, Part I

The perfect moment to visit Cuba is fast receding as "normalization" of Cuban-American relations rolls out, and ever larger numbers of US visitors flood the island. But do not dismay for, as Cuba gradually becomes "just another Caribbean island", you can experience revolution and transition in these two chapters.

Rum and Revolution, Part II

Now that we've met the Revolution, a Cuban cigar, "Guantanamera", the Soviets, the Castro brothers, and Che Guevara, here we'll talk about Cuban Spanish, architecture, the embargo, and a $4000 lobster dinner.

It's All Bubble and Squeak* to Me

Back in the good old Sacramento days when we weren't "good" and we weren't "old", my pals and I never tired of Mr. Daugherty's funny little rhymes that rolled off his tongue in oddly accented English that sounded like Eliza Doolittle's father in *My Fair Lady*: "Your rattles and jar, that's your car. Your trouble and strife, that's your wife. A hit and a miss, that's a piss. Dog's meat, that's your feet." Between chuckles and curiosity, I soon found out he wasn't making this stuff up, but rather carrying on the tradition of rhyming Cockney slang that's now almost two hundred years old.

The word *Cockney* has evolved in meaning over time from a reference to all city dwellers to a label for the residents and their speech in the Cheapside neighborhood of London, and now refers to the dialect and accent of working-class Londoners in general. It is precisely the speech that Henry Higgins (played by Rex Harrison) in the legendary musical *My Fair Lady* proposes to train out of Eliza (played by Audrey Hepburn) so he can win the bet with his linguist friend that he could coach a Cockney into speaking like a duchess. The musical is based on the 1913 play, *Pygmalion,* by George Bernard Shaw, who commented on English accents in the preface, "It is impossible for an Englishman to open his mouth without making some other Englishman hate or despise him." Cockney will never be spoken by the British Royal Family, but it has acquired status on the Isle as a valid English dialect and gained popularity among Americans (who always love a "foreign"

---

* To decipher the title, apply the rule of rhyme, and imagine what word sounds like squeak and fits this context of, "It's all _____ to me."

accent), thanks to the fame and now-familiar speech of celebs like Phil Collins, David Beckham, Michael Caine and, the voice we can't get enough of whether speaking or singing, Adele.

A very outstanding feature of the Cockney accent is the absence of the *h* sound: "Ow, me 'ead 'urts!" And yes, they really do say "me" instead of "my." You won't catch a Cockney saying, "*My* girlfriend broke *my* heart," but he might say, "The cheese broke *me* 'eart." "The cheese"?? Sure, you know—that rhyming thing again: *cheese and kisses,* that's your "missus" (wife or girlfriend). With a little practice, you, too can learn to speak Cockney-style! Just check out the online tutorial, "Learn the Cockney Accent with Jason Statham." Jason gets right *in your face* with his demonstration of the dialect, and that essential insouciance that goes along with it, for a spellbinding 7.27 minutes. At the end of that crash course, you could give it a try, but be forewarned for the British, and Londoners in particular, think we Americans sound "ridiculous-bordering-on-pathetic" when we try to imitate any of the accents of the Kingdom.

That said, why not spice up our speech with a few rhymes borrowed from Cockney slang? Some of them have already become so ingrained in American English that we have long forgotten they originated on the other shore of the "puddle." The Cockney rhyme for *money* is "bread and honey"—and I'd always assumed it was the hippies who'd creatively coined that usage for *bread* back in the sixties! To understand what's behind our expression, "getting down to brass tacks," we must think like a Cockney and get their rhyme of *tacks* with *facts. Chew the fat* is Cockney for "have a chat." A life coach might urge us to "blow a raspberry" at negative self-talk, and knowing this to originate with the Cockney slang *raspberry tart* (the rhyming stand-in for "fart"), that imaginary gesture suddenly takes on promising power.

What that "raspberry" demonstrates is that the slang starts out as a rhyme, but the rhyming word is often lost through familiarity. Hence, every Cockney gets that your *china*, short for *china plate*, is your "mate" (pal or friend). "*I still 'aven't got a Scooby*" leaves off the *Doo* of *Scooby Doo* but, rhyming with "clue," everyone knows you're still in the dark. *Use yer loaf!* shortens "loaf of bread," rhyming with "head." Your *tom* is your "jewelry" from *tom-foolery*. *Titfer* is slang for "hat" from Cockney *tit-for-tat*.

Indulge me through a few more classics: *dog* is the "phone" from *dog and bone*; *mincers* are "eyes" from *mince pies*. Picture yourself as a fly on someone's wall in Tottenham (Adele's home turf): "I couldn't believe me mincers! The cheese showed up with all that new tom, and I 'aven't even got the bread to keep me rattles on the Kermit. It'll be me Scotches carryin' me tomorrow." (Note: *frog* and *toad* = "road," and it's just a short leap from there to *Kermit*; *Scotch eggs* = "legs.")

As with all slang, there's constant coinage of fresh phrases that can be admired for their creativity. *Watch and chain* is Cockney-clever for "brain": "*Is yer watch a bit slow today?*" *Thick and thin* is "skin"; *field of wheat* is a "street"; and *Spanish onion* is a "bunion."

The word *Cockney* itself is traceable to *cockeney*, meaning a misshapen egg, and first used a few centuries earlier to refer derogatorily to city folk ignorant of real life (ironic, isn't it?). Oddly enough, it remains unknown how all this rhyming slang got started. Was it a linguistic "big bang" of spontaneous generation? Perhaps a game of wit that captured imaginations and tongues like terms of venery (see "The Herd Mentality")? Or, was it the conscious invention of a secret code meant to keep outsiders out of Cockney business, akin to the invented *Boontling* language of the Anderson Valley in Northern California; the original *Lunfardo* of the Buenos Aires underworld; or Bolivian *Machaj Juyai*, used to secretly pass medicinal knowledge from healer father to apprentice son? Some researchers suggest Cockney was originally the code language of thieves in London.

However it came about, we can be sure that standing on a busy *field* in Eastside London, listening to the Cockney world go by, we won't have a *scooby* what they're saying.

Lost (But Not Forgotten) in Translation

W hile working as a volunteer translator at a clinic in Mexico, my assignment in Surgery was to give post-op patients their discharge instructions in Spanish. This should have been a straightforward matter of handing them the page with boxes checked by the surgeon and adding a few verbal clarifications. But on closer look at the document, I was between horror and hilarity at the translation of the English directives into Spanish. It was hopelessly misbegotten, accidentally rhapsodic, and blastedly unintelligible (especially for the many folks with limited reading skills).

I give you in English a snippet of what the Spanish translations actually instructed the patient to do: "The look into your incision/wounds you every day. Of that which you see more redness, swelling, pus, drainage, or sangria, or if you make that a fever, turn around to see the doctor." To make matters murkier, the patient's wife consults the instructions for changing the bandage on his hernia incision, and discovers she is to "wash the hands well before putting the new preparation ablaze." In the section about when to remove the surgical dressing, here is a real head-scratcher, "You can take off the overcoat to dress in three days."

Among the dietary guidelines, the patient was instructed to avoid *bebidas suaves*, which to a Spanish speaker means "mild, gentle drinks." It would never occur to him that the injunction was against what we call "soft drinks" and, suffering the pain of that recent hernia surgery, he might just opt for a double whiskey. Nothing mild or gentle about that; just following doctor's orders! The surgical nurse was gratefully willing for me to rework the form and admitted it had been tacked together by a mish-mash of electronic translation, dictionary digging, and a few high school Spanish opinions thrown in for better or worse.

You might guess in what regard I hold electronic translators (e.t.), and you are correct, but truth be told, I do often use one to send Mariann a greeting in Swedish or wish Ludovica a happy weekend in Catalan. And I use online dictionaries to resolve arcane words and regional colloquialisms in Spanish. But when it comes to whole sentences, let alone paragraphs, the electronic translators falter despite huge improvements in recent years.

E.t can be a useful tool, but if you need to deliver a clear message, hire a human who gets paid for doing a very challenging job for which they have years of training and experience. (Written translation was one of my former professions and, frankly, I had to conclude it was just too hard.) Language is so deeply personal, cultural, and nuanced that we won't be saying farewell to real live translators anytime soon even, if e.t. does keep "learning" from its mistakes. In 2012, the US Department of Labor Statistics predicted that jobs for translators would expand by 46 percent by 2022 due to increasing globalization in all major sectors. Hence, the occupation of translator/interpreter will become the fifth-fastest growing in the United States, serving commerce, government, law, education, and especially, health care.

Translation missteps have been entertaining us for years. Surely you've seen the supposed gaffes of American corporate advertising abroad that have been circulating on the Internet for decades: that the Chevy Nova flopped in Latin America because in Spanish *No va* means, "It doesn't go"; that Parker Pens translated the slogan, "It won't leak in your pocket and embarrass you", with the Spanish verb *embarazar* (to make pregnant); that in Taiwan, "Come alive! Join the Pepsi generation!" was rendered, "Pepsi will bring your ancestors back from the dead." Yes, these and so many other favorites are the stuff of legends—spurious, and oh-so-entertaining *urban* legends. In fact, Chevrolet sold a lot of Novas south of our border, and sales even surpassed expectations in Venezuela. But before you label me a killjoy let me add that yes, Mazda did name a new 1999 model *Laputa* (the prostitute, in Spanish.) Nissan gave us more to hoot about with the 2011 release of a minicar they called the *Moco*, Spanish for "booger". And the American Dairy Association did translate "Got Milk?" as *Tienes leche?* which can mean, "Are you lactating?"

Let's see how English translation shows up abroad in our foreign hosts' attempts to keep us well behaved, safe, and making enjoyable menu selections. A sign in English upon entering a church in Spain: "We thank him to discover their head before entering this enclosure. This is a place of cult." (How it went south: *descubrir:* "to discover" as well as "to uncover"; *culto:* worship.) This sign in Spanish at a road closure, "*Peligro! No pasar!*" (Danger! Do not pass!) was translated for the safety of the foreigner: "I am in danger! Not to happen!" (and then perhaps interpreted by the English-speaking passerby as roadside existential agony). Those pesky words with multiple meanings!

In China, the translations into *Chinglish* are earnest, compelling, surreal, and all captured on camera. At a vista point we read the warning, "Beware of missing foot!" (Then we probably look down just to check and lose our footing on the steep hillside.) At construction sites: "Execution in Progress," "Erection in Progress," and "Beware of Safety!" The fire extinguisher in a high-rise office building is labeled, "Hand Grenade." Nokia's inviting slogan, which promised to connect people across the globe, was translated from elegant Chinese characters into an ignominious message: "Connecting Poopie."

When it comes to restaurant menu translations from Chinese

into English, the lexicon takes a turn toward the psychedelic. Consider these irresistible offerings: *The Palace Oil explodes the duck; Potato the crap; Six-roasted husband; The fragrant spring onion explodes the cow; Meat muscle stupid bean sprouts; Wang had to burn; Fries pulls out the rotten child; Chicken rude and unreasonable; F*** the duck until exploded*; and … hmmm, let me think it over while I nibble on my last protein bar. Indeed, we all have plenty on our to-do list, but will someone please fix that glitch in Chinese to English translators that persists in rendering the culinary term "dry seasoned" (among others) as "f***."

Despite all the Spanish language resources available in early twenty-first century America, the Exit Only sign in Starbucks was translated for the convenience of Spanish-speaking customers as Éxito Aquí (Success Here). In 2010, coming back from a trip abroad, I was surely hallucinating in front of a sign in Spanish pointing to Customs in the San Francisco Airport which spelled out, not *Aduana*, but *Costumbres*, as in "cultural practices."

Finally, two words of advice: Do *not* drop your Spanish class, and under no circumstances should you put your faith in an electronic translator and then walk into a salon in Argentina, Mexico, or Spain to request a wash and a blow dry. You'll get the wash, but it might be followed by a "dry" whack to the head delivered by a very puzzled but compliant beautician.

We Don't Have a Word for It, Part I

Our topic is fascinating foreign words that have no equivalent in English, so let's dig right into some of my favorite untranslatable terms from around the world. As you shall see, in each case we can string together enough words to create a passable definition, but though English speakers may have a concept of what the foreign term expresses, our language just doesn't have a word for it.

- **Schadenfreude** (German): Taking pleasure in another's misfortune. This is perhaps the most well-known and oft-quoted of the untranslatables for the obvious reason that the English language really *could* use a word for something we do all the time. "When the cop pulled the guy over who passed me going 85, I was glad it was him and not me. He had it coming!" In a word, *Schadenfreude.*

- **Age-otori** (Japanese): To look worse after getting a haircut. Who hasn't suffered this ignominy, albeit temporarily? Thank goodness and the gods of grooming that hair does, after all, grow back.

- **Forelsket** (Norwegian): The euphoria of first falling in love. Love songs since time immemorial have been trying to describe that feeling, but apparently it never occurred to us in English just to invent a word for it. It's easy to see how the Eskimos have lots of words for snow and the Fijians have but one, in keeping with their respective experience with the substance, but wouldn't you think that the universal experience of love would demand the generation of words for *all* its stages?

- ***L'esprit de l'escalier*** (French): This is usually translated as "staircase wit," but that doesn't nearly convey the frustration of coming up with the perfect comeback *after* the encounter is over and you're already headed upstairs to bed for the night.

- ***Meraki*** (Greek): This is what is generated when you put heart and soul, creativity, and love into what you are doing. It's what is created when a group of dedicated folks put on a fund-raiser to benefit the Boys and Girls Club; it's my niece, Lauren, writing a song to reach out across continents to a little girl from Northern Africa going to Colombia to be fitted with a prosthetic foot; and it's the spirit of all those who raised the money to make that miracle possible.

- ***Wabi-sabi*** (Japanese): This is the celebration of the impermanent, imperfect, and incomplete as essential elements of art and life. This Japanese concept of beauty is sweeping the nation just as *feng shui* did in the '80s. Not only is *wabi-sabi* a bed & breakfast in Maine, an art center in New York, the name of numerous restaurants (some featuring incomplete dishes of flawed food), and a popular name for pairs of kittens and goldfish, but according to author Arielle Ford in her book *Wabi-Sabi Love,* it's the way to find perfect love in an imperfect relationship. It could also characterize my style of gardening and housekeeping, as well as my computer skills, my understanding of finances, and the last soufflé I attempted.

- ***Hygge*** (Danish): Practicing the pronunciation of this word with Ida, my Danish exchange student, I knew that, even if we can't name it with a single word in English, I want more of it. It's a state of mind marked by cozy warm togetherness. Think of sitting by a crackling fire in snuggly slippers with glowing cheeks alongside your favorite companions, enjoying a wonderful vintage of your favorite beverage at the start of an endless weekend. Maybe someone has found a way to bottle the stuff because, although the Scandinavian winter days are long, dark and cold, Denmark dependably comes up as one of the happiest countries in the world.

- *Shinrin-yoku* (Japanese): Literally "forest bathing," it means improving one's health by spending time in nature amidst trees. There's science to back this up, and the practice is free and abundantly available to us all.

- *Gökotta* (Swedish): To go out early in the morning to hear the birds and appreciate nature. My Swedish friend, Mariann, confirms, "Yes, that is correct. *Gök* means cuckoo and *otta* early morning." Isn't that adorable?

- *Toska* (Russian): One cannot improve on Vladimir Nabokov's description: "No single word in English renders all the shades of *toska*. At its deepest and most painful, it is a sensation of great spiritual anguish, often without any specific cause. At less morbid levels, it is a dull ache of the soul, a longing with nothing to long for, a sick pining, a vague restlessness, mental throes, yearning. In particular cases, it may be the desire for somebody or something specific, nostalgia, lovesickness. At the lowest level, it grades into ennui, boredom." That's a lot of mileage in a five-letter word, and it rings of truth and that he knows of what he speaks.

- *Tartle* (Scottish): If you tartle, you hesitate while introducing someone because you've forgotten his or her name. Funny how some of our most universal and tenderly human foibles are the ones that embarrass us the most. Kudos to the Scots for giving this one a name. "He tartled for more than a few seconds while introducing his wife to his boss."

- *Torschlusspanik* (German): Literally, "gate-closing panic," it refers to the fear of diminishing opportunities with advancing age. German is a language where you can tack several nouns together to create a new concept in a single word, thus opening new gates to endless possibilities even while *torschlusspanik* reminds us that old ones are clanging shut.

- *Ya'aburnee* (Arabic): Literally, "You bury me," meaning, "I hope I die before you because I love you so much I couldn't stand the pain of living without you." Sweet? Selfish? Maybe both.

- *Yoko meshi* (Japanese): Yoko means horizontal, and meshi is boiled rice. You're going to love this one! It's the Japanese term for the stress of communicating in a foreign language, and could be roughly tacked together in English as "A meal eaten sideways." This term holds clever wordplay in the fact that Japanese is written vertically while most other languages are written horizontally. Even so, don't you think *all* languages, especially English, should have a word for that particular discomfort?

- *Korinthenkacker* (German): This rollicking word translates literally as "raisin pooper", and refers to someone who is too absorbed in nitpicky details and busy with petty trivia to be of any use. It makes me think of a restaurant manager who, in the chaos of the lunch rush, could be found in his office perfecting the peeling of an apple in a single, unbroken strip, or, better said, he sat at his desk pooping raisins.

- *Retrouvailles* (French): The joy of being back together with someone after a long absence.

And just turn the page, my dear reader, and we shall have a rush of *retrouvailles* when we reunite to delve into some Spanish words that have no direct translation into English: some delicious, some enchanting, and a few just downright practical.

We Don't Have a Word for It, Part II

"We were sitting around the patio table after the meal, talking with my kids' godmothers and my son-in-law's parents about how people in the United States worry so much about what other people will say about what they do. Lorna, who always loves to be pampered and made a fuss over, was wearing her new Coach tennis shoes for the first time. Her husband Louie, who has no hair on his head or face and is cross-eyed, announced it was time to go because he had to get up very early in the morning."

Now in Spanish:

> *Estábamos de **sobremesa** en el patio, platicando con **comadres** y **consuegros** de cómo los **estadounidenses** se preocupan tanto del **qué dirán**. Lorna, siempre **mimosa**, **estrenaba** nuevos tenis Coach. Su marido, Louie, **lampiño** y **bizco**, anunció que era hora de irse porque tenía que **madrugar**.*

English is considered economical with words when it comes to the number of them it takes to get your meaning across, but here it took almost twice as many as in the Spanish version. Of course, I planned it that way because we're talking about things that English simply does not have a word for:

- ***Sobremesa***: This is a lovely word for the time spent sitting at the table to chat after a meal. Of course, we do this with friends, but it has become an almost extinct custom among families in the United States because it requires that the household members first sit down to a meal together.

- **Comadre, compadre**: In Spanish-speaking countries, a child has multiple godfathers and godmothers (*padrinos y madrinas*) for every important life event: Baptism, First Communion, and Confirmation in the Catholic Church; graduations, *quinceañera*,[†] weddings, and so on.[‡] Thus, Spanish has a name for the relationship between the child's parents and the godparents: *comadres* (feminine, comother) and *compadres* (masculine, cofather). These two words are used more generally to refer to lifelong family friends.

- **Consuegros**: This is the word for your relationship with your married son or daughter's parents-in-law. Might have to diagram that one.

- **Estadounidenses**: Life would be easier if English had an unambiguous name for our nationality, such as "Unitedstateser." I know—too cumbersome! But what to do? Spanish has this official and unmistakable name for our nationality, though it is used mostly in official or formal contexts. Confusion ensues. We call ourselves Americans, and we can go to Spain or Italy as *americanos*, but in Mexico, they insist on calling us *norteamericanos (no capitalization of nationalities in Spanish)*. However, technically, they too are North Americans, as are Guatemalans,

---

†   *Quinceañera* is the celebration of a Latina girl's fifteenth birthday to mark her passage into womanhood. Traditionally, it begins with a Catholic Mass which is followed by a grand party. Similar to a wedding ceremony, the girl wears a long elaborate gown and is surrounded by her chambelanes (maids of honor and groomsmen).

‡   There are many godparents for a Hispanic celebration because all the extended family and close friends must be involved, and also because those *padrinos* and *madrinas* pay for the various aspects of the event. In a wedding, for example, there are godparents for the church, the reception hall, the flowers, the food, the music, the decorations, and many other features. For my student Cristóbal's wedding, I was asked to be *la madrina de la Biblia en español*, the godmother of the Spanish-language Bible. ¡Un honor! When my student Jaime graduated from Mendocino College with highest honors, he asked me to be a *madrina* for this important milestone in his life.

Hondurans, Costa Ricans, and so on, down to the end of the Isthmus of Panama. In geographical terms, there is only North America and South America, *Central America* being a portion of North America, and a useful demographic and political designation. North America includes Canada and Greenland, and ends at the border of Panama with Colombia. In South America as well, it is not acceptable to call ourselves *americanos* (because they are too—*sudamericanos*). We are *norteamericanos* or, more accurately, *estadounidenses*.

- *El qué dirán*: Literally, "What will they say?" This is the worry over what others will think and say about what you do. It shows up less these days in literature and media because, frankly, things are loosening up and folks are caring less about how the flies on their wall are reacting to their bad habits and peccadilloes. That said, if I'm visiting Mom in Bakersfield and a friend is dropping me off after an evening out, I'd better be in the front door within five minutes, or she will be deeply worried about the *qué dirán* of her neighbors.

- *Mimoso*: This is a person who loves to be pampered and made a fuss over. We might say "high maintenance," but there's a sweetness about *mimoso*/*mimosa* that would be lost.

- *Estrenar*: You could say "to debut," but we wouldn't "debut a pair of shoes." In Spanish, it means to show off something for the first time: a jacket, a dress, a car, a sassy attitude; also, to premiere a play.

- *Lampiño*: "Beardless and bald." Luckily for the follicle-challenged, this is a trendy masculine look in the early twenty-first century.

- ***Bizco***: Surprisingly, Spanish has single words for some physical differences (I'm trying to be PC here) that English must describe with a modifier to the body part. This one means "cross-eyed." There are more:
- ***Tuerto***: "one-eyed"
- ***Manco***: "one-armed"
- ***Zurdo***: "left-handed"
- ***Madrugar***: This means, as illuminated in our story, "to get up early in the morning."

Here are a few more, including some that budding bilinguals will recognize:

- ***Entrecejo***: This is the space between the eyebrows. Actually, there *is* a very arcane word in English for this area between (*entre*) the brow (*ceja*), and in this age of Botox, someone should invent a better name for it than "glabella."
- ***Chapuza***: "Shoddy work" or a "botched job." I think I stayed in a hotel of this name in Paraguay.
- ***Anteayer***: This is so handy! A single word to say, "The day before yesterday." And Spanish also has ***pasado mañana*** for, "The day after tomorrow."
- ***Lustro***: "A period of five years." Let's see, what would be your age in *lustros*?
- ***Tardar***: This is a verb meaning "to be late" or "to take a long time." Although the syllable count is almost the same, there is an economical elegance to *tardaron mucho en llegar* compared to, "It took them a long time to get here."

I've saved two of my favorites for last:

- ***Tertulia***: This is a meeting of like-minded individuals to engage in learned discussion of a particular topic at a regular time and place, usually a bar or café. Ernest Hemingway was a well-known participant in literary *tertulias* when he lived in Spain as a reporter on the Spanish Civil War in the late thirties. We sometimes have *tertulias* of Spanish speakers at my house, and while we definitely think alike (love food, wine, books, and travel), our discussions are often more lively than learned. *Tertulia* is a word that reflects a cultural aspect of Spain and some parts of South America but isn't widely known in Mexico. It's rather similar to a *salon* but usually held in a public place and not a private home.

- **Duende**: A *duende* is a magical creature such as an elf or goblin, but I include the word here because it's most often a kind of magic or charm, an ineffable and enchanting quality present in some people and certain works of art and literature. *Tener duende* is to have "it." *Wikipedia* has this to say about *duende* in reference to flamenco and art in general: "*El duende* is the spirit of evocation. It comes from inside as a physical/emotional response to art. It is what gives you chills, makes you smile or cry as a bodily reaction to an artistic performance that is particularly expressive."

May the spirit of *duende* reside in your heart and mind, and dwell with you always.

News from the World of Words

How would you like to undergo a medical procedure (brief, pain-less, no side effects) and wake up fluently speaking the foreign language of your choice like a native speaker? That would make for a great sci-fi linguistic thriller, but for now, it seems ridiculously impossible (though some of us long-term students of languages are already putting our names on the advance waiting list). It's just wishful thinking. Or so I thought until a news item about foreign language syndrome gave me hope. Pimsleur, one of the world's top foreign language teaching companies, describes these cases:

> In April 2012, a seventeen-year-old Malaysian student involved in a motorbike accident emerged from uncon-sciousness speaking four new languages: Chinese, Japanese, Korean, and Indonesian. In what was consid-ered to be an extreme form of this syndrome, the language changed on a daily basis, lasting for several hours at a time.
>
> In a bizarre twist on the theme of foreign language syndrome, a Croatian girl woke up from a coma speaking fluent German. As this was her second language, it was not a particular surprise. What was intriguing was the fact that she was no longer able to speak Croatian, which was her first language. Her ability to speak her native language had somehow been inhibited through her accident. (2010)
>
> In a third example, a Czech speedway driver who had just begun learning to speak English came to after a motorbike crash speaking fluent English to the astonish-ment of his friends, especially as there was no trace of an accent. Later, he could speak to an English reporter only through an interpreter. (2007)
>
> Other examples specifically related to (the) syndrome

include a British woman who began speaking with a French accent after a stroke. More unusually, an American woman who was put under an anesthetic for dental treatment woke up speaking with a curious combination of English, Irish, and other European accents. In one of the most extreme cases, a Norwegian women injured by shrapnel during World War II began speaking with a German accent. She was subsequently ostracized by her local community.

The rare phenomenon of foreign language syndrome, or foreign accent syndrome, was first reported in 1907 and has since manifested in over one hundred recorded cases. These most often resulted from damage to the brain (usually on the left side where language is processed) caused by stroke or other types of trauma as you see in the cases quoted previously. As of this writing, the most recent case of foreign language/accent syndrome was reported in early 2016. It involves a woman in Texas who had surgery on her jaw to correct an overbite and woke up speaking with a heavy British accent. All the cases of this disorder are inexplicable but hers is particularly rare because it was not precipitated by trauma to the brain. The online video featuring her case is compelling as we hear her tell that her only trip out of the United States was to Mexico, while we listen to her British accented speech *and choice of words*. (See references.) Despite all the scientific advances of the early twenty-first century, there is as yet no official explanation for any of these phenomena, and the brain continues to be a mysterious and many-splendored thing.

* * *

Continuing now with other news from the world of words:

In 2013, a Tennessee judge handed down a ruling (since overturned) that a mother could not name her baby "Messiah." In early 2015, a judge in France ruled that the parents could not name their baby "Nutella," the trade name for a popular chocolate-hazelnut spread, because it was against the child's interest. Where do you draw the line, and who should decide what is in the child's *interest*? I know of a woman who named her son "Blyth," and I feel for him. Facebook tells me there are many unfortunate males in the world named "Jay Walker," and another legion of them named "Pete Moss." Would Mrs. Butts end up before a judge defending herself for naming her son "Seymour"? My dear friend Pattie really wanted to christen her baby boy "Johan," but decided to name him just "J" and let the boy later decide for himself, since Johan di Maggio sounded like a bratwurst pizza.

* * *

Also in the news, languages are going extinct all over the globe. It is a phenomenon that has been occurring since the beginning of speech, but linguists note it is accelerating now because of globalization, the loss of rainforests, the movement of people out of rural areas and into cities, and of course, technology and the worldwide dominance of English. Renowned linguist, John McWhorter (*The Power of Babel*), and many of his colleagues estimate that one hundred years from now, only about six hundred of the world's six thousand or so languages will remain.

To learn that Sumerian died out in Mesopotamia before the birth of Christ, that the last speakers of Punic expired in North Africa in the early fifth century, or even that Latin became extinct in the 700s (but has achieved immortality as a *dead language*), does not bring sadness. But what poignant loss is felt to know that Klallam was forever silenced in the state of Washington with the death of Hazel Sampson on February 4, 2014; that there is no one left to speak Yurok in California after Archie Thompson died on

March 26, 2013; and that the 2011 passing of Brownie Doolan Perrurle signaled the end of Lower Arrernte in the Northern Territory of Australia. Over 50 languages have died out with their last speaker in the first decade and a half of the twenty-first century. Compared to the 170 that disappeared during the entirety of the twentieth century, we can see that the process is snowballing. If the trend continues with increasing speed throughout the twenty-first century, those linguists' prediction for a century hence will surely become reality.

* * *

To close this news report on an uplifting note, here's an item to gladden all hearts. In January 2014, a seventh-grader from Santa Clara, California invented Braigo, a braille printer, from a Lego robotics kit, printer parts, and a computer chip. How did it all come about? He saw a flier soliciting donations for the blind, and curiosity aroused, asked his parents, "How do blind people read?" They told him to google it, and he dove in. After finding out that a simple braille printer cost around $2000, Shubham Banerjee combined tech-savvy, Lego-love, and philanthropy to create a product that can be marketed for about $350. Intel provided funding for this young entrepreneur to take his seventh-grade science project to the next level, and he became a worldwide phenom. (Does the Nobel Prize have a junior division?)

Shubham was born in Belgium, and his family moved to the United States when he was four. I'll bet he speaks at least two languages: English obviously, plus he may have learned Hindi from his family, and Belgium is a bilingual country with Flemish and Walloons, dialects of Dutch and French respectively. Research proves overwhelmingly that children who are bilingual from their earliest years show higher development of problem-solving skills, multitasking, and logic, and more cognitive flexibility. And that news alone should revolutionize American education.

Speaking of Tongues

I n my early years at Mendocino College, the Dean of Instruction, Susan Bell, and her husband Neill were enthusiastic students in my beginning Spanish classes. The Bells threw great parties up on Black Bart Ridge. Susan was a fabulous cook, the guest list was eclectic, and the conversation always lively. The Bells and I had become fast friends, and having them in my classes was a delight. Susan took on Spanish with the same joyful enthusiasm that seemed to motivate her approach to life overall. Gregarious and uninhibited, she sought to practice Spanish with Neill and other students, with bilingual college employees, and out in the community every chance she got.

One day before class, she recounted what had happened when she engaged the owner of a local Mexican restaurant in conversation after finishing her lunch. First, she introduced herself and warned him that she knew *poquito español*. Fair enough. Then she began to tell him how much she was enjoying her *clase de español*. So far so good, and he complimented her pronunciation and her dedication. Susan loved conversation, and she was just warming up into this one—in *a foreign language* at that!

The pesky trouble with all lexicons is that a single word will often have multiple meanings. As Susan was going on about how much she loved the language, and *el señor* heard her say for the third time, "*Me gusta mucho la lengua*," he responded with, "*Un momento.*" He disappeared into the kitchen, and came out three minutes later with *un taco muy especial para la señora*, and placed before her with a flourish a very special taco of beef tongue made especially for the lady. As she chewed through this new culinary adventure, Susan pondered what had just taken place: Language? Tongue? Ah-ha! *Lengua* means both. There are two main words for language, and Mexican Spanish speakers almost always opt for *idioma* over *lengua*. Chalking up his bafflement to her "*poquito español*," the *señor* interpreted that she was professing her enchantment with beef tongue (*lengua*) and gallantly gave her the opportunity to sample his.

I had to take some responsibility for this communication snafu because I had given my students both *idioma* and *lengua* for "language", and you can see which one stuck, even though *idioma* is by far the preferred choice in Mexican Spanish. Susan laughed heartily over this misunderstanding (that resulted in a free taco) and waded right back into deep and unpredictable linguistic waters, always convinced that everything would turn out just the way it should and maybe provide entertaining moments en route.

If you are into sampling exotic tacos, some authentic Mexican eateries offer, in addition to *lengua*, *tacos de tripa* (tripe: lining of the first of the cow's three stomachs); *tacos de sesos* (brains; but why just beef? Are the pigs, sheep, and goats not smart enough?); *tacos de oreja* (pig's ear; with nothing left over for the silk purse); *tacos de rabo* (bull's tail); *taco de cabeza* (roasted meat from the cow's head); and lastly, *tacos de ojo* (eye) and *tacos de mejilla* (beef cheeks)—two specially prized parts of that head. As your mind's eye is already showing you, nothing is wasted from ears to tail.

At the mention of words with multiple meanings, *taco* brings to mind only one thing to all of us influenced by Mexico and its cuisine. But remember, there are twenty-one Spanish-speaking countries in the world, and for Spanish speakers from other parts, *taco* can mean a "plug," "wedge," "ramrod," or "blowgun"; a "calendar pad," a "gulp of wine," "confusion," a "dirty word," an "obstacle," the "heel of a shoe," a "short, stocky person," or a "pool cue." Welcome to the labyrinth of lexicon!

Our English word *tongue* has its roots in old German, Dutch, and Norse. It seems to be a word English speakers and learners alike don't like to spell and just might confuse with *tong* and *thong*. This is evidenced by Internet images of bakeries in America with hand-lettered signs instructing customers "Please use *tongues* to pick up cookies, not your hands," and "Do not touch bread with hands, please use *tongue*," and "Please do not touch with hands. Use bread *thongs*. Thank you."

I remember well a potluck with my Spanish-speaking friends in Sacramento in which the main dishes were *lengua* prepared in three very different ways. Zheyla from Ecuador prepared her country's version of tongue, as well as a second dish of *lengua a la italiana*, stuffed with a mixture of prosciutto, olives, and garlic. Lilia's was the famous Mexican version baked with onion, garlic, bay, mint, and salt, then chopped up and served with corn tortillas, tomatillo salsa, and lots of cilantro and lime. Previous to this culinary triple revelation, I had only sampled the Basque-style pickled tongue during my formative Bakersfield years, and I remained slightly prejudiced though (if the quantity of tongue I consumed that evening is any measure) very appreciative of these new lingual experiences.

What got me thinking about all this *lengua lore* is an ancient legend from the Afro-Cuban spiritual traditions that I used for years as a reading in Spanish classes because it is a simple but powerful story that relies on the very same play of the dual meaning of *lengua* as "language" and "tongue." To conclude this chapter, here is the legend in translation as best I remember it:

> Obatalá, the supreme god of all creation, observed that his secretary, Orula, was very creative, imaginative, and

unusually wise, despite his youth. Obatalá was wondering if he could lighten some of his workload and delegate a sector of responsibility onto Orula's shoulders, but knew he had to test the youth's maturity and judgment before giving him such a big job. So, Obatalá commanded Orula to prepare him the best meal possible.

Orula, obedient and willing, went immediately to the nearby market and filled his shopping bag with a bull's tongue and all the spices and ingredients he needed for a most worthy dish. When he presented it at Obatalá's table, the appetite of the supreme leader was sated, and licking his fingers, he asked his secretary why he had chosen to prepare *lengua* as the best meal. Orula replied, "It is with the tongue that praises are sung, virtue is exalted, good works are revealed and emulated, and that *aché*, the mystical energy of the universe, is manifested."

A short while later, Obatalá instructed his secretary to prepare him the worst meal possible. Orula gave no reply but went straight to the market and again filled his shopping bag with a bull's tongue and all the accompaniments. When he served the dish and his master saw the same plate before him, Obatalá said, "How is it that you serve me the same meal as the best as well as the worst of all dishes?" Orula replied, "I told you then that it was the best, and now I tell you it is the worst because with the tongue reputations are destroyed, slander ruins lives and whole populations are lost; with the tongue, the most vile acts are committed."

Amazed and pleased at the intelligence and wisdom of his secretary, Obatalá gave Orula rule over the World.

And we've been speaking, eating, and wagging tongues ever since.

Pigments of Our Imagination

What's your favorite color? What hues make you feel energized, tranquil, optimistic, or elegant? Have you ever pored over chips at the local paint store and wondered who dreams up names like Cozy Cover, Copper Beach, Taffy Crunch, Swiss Coffee, and how much they get paid for doing this? Is there any doubt in your mind that at a traditional wedding, the bride wears white, and you should not show up in black? What color is your envy as you watch your neighbors leave for a tour of Tuscany, you waving *arrivederci* from your ladder while painting the exterior of your house *Stonegate* taupe in the August sun? Is there a color for your mood at the end of a week of Maui surf and sunsets as you fly home to face a pile of bills and the morning roll call at the office? Would you wear your green pants and red sweater to a party after the month of December has passed? What color were your "gills" on the fishing boat in the rocky bay? And when you realized what the dog did to your fine Italian leather shoes, what color did you "see"?

A single color (pink vs. blue on a baby announcement) or color combo (orange and black in the fall) communicates unmistakable meaning via our culture and conditioning. Color is a form of language. It evokes reaction, creates mood, and expresses experience. This is true all over the world, but what is evoked or expressed by the color yellow to a German might seem as foreign to us Americans as their word for the color itself: *gelb*. While most countries in the West (the United States, Canada, and Western Europe) associate yellow with optimism, warmth, and good cheer (as well as cowardice!), Italians, Germans, and French are turning yellow with envy alongside our American green. In Egypt and Burma, yellow is a color of mourning, and for the Cherokee Nation, yellow is a symbol of conflict and strife.

In Western countries, white is the color of purity, peace, safety, and health, and let's not forget that good guys used to wear white ten-gallon hats and ride white horses—"Hi-ho Silver, away!" (Heroes of the twenty-first century mostly prefer the power and intimidation of black.) Food is perceived to taste better and be fresher and healthier if served on a white plate. The bride's dress and flowers are white and so is the frosting on the wedding cake. But as we go East, while white will still suggest peace and purity, it begins to speak a very different language of sadness and mourning. In China, Japan, Korea, and other Eastern countries, white is the color of death and funerals. In India, it is traditionally the only color a widow is allowed to wear.

Red is a bold color that can suggest excitement, passion, danger, love, anger, and "Stop!" Studies show that sports teams wearing red gain a competitive advantage and that the color actually makes people stronger during competition. Western countries have red- light districts of prostitution and sex paraphernalia shops. However, if we "paint the town red," we might wake up hung over but probably just had a night of good, clean fun. In the East, red denotes good fortune, prosperity, and festivity. It's the color worn by brides in China and India, but in South Africa, it's the color of mourning. Superstition compels Spanish bullfighters to shun yellow, green, and purple, but to wear hot-pink stockings for good luck. As for the matador's red cape, all cattle are color-blind, and the bull will charge anything that's waved in his face.

America has exported "the blues" worldwide, and while the color can stand for depression and sadness, it also communicates calm, trust, and authority. American financial institutions inspire trust, suggest strength, and promise success with logos of blue. In the West, it's a masculine color (and most men's favorite); in China, it's a feminine color. And on the subject of color and the sexes, although it's almost impossible to imagine anything but pale pink for little girls and powder blue for baby boys, it was just the opposite in Belgium until recent decades.

In many countries, blue is the color for pornography, as in the now-outdated American reference to "blue movies." (In Italy, those racy movies are red.) Another bygone American expression, "to turn the air blue," meant to swear up a storm. What people used to call "blue jokes," we now just call "off-color" or "dirty." But in Spanish, it's the color green that suggests risqué behavior, so a "dirty old man" is a *viejo verde*. In Australia, if the couple next door is "having a blue," they're having a fight; and "he made a blue" means he made a mistake.

The bright red of Coca Cola's signature and Target's bull's eye suggests excitement, youth, and energy. In America, orange is a cautionary color (think road hazards) as well as one of good cheer, confidence, and approachability (Nickelodeon, Gulf Oil, and Hooters). Orange doesn't give a "hooter" about trying to be subtle or sophisticated. It's the preferred color for fast food joints and discount retailers (McDonald's, Burger King, and Payless anything). Just as McD's customizes its menu to offer McLobster rolls in New England, McZpacho chilled tomato soup in Spain, and McKastsu sandwiches in Japan, the megaretailer also adjusts its website and color strategy for specific areas of its worldwide market. While staying heavy on the red/orange/yellow color scheme, there's a celestial blue background for most of the Middle East (virtue and protection) and a green one for Europe (luck, health, and environmental awareness).

In Holland, orange is the color of the royal family (House of

Orange), and whenever the Dutch are vying for the World Cup, the entire country drapes its farmhouses and gabled buildings in bright-orange fabric. There will even be an occasional sighting of orange cows. When the big, fluffy marigolds bloom in Mexico, orange speaks of death as people celebrate *el Día de los Muertos* (The Day of the Dead) in early November.

While Americans go green with envy, the French are green with fear. With hair standing on end, an Italian might be blue with fear, but green with rage. In US print and publishing, the color yellow alerts one to sensationalist journalism rife with scandal and exaggeration. In Italian publishing, a "yellow", *un giallo,* is a detective thriller. A "white night" is a sleepless one in French, Italian, Spanish, and other Romance languages.

In my high school sewing class, Sister Mary Harrold rhapsodized about the existence of five hundred different shades of black. We were unimpressed because that, along with white, was the only color she ever got to wear, and we were just kids in uniforms dying to sport *anything* but the requisite forest-green plaid skirts and crisp, white blouses. The possible shades of blue and green could be infinite. Only fifty shades of gray? How unimaginatively dull in a world full of colors and the foreign languages they speak.

Between the Sword and the Wall

A s I started to write about this delightful but vast and slippery subject, I felt rather backed up against a wall with a sword at my throat, wild-eyed yet engaged at the prospect of a challenging duel of words between Spanish and English. Our American expression, "between a rock and a hard place," comes close, but doesn't nearly suggest the pounding heart and darting eyes conveyed by the Spanish predicament of being *entre la espada y la pared* (between the sword and the wall). Proverbs and popular expressions provide insights into the deep, cultural conditioning of attitudes and beliefs, and of course, they come and go with changing times. Thankfully, we no longer hear Spaniards spouting the order of things as, "*El hombre en la plaza y la mujer en la casa,*" (The man in the plaza and the woman at home) any more than we hear the phrase "barefoot and pregnant." Thank goodness and amen to that.

The vastness of this topic of proverbs and expressions also stems from the fact that there are twenty-one Spanish-speaking countries, each with a unique culture and individual linguistic style. You've invited all your international friends to party on your yacht in the Mediterranean for a month, and to express our approval and excitement, we say: "Cool!" (Americans), "*¡Chido!*" (Mexicans), "*¡Chévere!*" (Ecuadoreans), "*¡Regio!*" (Argentines), "*¡Guay!*" (Spaniards), "*¡Pura vida!*" (Costa Ricans), "*¡Genial!*" (Peruvians), and "*¡Enpingao!*" (Cubans). With all that spicy variety, we're going to have a grand time!

You don't have to be bilingual to appreciate the similarities and differences between English sayings and their Spanish counterparts. Some are even exactly alike, though we won't claim that one language poached and translated the expression from the other. Sometimes, the two languages say the exact same phrase. We say, "A rolling stone gathers no moss," and Spanish says, *Piedra que rueda no cría moho*; "Better late than never": *Más vale tarde que nunca*; "Love is blind": *El amor es ciego*. Tempting as word-for-word translation is, it almost never works. Try commenting to a Spanish-speaker that it's raining *gatos y perros* ("cats and dogs") and they'll think you've got "bats in the belfry," or as they might put it, *ratones en la azotea:* "rats on the roof."

When the subject of your conversation unexpectedly walks into the room, don't translate "Speak of the devil," for it is *el rey de Roma* ("the king of Rome") you were talking about. Forming a direct translation of "wet blanket" won't transmit the image of a party-pooping friend, even though there *is* "water" mixed with "party" in the term *aguafiestas*. All that said, from here on, I will translate the Spanish expressions into English as exactly as possible, even if it comes out a bit awkward, so that you can match up the words in the two languages.

There are sayings that carry basically the same elements, but include slight differences that might raise our eyebrows. "A bird in the hand is worth two in the bush": *Pájaro en mano vale cien volando* / "A bird in the hand is worth a hundred flying." In a rash act, he "jumped out of the frying pan and into the fire," but the Spanish speaker says some variation of, *Por huir del fuego, dio en las brasas* / "Fleeing the fire, he fell into the hot coals." Another way to say, "To go from bad to worse" is *Salir de* (to leave*) Guatemala para entrar en Guatepeor*, not complimentary to that country, but clever word play, switching out *mala* (bad) for *peor* (worse). In Spanish, you're not "pulling my leg," you're "pulling my hair": *Me estás tomando el pelo*.

It gets fun and colorful when the expression communicates basically the same idea but with totally different imagery. We have the boring old adage, "Silence is golden," but Spanish instructs that *En boca cerrada no entra mosca* / "In a closed mouth, the fly doesn't enter." We attempt to brighten a difficult time by saying, "Let's make the best of it" or "Every cloud has a silver lining," but I am far better cheered by the Spanish saying, *Ya que la casa se quema, calentémonos* / "Since the house is burning down, let's warm ourselves up." Talk about black(ened) humor!

One of my mom's favorite retorts to my missteps has always been, "It serves you right!" The *mamá* of another land might say, *Quien con perros se acuesta, con pulgas se levanta* / "One who lies down with dogs, gets up with fleas." That certainly offers more color if not more consolation. Another of mom's favorites in my childhood, "Go fly a kite" is *Vete a freír espárragos* / "Go fry asparagus." "To each his own" (with a roll of the eyes) is the beloved expression in Spanish, *Cada loco con su tema* / "Every nutcase with his theme." That reminds me of one of my forever favorites that hasn't a match in English: *De médico, poeta, y loco todos tenemos un poco* / "Of doctor, poet, and nutcase, we all have a little." That's a simple philosophy about the human condition that probably hold true for all.

This next one is very Mexican with its reference to the famous dish called *mole*. If something is "a dime a dozen," they might say *Es ajonjolí de todos los moles* / "It's the sesame in every mole." While we "sweat bullets," someone somewhere farther South will "sweat ink" / *sudar tinta*. We might be left "holding the bag," but pity the unlucky guy who has "to carry the cadaver"/ *cargar con el muerto*. What costs me "an arm and a leg," to Lupe will extract *un ojo de la cara* / "an eye from the face." Big decision to make? Time to *consultar con la almohada* / "consult the pillow" while you "sleep on it."

I love the facile rhythm and rhyme of some Spanish sayings. To be "two-faced" is to have *cara de beato y uñas de gato* / "face of piety and claws of a cat." "You snooze, you lose": *Camarón que se duerme, se lo lleva la corriente* / "Shrimp that falls asleep gets carried away by the current." "Look before you leap": *Antes que te cases, mira lo que haces/* "Before you get married, watch what you're doing." "You can't make a silk purse out of a sow's ear": *Aunque la mona se viste de seda, mona se queda/* "Even if the monkey is dressed in silk, it's still a monkey."

Two more favorites: "A horse of a different color" is *Harina de otro costal /* "Flour from a different sack." "To run off at the mouth" is *Hablar por los codos* / "To talk through your elbows." (Do you get that one? Neither do I, but it's said without regard to logic.)

I've found that the fastest way to extricate myself when I'm "between a rock and a hard place"/ *entre la espada y la pared,* is "not to have hairs on my tongue"/ *no tener pelos en la lengua,* that is, to "speak my mind truthfully." If talking my way out fails, I might have to *echar la capa al toro* / "throw the cape at the bull" in a last-ditch effort to get out of those proverbial *calzas prietas /* "tight britches" or "hot water" as we know it all too well this side of the Atlantic and the Rio Grande.

The Language Police

In a previous title or two, I have mentioned the "Grammar Powers That Be in America" (GPTBiA) with tongue-in-cheek yet half expecting that some wise English professor will descend from the ivory tower of a prestigious university to enlighten me that *of course* there is a language police for English: some single body of sage grammarians and lexical heavyweights to adjudicate the dangling of prepositions and splitting of infinitives, to definitively establish the true meaning of a "bromance," and if "selfie stick" is hyphenated. But said professor has not materialized, and the only thing my research has definitively established is that no such organization exists for English either in America or the UK. So the question remains: Who/What/Where is the mysterious power over our language that gave us the green light to tag a preposition to the end of the sentence after centuries of torturing us into repeating, "This is the moment *for which* I have been waiting," and, "*With whom* are you going to the prom?"

In the United States, there simply isn't an officially recognized authority invested with decision-making powers over grammar and the lexicon. So where in the world *is* there such a thing? Spain has The Royal Academy of the Spanish Language, which was founded in 1713 and has followed the same motto for over three centuries: *Limpia, fija, y da esplendor*. My best loose translation of that charge is: "Keep it clean, regulate it, and make it shine." Today, there are twenty-two branches of the Real Academia Española (RAE) sworn to maintain the legacy and integrity of Spanish: the mother academy in Spain, one for each of the other twenty Spanish-speaking countries of the world, and one for the

Spanish spoken by an additional forty million or so people in the United States. Of course, there are dialectical differences between the Spanish of Peru and that of Cuba, and between the pronunciation and some of the vocabulary of Equatorial Guinea (an officially Spanish-speaking country on the West Coast of Africa) and that of Argentina. Despite regional variations, populations of all twenty-one countries plus the United States can intercommunicate pretty darn well with only minor glitches.

Glitch sample A: a *guagua* is a toddler in most of South America, but in Cuba and the Canary Islands, it's a bus. That could be a deal breaker in romantic communication for the Cuban suitor boasting to his *novia* (fiancée) about his fleet of a half-dozen *guaguas* when she understands him to be the father of six toddlers.

Glitch sample B: In most countries, you can use the handy verb *coger* to "catch or grab something": *coger un taxi*; *coger un resfrío* (catch a cold), but don't utter that verb in Mexico or Argentina where it's a sexual vulgarity, for you'll scandalize your listeners, or at least give them a good laugh after the shock wears off.

This intercommunication in Spanish among twenty-one countries and the United States is unique and remarkable especially when we consider that in many countries of the world, linguistic differences are so radical as to prevent communication altogether. In Germany, which is slightly smaller than the state of Montana but boasts as many as 250 different dialects, folks from one area can't *sprechen* with those from another region reliably at all. China, with an area slightly smaller than that of the United States, has 297 *living* languages according to *Ethnologue*; and just for the record, India has 122 major languages and 1599 others.

In the United States, there *is* regulation of Spanish (by the RAE), Yiddish (by the YIVO Institute for Jewish Research), and Cherokee (by the Council of the Cherokee Nation), but neither the United Kingdom nor America has any official say over English worldwide. The only English-speaking country in the world with a language academy is South Africa.

According to *Wikipedia*'s list of language regulators, there are 130 organizations, as the three mentioned in the above paragraph, which exert control over 110 languages in 187 countries and regions. Do they rule with an iron fist? A jerk of the chain? A wave of the hand? A shrug of the shoulders? I won't accept that vast research assignment unless it comes with a limitless travel budget, but we'll at least look into some of the recent regulatory activities in Italy, France, and Spain.

The highly respected Dante Alighieri Society, promoter/protector of Italian language and culture, has "asked" Italians to stop using so many English words when a perfectly good one in their own language will suffice. However, for the most part, Italians continue to look forward to *il weekend* as a time to relieve *lo stress*. And that's just during their free time! In the workplace, *Anglitaliano* has become so ingrained that one might assume no business could be transacted without English words: *Il manager italiano* deals with *il marketing, lo staff, il brand,* and *la competition*. Daily *multitasking è un must!* I have studied at the Dante Alighieri Institute in Siena, Italy and deeply admire their mission and dedication, but can they win the battle against ever-more English creeping into Italian? È impossibile!

The French are determined and heavy-handed. They have done more than "ask." They have *outlawed* the use of terms like "e-mail" and "hashtag" in official documents and decreed they must be expressed as *courriel* and *mot-dièse*, respectively. The Académie Française is a powerful council of the French government that rules on all matters linguistic and rails against the sullying of the language with English words. The Académie and the French

Ministry of Culture continue to resist the invasion of *le weekend,* "blog," "Twitter/tweet," "e-book," "parking," "chewing gum," and dozens more. The rejection of many terms like "fast-food" and "binge drinking" is every bit as sociocultural as it is linguistic.

In Spain, the RAE has declared war on the gratuitous use of English words in advertising that the purchasing public perceives as sounding more powerful, beautiful, sexy, valuable, affluent—you get the idea—than their native Spanish. The anti-English-in-advertising ad campaign created to appeal to women shows a come-hither beauty with flowing blond hair moving provocatively as she holds a pink rosebud against her cheek. In the background, a sultry female voice in Spanish promises, "new fragrance, new woman," sensually repeating the name of the perfume, "Swine." In a follow-up commercial, the same model again gyrates in slow motion, the disembodied voice returns with her sexy Spanish whisper, now revealing to audiences, "Swine, the perfume whose name in English tells you that you smell like a pig, but since it was in English, you smelled like Swine: a fragrance of pigs that penetrates your dreams. It sounds very good, but it smells very bad." In the final scene, she's in the arms of Mr. tall-dark-handsome, and they are looking at each other with knitted brows as the realization of the stink they're in begins to dawn.

There is a second ad for men also designed to combat the tsunami of English words in Spanish publicity: After donning a pair of dark glasses called "Sunset Style with Blind Effect," the debonair man in the elegant black suit proceeds to knock over the chess game and crash into a room divider while the suave, male voice purrs in Spanish, "The only glasses that don't allow you to see anything. Dark, like all the words in English, put there just so you can hear them in English. Did you see that clearly, 'great man'? It sounds good, but you can't see a thing."

This campaign was launched in May of 2016 and, as of this writing, there has been no report on the reaction of the Spanish purchasing public or any change of linguistic direction on the part of advertising agencies. The tone of both ads seems almost intentionally hokey, and it may be just that dash of corny over the veneer of elegance and beauty that captures imaginations and creates two viral cult classics. Obviously, the RAE has put not just mouth but a lot of money into these productions. Being somewhat of a linguistic purist myself, I admire the organization's passion and commitment to maintaining the integrity of the language. They might be successful in diminishing the use of English words in Spanish ads (*disappearing* is out of the question), but I won't bet on it. With the world's embrace of English growing ever larger, that would be like going to a bullfight in Madrid and betting on the poor *toro* coming out alive.

At the beginning of the eighteenth century, Jonathan Swift of *Gulliver's Travels* fame proposed establishing an academy of the English language in Great Britain because, in his words, "our Language is extremely imperfect...its daily Improvements are by no means in proportion to its daily Corruptions (and) in many Instances it offends against every Part of Grammar." The idea died with the demise of Queen Anne, his most enthusiastic and influential supporter. In the following century, a bill to establish a national academy of American English was unsuccessfully introduced into the US Congress in 1806. In 1820, the American Academy of Language and Belles Lettres was launched with John Quincy Adams as president, but it failed in short order after receiving little support from the government or the American people.

It's unlikely we'll see another attempt at the formation of an English language policing agency any time soon. I believe that's a good thing because English is a world language, and the fact that it now has more non-native speakers than native speakers will make for even greater absorption of outside influences. The American dialect in particular is so embracing of foreign words and welcoming to trendy inventions that it seems destined to continue its wild romp along the linguistic trail, and would not respond well (or probably at all) to a heavy hand that tried to rein it in.

Rum and Revolution, Part I

M arch 22, 2015. It was my last day in Cuba, and I was savoring every step of a solo walk around Old Havana when I locked eyes with a skinny, wizened old man savoring a magic moment of his own as he pulled deeply on a fat, six-inch cigar. He regarded me with a twinkling gaze as he blew out the smoke—unhurriedly, obviously savoring that phase of the breath as well. *"¿Canadiense?"* When I shook my head and said, *"Norteamericana,"* he snatched the cigar from his lips, threw his arms straight up to the sky, and did a happy dance right there in the street. I couldn't help but do the same! Tourism (especially from Europe and Canada) has been under development as the golden egg of the economy since the collapse of the Soviet Union in 1991. Cubans would naturally assume we were Canadians, but when they found out we were Americans, they would be invariably welcoming and curious.

The group I signed on with was organized through the junior college in Santa Rosa, California and sponsored by Global Exchange, an international human rights organization dedicated to promoting social, economic, and environmental justice around the world. Our official mission was the study of Cuban nature and culture—quite flexible, but still structured to comply with US law. Our group had several people-to-people meetings scheduled for us that were informative, warmly personal, and mostly satisfying, each in its own way. I give the trip A+, not for the comforts, cuisine, or amenities but because of everything I experienced and learned; everything that challenged, delighted, or worried me; and every person that I got to meet along the way. We traveled by tour bus (twenty of us mostly from Northern California) with our dependable driver, Boris, and superb guide, Tatiana. Their names were a surprise, but she told us that with the profound Russian influence in Cuba prior to 1991, it was trendy to give children Russian names. So, it's not uncommon to find people of a certain age with names like Vladimir Moreno, Natasha Álvarez, Svetlana Valdez, and so on.

The Revolution is still alive and well in Cuba, though given the shambles of the economy, it seems undeniable the Communist experiment has failed in the most fundamental ways. On February 23, 2015, a month before we left, the *Associated Press* reported that 150 to 200 dissidents had just been imprisoned in Cuba. The timing seemed dreadful given that in January, Obama called upon Congress to lift the embargo and travel restrictions. I had a feeling there was a back story but wasn't able to dig it up before departing. Neither our very knowledgeable guide nor any other Cuban I talked to had heard about what had been reported in worldwide press as an obvious violation of human rights. At a meeting with an international relations official of ICAP (The Cuban Institute for Friendship Among Peoples), she knew nothing about it either but assured us that nobody is ever arrested for speaking out against the government, though if they commit subversive or criminal acts, then they will be imprisoned. Knowing that a few dozen of the arrested dissidents were women who regularly demonstrate against the government by marching in Havana, I had to wonder about the revolution's definition of "subversive and criminal acts."

It was already dark when we arrived at the appointed hour to a very small rural town called Polvo Rojo (Red Dust) for their monthly assembly of the Committee for the Defense of the Revolution. I was expecting a political meeting of sorts, perhaps with militant exhortations of the kind Fidel Castro made famous in his hours-long speeches. We learned from Tatiana and our group organizer from Santa Rosa JC, Professor Gino Muzzatti, that every community has such a *comité* as the guardian of the social order at the local level. One website I checked says these committees are charged by the regime to promote social welfare and report on counterrevolutionary activity; that they are, in effect, the "eyes and ears of the Revolution." In this case and throughout the entire evening, not a revolutionary word was spoken. The whole town had turned out with a big table of food in the middle of the road and salsa music provided by two boombox deejays on a nearby front porch. We added our contribution of several bottles of rum, and everyone proceeded to meet and mingle, eat and drink, dance and make memories into the night at this rural Cuban block party.

The teachers at the elementary school where we spent an afternoon said they had never been visited by an American group before. That meant the kids were seeing their very first Americans, and I couldn't but wonder if they had been worried we might be brutes with horns and surprised that we looked so *normal*, smiled a lot, and applauded their performance with genuine enthusiasm. One classroom had ten computers, but only two still worked because repairs and replacement were not an option. The children sang patriotic songs for us, including "Guantanamera" (from the poetry of the Cuban national hero, José Martí), and a homage to the national hero, Che Guevara. Afterwards they presented us with their drawings and poems. One little boy, shy and proud with shining eyes, gave me a big blue origami bird. It was a sweet and satisfying afternoon, and the whole experience will always stay in my heart.

We passed a slow-motion afternoon in the colonial city of Trinidad, a UNESCO World Heritage Site in central Cuba, its charming cobblestone streets and pastel-colored houses built on the eighteenth- and nineteenth-century commerce of sugar and slaves. Then there were three days in a mountain reserve called Topes de Collante where we took nature walks (including deep into a cave), met and talked with locals, bought coffee beans, and of course, as with everywhere we went, got to hear salsa music. How can you hear that beat and not *move* to it? My fellow traveler and good friend, Titus, had been taking salsa lessons in Santa Rosa, so we had fun dancing together on a few occasions. At our hotel in Topes, the talented Trio Tradicional was playing to just a few of us in the lobby, and I grabbed my three minutes of fame and adulation when I got up the nerve to take to the microphone and sing along to the old Cuban standard, "Quizás, quizás, quizás."

In Santa Clara, we visited the memorial where the remains of Che Guevara and twenty-nine of his *guerrilleros* were sealed in vaults after being returned from Bolivia where they had been killed in 1967 while fomenting armed revolution. The museum with photographs of Che and company in the Cuban Revolution against the Batista government in Cuba and in the Bolivia campaign, plus the display of documents and personal belongings, moved and fascinated me. Che remains the most romantic, dashing, and saleable icon of the Revolution. Countless books about him are for sale on every plaza, and his is the most frequent image on postcards, billboards, and refrigerator magnets. Of course, there are huge images of Fidel Castro everywhere, too, accompanied by his best-known revolutionary pronouncements. After the Che mausoleum, we met with families at a nearby cooperative farm who had laid out a bounty of almost surrealistically huge and colorful fruits and vegetables from their harvest for us to feast on with eyes and palates. As with everyone else we encountered, they welcomed our presence and encouraged the dialogue.

Many of my friends thought I would see all of Cuba from East to West, but if we had set out to do that, in ten days we would hardly have had time to leave the bus! Cuba is approximately the same length as California, but since it's an island, one tends to assume you can drive around it in a day. It is the largest country in the Caribbean and includes over four thousand smaller islands and "keys", *cayos* in Spanish. During two days at a resort in Cayo Santa Maria on the Atlantic Ocean, we basked on an exquisite beach of fine white sand and crystal turquoise waters. That made up for the fact that the resort was huge, all-inclusive, and packed with Europeans and Canadians on package holidays. Though it was fun to take in a little glitz, mojito in hand, I was happy to leave that scene and head back to the *real* Cuba for our last three days in Havana.

It's a long bus ride, so here is a lexical note as we bounce down the highway: How did Ernesto Guevara come to be known as "Che"? If you saw *Motorcycle Diaries* (highly recommended) you'll remember that he was originally from Argentina where *che* is the most frequent word they utter. It's untranslatable but kind of like "look"/ "hey"/ "dude"/ "wow"/ "like"/ "y'know" at the beginning of a sentence to get the listener's attention and also might pop up elsewhere as a filler word ("so, well, uhm..."). Hearing him say "che" a hundred times a day, how could his non-Argentine pals have called him anything but?

Turn the page for adventures in Havana, crumbling architecture, reflections on the economy (a 30-cent taxi ride and a $4000 lobster dinner), and those fabulous old cars. *Hasta pronto...*

Rum and Revolution, Part II

The streets of La Habana (lah-BAH-nah) were full of rickety bicycle cabs, the occasional farm animal burdened with produce, and really old cars—a few of them cherry, but most wearing every rip, dent, and wrinkle of their fifty-plus years. We had to pinch ourselves to remember it was 2015. Marcos, my Cuban friend back home, said when you look under the hood of one of these pre-Revolution relics, you not only won't see original equipment, but most of what's there won't even be an actual car part!

Before my trip, I bought *A Quick Guide to Cuban Spanish* and even had Marcos come over to practice some of the slang with me. When I told him I didn't anticipate trouble understanding Cuban pronunciation, he just smiled, rolled his eyes, then set me straight. As he had predicted, when people were speaking directly to me, I could understand everything, but to capture even the gist of a conversation between two Cubans—forget it! They break all speed records of speech, and I would have needed that entire book of Cuban slang committed to instant recall memory to even catch the drift.

It's well known that in Cuban Spanish, the *s* isn't pronounced in some positions, especially at the end of a word. So while I am still "Susanna," Marcos is *Marcoh* when he visits his family and friends. *Los amigos* comes out as *loh amigoh* in Cuba and other parts of the Caribbean. This isn't likely to inhibit understanding, but I had to giggle when the speaker from the Ministry of Science and Environment was talking to us about *pescadores* (fisherman) but, with the first *s* disappeared, kept referring to *pecadores* (sinners)—a welcome moment of lexical levity in an otherwise dry discourse.

Well-known architect and professor at the University of Havana, Miguel Coyula, was very young when dictator Fulgencio Batista escaped with his life and a ton of money as Fidel Castro and the revolutionaries took power on January 1, 1959. Under the new Socialist order, housing as a business was declared illegal. Everyone was allowed to move into houses and apartments that had been abandoned by Batista supporters fleeing the country, but no one could own an apartment building or charge rent to others. A space that used to house one family was now occupied by several. My understanding is that people would pay rent to the government for a period of time and then be declared the owner of whatever they called "home." However, in the absence of landlords, nobody was responsible for repairs and maintenance. All over Havana, we saw crumbling, overcrowded, filthy-looking buildings alongside lovingly tended residences and many buildings of great architectural beauty. The most shocking thing Mr. Coyula told us is that 3.1 buildings a day collapse in Havana. He didn't address the personal cost in sudden homelessness, to say nothing of injury and death, but one can only imagine!

Despite seediness, power outages, and shortages of what you and I consider essential, La Habana seduces with vibrant flavors, colors, and rhythms that lead you through winding streets and keep you turning yet another corner to discover more. I knew three nights would not be enough to even scratch the surface. Yet my experience of the city was especially memorable because I was able to meet Marcos's cousin, Jorge, and see Old Havana through his eyes, and view the economy from his perspective.

What is accessible to a tourist and what a Cuban can afford are so far apart the mind can hardly compute. Some actual figures, given in dollar equivalents, will illustrate what I mean. A Cuban professional makes the equivalent of $20 a month. (Doctors' salaries were recently doubled to around $40.) University education under the Castro regime has always been free and used to be accessible to everyone, but now applicants must pass entrance exams. The country's twenty-five universities continue to turn out massive numbers of doctors, lawyers, architects, teachers, and so on. These waves of newly minted professionals face a big challenge to find a job in the first place and then to live on the meager salary once they do. I spoke with Cubans working in restaurants and hotels or selling crafts in the plazas who had given up their professions to work in tourism for a better living. I'll wager that even a hotel maid can finish out the month with more than $20 in wages and tips combined.

Jorge and I made plans to have dinner in Old Havana at the restaurant where our group had eaten the night before because the food was great, the prices very reasonable, and it didn't seem touristy. At $12.50, the most expensive item on the menu was the divine "Trio" of lobster, shrimp, and octopus, which I recommended to Jorge. Add to that a glass of wine, a *cafecito*, and a tip, and one diner has just spent the whole month's Cuban salary. Granted, I paid the bill, but can you imagine spending your month's income on a single meal? Picture yourself sitting down to a $4000 "Trio" with a glass of wine and a coffee. Feeling the impact of this economic disparity, you're probably choking on that lobster.

Unlike ten to twenty years ago, Cubans can now frequent any restaurant or hotel in their country, but it's mostly moot because, for someone paid in Cuban pesos, these places might as well be on another planet. The next night, fellow traveler Titus and I walked for hours with Jorge along the sea wall, the Malecón, Havana's favorite 'round-the-clock hangout. At midnight, we unanimously opted to have a taxi take us back to our hotel and then take Jorge on to his suburb. It didn't even occur to Titus and me that there was an alternative to the tourist taxis we'd already taken around town and we started waving our arms at the passing traffic. But Jorge was adamant: it was unthinkable to pay the exorbitant $7 fare. We walked four blocks inland to a busy corner where loaded taxis—very beat-up '40s and '50s vintage cars—were whizzing in both directions. One stopped to let off three of its five passengers and we hopped into the back seat. It cost ten Cuban pesos per person (about 30 cents) to go anywhere in the city. That's dirt cheap for us Americans, but still an extravagance for a Cuban making a maximum of $20 a month.

Toward the beginning of the trip, we arrived at a rural hotel only to be unexpectedly switched to inferior lodgings with torn curtains and crumbling cinder blocks, "basic" at best. In our first two hotels, I could only get vaguely lukewarm water in the shower. Vegetables served in restaurants were almost always overcooked and often canned. In moments of disappointment or frustration, as well as celebration, our ebullient group organizer from Santa Rosa JC, Professor Gino Muzzatti, would prescribe a dose of vitamin R: Cuban rum, preferably Havana Club, aged 7-15 years.

Our Cuban guide for Global Exchange, the delightful Tatiana with the unforgettable smile, taught us the principle of TIC: "This is Cuba (and that's just the way it is)." She said Cubans have a way of laughing and making jokes about reversals, shortages, and loss, not out of optimism but as a survival mechanism. They live with such daily hardship over aspects and objects of life we in the United States take so completely for granted, that cheer and a chuckle in the moment may be the only thing between them and despair. That discussion put torn curtains and soggy vegetables into perspective.

Many Cubans I spoke with were excited and optimistic about their future without the embargo and travel restrictions against Americans, and hoped to better their economic lot as a result. Some were proactively converting part of their residences into B&Bs or planning other ways to profit from the increase in tourism from the United States. Everyone was waiting for the influx of products to the island, from essential medicines to luxury electronics. It could be a long wait. Legislation holds the US trade embargo in place, and that alone could take years to untangle. Congress must vote to lift the embargo, and the Republican Party remains strongly anti-Castro.

Progress was made in April of 2015 when Presidents Raúl Castro and Barack Obama met at the Summit of the Americas in Panama City. Three days later, Obama announced that Cuba will no longer be on the United States list of nations that sponsor terrorism. In December of 2015, the two governments reached an agreement to allow commercial airline service between the US and Cuba. In May of 2016, the *Adonia* docked in Havana, the first American cruise ship to do so in fifty years.

At this writing, according to US law citizens still cannot travel freely to Cuba for vacation or sight-seeing. They must provide a clear motive that falls acceptably within the government's twelve authorized reasons for permission to travel to Cuba. The authorized areas include family visits, sanctioned academic programs, professional research or journalism, official religious activities, and participation in artistic performances or athletic competitions. (See the full list of permissible capacities in References.)

When the embargo and travel restrictions are finally and completely lifted, may there be more positive outcomes than negative ones, and may the resistance to widespread "Starbucksification" and "Walmartizing" in the consumer sector stand firm. I'm no economist, but it seems to me that no matter how many new things there are to buy, $20 a month won't stretch any further than it already does. The Socialist government is subsidizing everything, including salaries, and isn't likely to be giving significant raises. And won't a huge increase in American tourism drive the prices in restaurants, shops, and hotels even higher and further out of reach for the average Cuban?

Tens of thousands of Cubans have decided not to wait around for the answers or invest any more years hoping their economic lot will improve. Forty-five thousand left the island in 2015, most making their way to the United States via other Latin American countries. The estimates for the 2016 exodus are even higher. The great majority are young people looking for a future and willing to leave behind their beautiful island and beloved culture because life there is simply too hard and the dream of real progress too hopelessly distant in their lifetime.

In 1995, the two countries negotiated migration agreements stating that the U.S. will accept up to 20,000 legal immigrants a year, and return to Cuba those attempting to enter illegally by boat. A year later, the United States took a unilateral leap, permitting all Cubans who arrive to the country to remain for a year under a status called *parole*, and then be eligible to apply for permanent residency. There can be no doubt that the stampede of Cubans taking flights out of Havana and then traveling for weeks by land and over water through various parts of Latin America to reach American soil is fueled by fears that warming relations with their country will prompt the United States to close those generous open arms which still beckon to Cubans, but do not extend the same largesse to any other nationality of the world.

CHAPTER FIVE

The Wonders of the Bilingual Brain

Riding the Silver Tsunami

Baby Boomers grab your surfboards! We'll see what being bilingual can do for aging brains, and find out some good news about regenerating neurons, self-repairing dendrites, and 100 ways to protect against Alzheimer's.

The Best Brain Elixir

What are London cab drivers and some Swedish military recruits doing to grow bigger brains? Do infants remember sounds they heard in the womb? Why do some children show accelerated development of problem-solving skills, reasoning, focus, and memory?

The Baby Brain Bloom

The benefits of bilingualism accrue throughout life and it's never too late to start learning a foreign language. Of course, considering that a baby at birth can distinguish all 800 sounds of the world's 6500 languages, the earlier the better!

The Tongue May Falter, But the Brain Purrs

You took language in high school and now you've "forgotten everything." Is that possible? Here's the secret to where it is and how you can get it back, plus, the four big myths about learning a foreign language—revealed and debunked!

The Job Seeker's Competitive Edge

What is the single most overlooked job skill—overlooked and underrated by the applicant, but avidly sought by the employer? Here's how to capitalize on it and earn up to 20% more over the course of your working life.

Riding the Silver Tsunami

I will not be coy with you, dear reader. This is about Alzheimer's disease, and although there is very good news herein, some of what you'll have to read to get there is not pretty. Fascinating, yes, just not pretty. The lack of photos and pie charts on these pages is a plus because you'll be using your imagination, and that in itself is excellent anti-Alzheimer's exercise.

For starters, picture the holes in a chunk of Swiss cheese. A slice of Alzheimer's brain actually does look like a piece of Swiss, with gaps in the tissue caused by (in highly simplified language that this author can understand) abnormal deposits of neural "gunk" that prevent neurons from transmitting and receiving messages and eventually triggering an autoimmune attack on the brain itself. Assailed by inflammation, neurons die, holes form, the brain shrinks, and the outward manifestations of the disease increasingly express: inability to remember, think clearly, compute, recognize loved ones, manage emotions, and live independently. This degenerative pattern has become all too familiar as we and our friends care for aging loved ones.

We're still on this page together, so let's take an early reward in the form of some good news. The lifelong prognosis for humans, though still ending in death, is not nearly as bad as most of us grew up thinking it was. Until very recently, science firmly held that brain cells could not regenerate. Do you remember the sinking feeling that came with that "knowledge"? Now what researchers have discovered is that new neurons are continually being added to the cerebral cortex, the brain center responsible for learning and higher decision making. What a welcome revelation! The brain *can* grow new cells and repair itself, and there *is* hope for future effective treatment of brain disorders and injuries. But for now, while a good orthopedic surgeon and about $3 of titanium can give you a new knee or replace a hip, partial- or full-brain transplant is not an option, and we are best served to dedicate ourselves to coddling—not curdling—the one we've got.

Engage your long-term memory once again and recall your high school or college biology class in which you learned that the average adult brain has some one hundred billion neurons. Some of you might also remember making mental review of the "fact" that each shot of alcohol kills about a million brain cells, and then doing the math at the end of a particularly wild weekend.

More good news: In 1993, scientists making cell counts of alcoholic vs. nonalcoholic brains had to conclude it just isn't so. Yes, large amounts of alcohol *do* impair the brain, though not by killing cells but rather by damaging the dendrites, those branched extensions at the end of the cells, thus inhibiting neurons' ability to communicate with each other, causing loss of coordination, garbled speech, and scrambled thoughts. Even though dendrites can self-repair, it's still not advisable to pour a martini, light up a smoke, and camp on the couch, confident that genius scientists and profit-motivated drug companies will soon produce the magic pill or potion to disappear the plaque that causes the Swiss-cheese effect.

Before we get to the best news of all, let's first investigate the numbers because all of us, whether we're the surfers on the so-called silver tsunami of aging baby boomers or young, buff bystanders on the beach, will see our lives affected in some way by Alzheimer's. Many of the seventy-six million boomers (defined as babies born post-WWII between 1945 and 1964) have already turned sixty-five, the age after which most cases of the disease begin to manifest. The Alzheimer's Foundation reports one in nine people sixty-five and older (11 percent) has Alzheimer's disease. Today's count of nearly five and a half million sufferers could explode to fourteen million by 2050 when the number of senior citizens will have doubled in the United States. Imagine the traumatic impact that will have on families, nursing homes, and the Medicare budget.

How to turn the tide? Neuron by neuron, one brain at a time. A friend recently recommended a book entitled *100 Simple Things You Can Do to Prevent Alzheimer's* by Jean Carper. Her search for simple but scientifically-backed ways to do what the title says was motivated by the discovery that she is among the 25 percent of Americans who carry the ApoE4 gene, making them more susceptible to Alzheimer's. Realizing that this means *vulnerable* but not *condemned*, she applied herself to devising a game plan and probably created a billion or so new neurons in the process. Here are titles of some of her one hundred, very readable, two-page chapters:

"Be a Busy Body"
"Say Yes to Coffee,"
"Grow a Bigger Brain"
"Eat a Low-Glycemic Diet"
"Check Out Your Ankle"
"Learn to Love Language"

Given as I am to loving language and promoting bilingualism, I am drawn to this topic in the first place because of how the manipulation of words and language enhances the brain, strengthening the structures and processes that will keep it firing fresh and fast for the rest of your life. Carper exhorts, "...read widely and write extensively to express your thoughts," and states that "handling more than one language constantly exercises and strengthens the brain." Every list of anti-Alzheimer's strategies gives high ranking to learning another language, and if you've ever tackled one, you have firsthand experience of why this it so. You can almost feel those neurons pushing out their little dendrite branches as your brain, forced to reject its easy path to the English word "neighbor," darts down endless corridors and turns away from numerous fruitless dead ends in the mind-maze before it finally produces—Eureka!—the Spanish equivalent, *vecino*. It's a beautiful and wondrous process and a highly frustrating one if you are that struggling foreign language learner.

The case for learning a foreign language is compelling. Scientists using MRI technology examined the brains of people who were studying foreign languages and those of others who were studying non-language subjects with equal dedication. Scans showed increased brain size in certain areas (posterior hippocampus and cerebral cortex) among the language students but not in the brains of the control group. Studies have established that speakers of more than one language score higher on academic tests in both math and reading, and they are better able to tune into their surroundings and focus on important facts. Do you have to speak your second language fluently in order to reap the brain benefits? My decades of experience teaching foreign language to English-speaking adults tell me your cerebral cylinders might be firing even more enthusiastically if you're struggling.

Since I dedicate my professional life to helping people become bilingual, I want to come back to the subject of frustration that we touched on briefly in the previous paragraph. For the vast majority of us, frustration is simply an unavoidable and permanent feature of speaking a language that you weren't born into. Yes, I am saying that frustration will *always* be a part of your bilingual experience in varying degrees of intensity. Once accepted, that's actually great news, because now you know to embrace it, dance with it, live and breathe it—do anything except fight it. Remember, too, as we've already seen, dealing with unfamiliar challenges is all part of the brain's healthy and regenerative impetus toward new neural production.

If you *are* bilingual, become even more so by honing your reading and writing skills. If you dream of speaking a second language, you've put it off long enough in the hopes of finding the "right time." Just start now already. The brain loves big challenges, fruitful frustrations, and bold new beginnings.

The Best Brain Elixir

D id someone say "brain elixir"? Let's make it something we can drink, especially if it tastes like piña colada. Or eat, preferably with the flavor and texture of fine, dark chocolate. Lacking that, at least give it to us in pill form because this is, after all, twenty-first-century America where we expect things to be fast, effortless, and effective. No pill? Okay, then, how about a surgical procedure? You know—risk-free, quick recovery, and lift this saggy jowl while you're at it.

Actually, there are many substances we can drink, eat, and pop that might benefit the brain. Ginseng is tops among several herbs said to improve memory and mental performance. Gingko biloba is another, known as the memory booster, and widely used in Europe to treat dementia. The list of "brain foods" tacked to your refrigerator door probably includes blueberries, wild salmon, avocados, nuts and seeds, leafy greens, whole grains, and yes, dark chocolate. (Finally, a guilt-free obsession!) It could be that coffee and tea can not only improve mood but also memory and general cognitive function as well. There's wheat grass versus brain fog, pomegranate juice versus forgetfulness, and of course, exercise as one of the very best, as well as cheapest and most accessible, ways to maintain brain health into old age. Studies show that people who walk just five miles a week increase their brain volume and show less development of Alzheimer's and other forms of dementia. Along with that green light for dark chocolate, here's a welcome piece of news for aging knees: Some studies indicate that brisk walking is preferable to heavy aerobic exercise.

The subject of growing a bigger brain captured my attention

when I read a BBC report about a scientific study of the brain size of London cab drivers. Interns undergo three to four years of intensive training and then take a test of the accuracy of their mental map of the city's twenty-five thousand streets and thousands of landmarks, and their ability to quickly calculate routes and avoid jams. Only about half of them pass to become taxi drivers in one of the world's busiest cities and craziest street grids. In each one of the individuals in the test group, MRI imaging showed that a specific part of the brain, the posterior hippocampus, had grown remarkably and continued to develop as the cab driver spent hours each day behind the wheel mentally mapping the quickest route between two points.

There was another recent landmark study in Sweden using recruits in the Swedish Armed Forces Interpreter Academy who were tested before and after a three-month period of intensive foreign language study. Compared to the control group, the language students showed growth in the hippocampus as well as in three areas of the cerebral cortex. Since the hippocampus is responsible for learning new material and spatial navigation, and the cerebral cortex is related to language learning, the findings in both studies seem logical in retrospect, but it is stunning to realize that the brain actually behaves like a muscle, increasing in size and strength with mental exercise.

Let's focus closer on foreign language learning and bilingualism, and go deeper and further into the past. In fact, let's go all the way back before birth, into the womb. In years past, science assumed that a baby was born as *tabula rasa*, a "clean slate," able to be imprinted and to begin to learn only *after* birth. More recent studies overwhelmingly demonstrate that at least during the last three months of pregnancy, unborn babies are tasting, smelling, and feeling their way around, perhaps seeing changes in light, and for sure hearing, remembering, and responding to sounds, espe-cially those of Mom's voice vibrating into her body from her vocal cords as well as passing through her abdomen into the womb.

Testing of newborns' brain waves showed that they recognized an invented word, *tatata*, which had been recorded and played to them thousands of times in the last trimester of pregnancy. An early study showed that the theme song of Mom's favorite soap opera was imprinted on her newborn's brain. Moms-to-be started putting headphones on their bumps to play Mozart, Berlitz language courses, and recordings of *The Great Books*, but the medical field says this amplification is *too much noise* and could actually be unhealthy overstimulation to the fetus's developing organs.

There is no longer any doubt that language *is* imprinted on the fetal brain, and landmark studies counting the frequency and speed of sucks on a pacifier connected to a recording show that babies in their first day of life outside the womb can distinguish between Mom's voice and an unfamiliar female voice. Amazingly and within minutes, they adapted their sucking pattern to connect with the sound of their own mother's voice. Pacifier experiments also suggest newborns can distinguish between native language and foreign language. In another study, Swedish babies sucked harder on pacifiers to hear more of the unfamiliar American speech sounds, and American babies did the same to hear more new sounds in Swedish. I've yet to find the study where the fetus was exposed to the two native languages of a fully bilingual mother, but you can already guess I would be betting on newborn recognition of *both*.

Now, let's say at least one of the parents *is* bilingual, and the newborn infant, far too young to utter a word, is sponging up the sounds of two languages because Grandma has come to live in America, and there's regular Skyping with relatives in the "old country." Researchers say that just growing up in a multi-language home can produce enhancements of memory, problem solving, reasoning, creativity, interpersonal relationships, communication, and of course, language development. If that's just passive exposure, imagine what happens to brain development when the child starts *speaking* a second language! Then there is there is a whole category of neurological-based skills, called *executive functioning,* now actually being studied in infants and found by researchers to accelerate in development as well. These include: impulse and emotional control, flexible thinking, working memory, planning and prioritizing, and task initiation and organization. If the bilingualism is maintained and developed, neurological benefits continue to manifest throughout life.

Being bilingual is no guarantee of higher intelligence, let alone happiness or success, but it undeniably can offer the proverbial "leg up" in life from babyhood onward. We've looked at some of the benefits that have been observed and measured during infancy and childhood, and now we'll take a speed ride through the next phase of life.

The Blooming Brain

A s we hover in space, far above Earth, we look down on our planet from a great distance and listen in with very powerful audio to 7.4 billion people speaking about 6500 different languages. Our computer deciphers them into individual sounds, and we discover that there are around 800 of these unique "phonemes" that produce all the languages of the world, and that each language is composed of about 40 distinct units of sound. In a compelling study by research scientist Naja Fernan Ramírez at the University of Washington, I learned that babies at birth can distinguish all 800 of these sounds. That seems impressive, but it is simply essential because every baby must be able to learn whichever of the 6500 languages it is born into. If this malleability persisted through life, we would all be able to learn any language quickly and produce it with a perfect accent. Alas, it is not so!

Did you ever struggle to get the Spanish 'j' sound from the back of your throat, or the French 'r' with just the right balance of palate and uvula? Have you ever noticed how much trouble some ESL learners have with the 'th' of *this* and *that*? My Dutch father (*vader*) had perfect grammar but said "dis" and "dat" his entire English-speaking life. The click is one of the most common consonants in many Southern African languages. If you've ever heard it in speech, you know it's not a sound the English-speaking mouth can easily reproduce.

By the time infants are twelve months old, they have become specialized in the sounds of the language spoken around them and they are well on their way to losing the potential to distinguish the other 760 or so. Predictably, babies in bilingual households can process the phonemes of two languages, but what about exposure in the form of recordings? It seems logical that hearing the sounds of other languages in any form at a young age would afford at least some linguistic advantages. No hard science here, but I can share some personal reality.

Not only did Dad and Grandma *spreken* Dutch throughout my childhood, but the family's favorite (and only) Christmas album was traditional songs in several different languages that we played endlessly from Thanksgiving through New Year's. Mom remembered a few Neapolitan folk songs from her childhood, and she'd sing them to us when Grandma wasn't around. Between church, school, and choir, there was a soundtrack of ecclesiastical Latin running in the background for the first fifteen years of my life (until Catholic Mass was said in English). I didn't pick up Dutch despite all my visits to the aunties, but Romance languages do come easily to me (and in the case of French and Portuguese, disappeared pretty quickly, too for lack of practice). When I was in Tanzania, it was great fun to learn some Swahili. Ida, my exchange student from Denmark, commented that my mimic of a long, gnarly Danish word was the best she'd ever heard from an American mouth. I attribute that to my Dutch *vader* and *grootmoeder*, my Italian mamma, the Catholic liturgy in Latin, and of course, Mrs. Domínguez, my high school Spanish teacher.

Undeniably, growing up in that petri dish of language sounds has given me some sort of advantage, but even so, and in the same category as my longing to be able to dance, ski, type, and play the harp, I deeply wish I'd started second language learning in my very early years. As we have already seen, ample research reveals the marvelous benefits to the brain resulting in improved communication and interpersonal skills, creativity, focus, higher reasoning, and memory. All the revelatory research on what's called the *bilingual advantage* begs a big question: In the United States, why does foreign language training usually not begin until the teen years, *if even then*? It's depressingly worth noting that a large majority of states do not require any foreign language in high school at all, and that the Modern Language Association (MLA) reports a 6.7 percent drop in foreign language enrollments since 2009. That's bad news in the long-term economic and political pictures, but it can mean good positioning for the students who *do* gain a degree of fluency and the bilingual-born children who keep up their speaking skills and also learn to read and write well in their home language.

Having second language ability may not be a sizeable advantage with college admission, but if the student has tutored or used the language in some capacity to help others, it *will* be a boost. The benefits of being bilingual in the job market are undeniable. What many applicants don't realize is that second language ability is what employers in both the public and private sectors are screaming for. Federal agencies especially need speakers fluent in Eastern and African languages, but local and state governments and private businesses still can't find enough qualified Spanish-speaking staff. Here is practical advice to high school and college students: Pour on the coals in your foreign language classes like your professional life depends on it. It's not easy to become bilingual, but even starting at high school (like I did) isn't too late. Find opportunities outside of class where you can practice speaking in "real life," and sign up for a total immersion program, preferably in another country. Expensive? Not necessarily. Scary? You bet! But only until you actually dig in and begin. *That's* when the second language starts to come alive, and you'll have a life-changing experience and fun in the process.

I'll never forget how terrified I was moving in with a family of total strangers in Guadalajara for a two-week immersion program after four years of high school Spanish. I couldn't understand a thing they were saying until finally I heard "tacos" and "tamales" and realized the *señora* was asking me which I preferred for my first meal in her home. I was perfectly happy with either, and that's what I thought I'd told her, but her quick step backward and rather shocked look made me think it hadn't gone well. It took a while to unravel my mistake, and lunch was further delayed while she taught me what I *should have* said instead of that I didn't give a hoot whether she served one or the other.* It sure wasn't my only embarrassing moment, but I survived and even thrived outside the classroom comfort zone. Two challenging weeks improved my speaking ability by at least 100 percent and gave me my first deeply satisfying feeling of, "Wow—I can't believe I did that!"

---

* I said, "No me importa" (It doesn't matter to me what you serve) when I meant to say something more gracious like "Me da igual" or "Me gustan los dos." (I like either/both.)

The Tongue May Stumble, but the Brain Purrs

The most common claim I heard from students showing up to the first day of class was, "I took Spanish in high school, but now I've forgotten everything." A former student remarked to me that he wanted to get back into Spanish, but what he had gained those several years back was now "all gone."

In fact, a lot of it is still there in something like suspended animation, just not on the tip of your tongue anymore due to lack of recent exercise. So class starts, and you pour some magic elixir (in the form of simple *exposure* to the language) on the stuck hinges and—lo and behold!—the door swings open, though creaky at first. Words and phrases in that "forgotten" foreign language start springing back to life into your memory and onto your tongue. This happens almost comically sometimes when a student took, say, French in high school, has "forgotten everything", now decides to take up Spanish a few years later in college, and is shocked that for the first few weeks every time she intends to say *Sí* it comes out *Oui*, and every morning starts off with "*Bon jo*...oops, I mean *Buenos días*."

So often, I hear something that goes like this, "Oh, I think I'm too old for that; my memory just isn't what it used to be." Is it really true that one can learn language at any age? We *all* wish we'd started in early childhood, but there are also advantages for adults: we can apply preexisting knowledge to any new subject, choose from and combine a variety of learning methods, and have access to travel and other ways to apply and practice skills. Adult language students are also highly likely to be able to read and write what they are learning to say with a minimum of additional effort.

In addition, research points in the direction of the "failing" memory *needing* and responding to stimulation like language learning to stay sharp and functioning. Scientists are seeing anatomical changes even in the brains of elderly people who are exercising the body and the brain. Important research has been carried out on adults with Alzheimer's that indicates that being bilingual is a powerful buffer against the disease and could delay its onset by four years or more, as well as slow its progress if it has already manifested. This has intriguing potential and, since it has very recently come under challenge by another study, research dollars will flow in and it will doubtless be studied and tested further in coming years. Wherever the "proof" lies, I'll wager there's great truth in that canned message I recently saw taped to a friend's wall: "You don't stop learning because you get old; you get old because you stop learning."

Years ago, I coined a saying inspired by the number of times I was asked but could not answer the question: "How long will it take me to become fluent?" My adage, *"No hay destino, sólo camino"* translates: "There is no destination, only the road." There's no place to "arrive"; it's always an ongoing process.

Every one of us is already fully multilingual with at least one hundred words from several foreign languages, words that we have heard and repeated so many times that they have become fully *ours,* and they materialize from mental concept straight to tongue without the intermediate stage of translation into English. That feat is what is called "thinking in a foreign language," and we do it all the time. In addition to *tacos, tamales, salsa*, and *enchiladas*, witness *sushi, harikari, à la mode, baguette, cappuccino, biscotti, arrivederci, wiener schnitzel*, and *Gesundheit*. In effect, when we say these words, we are thinking in a foreign language, and that's "fluency." Mastery of a language is the repeated act of becoming "fluent" with more and more words, expressions, phrases, and language patterns. Sure, it can feel hard, frustrating, and slow going—if that's what we focus on. But why suffer and rush if the process itself can be fun, enlivening, and delicious? Why not *savor* becoming bilingual throughout life?

Once and for all, let's debunk the four big myths about learning a foreign language that have just been begging to be blown out of the water:

1. *It costs too much.* Debunk: Yes, private tutors and the Rosetta Stone program are pricey, but there are good online language programs (like Duolingo) that are free. Community college classes are still a bargain, and language immersion courses in other countries can be quite afford-able, to say nothing of fun and deeply rewarding.

2. *I just don't have enough time.* Debunk: Even five minutes a day of doing *anything* in the target language will keep it alive and accessible, and keep you progressing. It's the *daily* consistency that makes a dream come true. (See "The Secret to Everything.") For example, one Duolingo lesson takes about ten minutes, but be sure to practice everything *out loud* because that triples the value of your lesson time. The more *active* your activity, the better. A three-minute conversation in fractured French with hands flailing to make up for your lack of words could boost your skills more than an hour of staring at pages of grammar expla-nations. Sing along with Andrea Bocelli in Italian, make your ATM transaction in Spanish, order your meal in your new language, chat up the German lady around the

corner. Mix it up, do something fun every day, get out of your comfort zone.

3. *I'm too old; my memory isn't what it used to be.* Debunk: Enough said!

4. *I don't have that "flair" for languages.* Debunk: Like there's a hit of linguistic angel dust visited upon him but not upon you? There is no "foreign language gene." Some people do better in math, and others gravitate more toward language. The real deciding factor in who becomes functionally bilingual and who does not is this: The bilingual person sticks with it, and the other person doesn't. No judgment there, just factors like motivation, need, perseverance, and personal circumstance. The hard truth is many people just give it up because they're expecting some magical osmosis to happen without nearly enough exposure to and repetition of the language on their part.

There is great excitement over studies demonstrating that *plasticity*, the brain's ability to change throughout life, is available, yes, *throughout life* with good nutrition, adequate sleep, regular exercise, and the amazing elixir of creative and communicative powers that activities like playing a musical instrument, speaking foreign language, and even learning to swing dance feed to the brain. This has tremendous implications for children throughout their developmental years, for adults as parents and professionals, and for seniors who want to remain vibrant and productive for *all* their years.

It's best to start your foreign language learning as early as you can. That would be right now—at any age. And just have some fun with it! Successful bilinguals don't wait until they're "good" at it to use their language in the world. As Ralph Waldo Emerson exhorted, "Do the thing and you shall have the power."

The Job Seeker's Competitive Edge

L et's say you're a recent graduate, or you've gotten laid off from a job, or you've simply decided to look for a better one. In other words, you're in the job market and need to maximize every advantage possible: any and all volunteer work and community activity, organizational experience you gained while planning the family reunion, or training skills you developed with the new family dog. Just kidding about that last one, but don't overlook a thing, especially if you're young with a slim resume.

Oftentimes, students of mine, after gaining intermediate language abilities, leave the application blank when asked, "What other languages do you speak? read? write?" They are afraid of overstating their skills, shy about over-representing themselves since they aren't fully bilingual. I say *always* toot your horn, but be truthful. You may not be "fluent," but you can be "functionally bilingual," meaning you may make a lot of mistakes but are able to use a second language effectively in life's ordinary situations.

On a trip to the local emergency room with a sprained ankle, I sat first in the waiting room and then in the treatment area in great pain but immense joy as I listened to three of my former students effectively handling the needs of Spanish-speaking patients. Regardless of whether or not they could navigate a cock-tail party in their second language, they were being *functionally* bilingual on the job. Was their ability attributable to my Spanish classes? Only in small part, for their skill and confidence came from seeing a need, being willing to step in, and then as with most jobs, repeating the same words and phrases time and again.

In a past life, I interviewed many applicants for jobs in food service, and I often think how powerful it would have been for an interviewee in *any* field to say to the manager, "I took X foreign language in school. I'm not fluent yet, but I speak, read, and write it enough to get my point across, *and* I'm on a daily study and practice program to continue to develop my abilities. I'm committed to being bilingual, and I know I can be an asset to this company with my advancing language skills and my understanding of another culture."

And I would have said in response, "¡Bravísimo! You're hired, and furthermore, within six months, I'm going to start you on an advancement program to get you that 20 percent additional pay that you, as a bilingual person, have the potential to earn over the course of your working life."

If you are one of the lucky people with the immense advantage of being born into bilingualism with a foreign language spoken at home, capitalize on this gift by developing your reading and writing skills to match your fluent speaking skills so that the dream job market will be calling *your* name, and that additional 20 percent of earnings will be in *your* bank account.

No matter your age, if you've taken even one class of foreign language, amazing changes have occurred in your brain, so don't stop now! Your gray matter is becoming more dense (for better muscle control, sensory perceptions, memory, emotions, speech, decision making, and self-control) and your white matter (which connects the gray matter areas and carries nerve impulses between neurons) is being strengthened. You see, it just keeps getting better, but *you* have to keep it up. A foreign language learning curve should be a nice, steady forward trajectory that goes gradually upward. (So it's slow and bumpy—who cares?!) Unfortunately, most trajectories look more like a roller-coaster ride of fits and starts and stops as the language center of the brain lights up (new class! online program! travel!) and shuts down (end of class; forgot about program for two weeks; no money to travel; oh, what's the use?).

There's a simple trick to even out this craziness, keep that learning curve on a steady rise, and ensure a snappily firing brain, to say nothing of move us in the direction of our goal. My goal is to be ever more fluent in Italian, so I spend a few minutes a day with the free online language program called Duolingo. There's a daily e-mail reminder, and I earn "rewards" by staying on a learning streak of one lesson every twenty-four hours. It takes about five minutes to do that. I triple the value of my short sessions by repeating everything I hear and reading everything I see *ad alta voce* (out loud). Of course, more is always better, but make no mistake—that five minutes a day is more valuable to my brain and tongue than thirty-five minutes every Saturday afternoon. The language learning center in my brain with the word "Italian" on the door always stays open with the lights on. That's the physiological advantage of the daily practice rule. There's also the added psychological benefit that, as long as I keep this up, I never feel like I've taken a linguistic backslide and lost ground through inactivity.

With high school and college graduations happening every spring, I wonder where all the students with one to four classes of foreign language will be in five years. I am passionate about making language learning a lifelong practice, just like physical fitness, eating a good diet, or getting enough sleep. Notice I picked three things that are highly desirable for a vibrant life but also challenging to maintain in our busy world. Let's compare daily language practice to putting a few dollars into a savings account every month:

1. It's not easy to start the discipline and stay consistent with it.
2. Sometimes you "fall off the wagon" by cashing out all your

savings or dropping out of your daily language routine. (I have firsthand experience at both!)

3. You can always begin again, the difference being a zero balance in your savings account compared to a bilingual brain bank that has stored much of the learning and can't wait to dust it off when you begin again.

4. If you follow through with your savings plan, at the end of a year, or ten, or fifty, you'll have a significant amount of money in the bank. A few minutes a day of foreign language compounds into bilingual abilities that are personally and professionally enhancing.

With a clear commitment and consistent deposits to your savings account or your bilingual bank (hopefully both!), you'll have very concrete results to show and much to be proud of. The only ingredients to add to the mix are a dash of acceptance for wherever you're at in the process, and lots of encouraging self-pats on the back.

CHAPTER SIX

A Life in Words

Make Love, Not War

A bittersweet flashback to the fifties, sixties, and seventies: the Cold War, the Iron Curtain, backyard bomb shelters, the Cuban Missile Crisis, Women's Lib, Kennedy's Camelot, Vietnam, and more.

Don the Noose for Biscuits

If you can relate to being a kid learning to sing the traditional hymn, "Gladly the Cross I'd Bear", and feeling somehow cheered there's a church song about *Glady, the cross-eyed bear*; or singing along with the Beatles to "Lucy in the Sky With Diamonds", always baffled at the part about *the girl with colitis goes by* ("the girl with kaleidoscope eyes"); then this one's for you.

All about Me (The Sequel)

This is the story of how I left my freeway flyer life of multiple part time jobs in Sacramento for a small city in northern California where the dearth of malls and restaurants didn't bother me, but

I found some street signs, place names, and roadside images truly worrisome.

All about Me (Prequel I)

Perhaps my linguistic trajectory through life was launched in my childhood, but we begin this prequel before I was even a twinkle in my parent's eyes.

All about Me (Prequel II)

Eight years of foreign language, a B.A. degree in Spanish, and now I'm in a grad program with native speakers from all over the world, and I can't carry on a simple conversation. I could have quit. It could have killed me. But since neither happened, I became bilingual.

Ez Dakite Euskaraz Hitz Egiten Duzu?

No, I don't speak a word of Basque, but I feel as close to this culture as to the Italian and Dutch of my own heritage. Beautiful people, fascinating history, delicious cuisine (but I'll pass on the pigs' feet), and a language that remains one of the great linguistic mysteries of the world.

The Cure by Feeding of Earworms

They worm their way into your skull without reason, but often with rhyme and a catchy tune. Then the same few bars keep playing in your head for hours, perhaps days, or as some sufferers report, for years. Is there a brain wash to eradicate the earworm?

In Megahurtz, But Not for Long

Does thinking of half a large intestine as one semicolon make you groan or grin?
It wasn't writer's block but a fractured wrist that derailed me from my author's tracks. So, I got creative—with other people's material.

A Girl (Not) Named Sue

Can you imagine a twenty-first century baby named Ethel or Gertrude, Gaylord or Ambrose? A first name can be inspired by genealogy, religion, tradition, trend, or simply choice. Mine seems to still be a work in progress.

Behind Closed Classroom Doors, Part I

Spanish classes without food? –Unthinkable. But did we take it too far with inky squid, flying eggs, and possibly poisonous mushrooms?

Behind Closed Classroom Doors, Part II

Cigarettes, alcohol, a near-brawl, and thousands of counterfeit bills changing hands. Was this a college Spanish class or a den of iniquity?

Behind Closed Classroom Doors, Part III

Simulating imprisonment and torture and contemplating disaster on a massive scale are weighty matters. Nothing like some explosive pyrotechnics to lighten things up.

Make Love, Not War

L ooking back at my childhood in America of the 1950s and 1960s, specific words come to mind with the emotions and confusions they evoked then, along with the impact of history they provoke now: *Sputnik, Cold War, atomic bomb, Iron Curtain, USSR, Communism, space race, JFK, Bay of Pigs, Cuban Missile Crisis, hippies, Vietnam.* Each term is loaded with metaphoric meaning for an era, a way of life, and for how we've grown up to be who we are today.

I will add to this list the term *sonic boom*, even though most folks weren't nearly blown off their feet in their own backyards twice a day unless they lived near an air force base. It's been decades since I've heard a sonic boom, but living in Bakersfield just eighty-three miles from Edwards Air Force Base, we got used to frequent deep-shattering *booms!* as just part of the landscape (or, more precisely, the skyscape). Visitors to the area would either be paralyzed with shock, run for cover, scream hysterically, or do all three at the same time.

I was a happy kid in a great home in a friendly town. I believed in Santa Claus and the Easter Bunny and knew my guardian angel was watching over me and that my parents would always protect me. But there were two inescapable fears weighing heavily on my scrawny shoulders: fear of eternal damnation in hell and fear of nuclear annihilation. By early Saturday afternoons, I was already nervous about the weekly trip to church at 5:00 p.m. to confess my sins and pray for my penance, this being the only protection from spending Eternity burning in hell, except for ceasing to sin altogether. As an aspiring saint, I tried that route but quickly gave up on perfect angelic behavior as an unrealistic option. There were just too many opportunities to be "unkind to my brother and sisters" and "disobedient to my parents." Saturday afternoons in the confessional were dreaded but essential purges to hold on to at least a reasonable shot at gaining a place in heaven.

On those Saturday afternoons before my weekly confession of "Bless me Father, for I have sinned ..." the neighborhood gang would gather in our front yard to play the new game we'd invented called *Sputnik*. The Soviets had launched the first satellite of that name on October 4, 1957, and by the time my sister Margie turned five twelve days later, it was a household word even to us kids. The game was simply all of us in a circle taking turns to see who could throw the basketball straightest and highest while the rest of us yelled at the top of our lungs, "Sputniiiiik!" We'd inducted the term into our lexicon of play and into our mental bank of fears that dangerous things could destroy us from the skies. We were just regular kids playing games, going to school, riding bikes, and blasting up and down cracked sidewalks on metal skates without a care in the world—except for the threat of nuclear war.

My dad was spending *his* Saturday afternoons sandbagging the basement of the house on *V* Street and then stocking it with nonperishables in the event we'd have to take shelter below ground from bombs falling nearby, or more likely, their fallout from afar. I stood in the doorway of that basement one sunny afternoon when I was not much taller than the doorknob and asked him—just to make sure—if our dog, Spotty, would get to come, too. When he said no, that we couldn't bring the dog into the bomb shelter, I was overcome with anticipated loss and feelings of dread. A few months later, we'd had a happy family vacation camping in Yosemite. I was sitting in the back of the station wagon watching the park recede from view, feeling a hopeless conviction that nuclear bombs would destroy everything, and I'd never see Yosemite again.

At school, we had regular atomic bomb drills, and when the alarm bell sounded with a certain pattern, we knew to slide off our little benches and crouch on the floor under our desks with our arms over our heads (as if!). My friend, Susan, remembers doing the same drill at her grade school in San Francisco and worrying desperately about how to get home to her mother when the attack came. *When,* not *if.* I know it sounds contradictory, but we were happy-go-lucky children living with a sense of impending doom. I was too young during the Cuban Missile Crisis to understand the circumstances and the potential consequences, but I clearly remember seeing the look on Dad's face and knowing this was *dire.*

When I was in high school, the side yard of our big corner lot was excavated, and a sixteen-foot, cylindrical metal tank with air filters and a spiral stairway was buried alongside the house. We were the first family in America to have this model of bomb shelter because my father had designed and built it at the steel company he worked for. The local TV news team showed up to photograph the event and interview my dad. By then, the Cold War was such a given in the fabric of life that I was more interested in how my flip hairdo looked for the pictures than in the threat of nuclear annihilation.

When President Kennedy was shot on November 22, 1963, the nuns led us in prayer that he would recover. I had grown up on TV hospital dramas like *Doctor Kildare* and *Ben Casey MD* and I was sure he would be saved. Besides that, the president was Catholic, and I still believed that God favored us as the true chosen ones. In the early afternoon, the teachers told us he had died, and we were stunned. I remember watching the reactions of some of the upper-class students and feeling confusion and wordless anguish. All I remember after that is being at home in the late afternoon while Mom was cooking dinner and Dad had locked himself in the hall bathroom because he couldn't stop crying. Maybe we hadn't *really* believed in Camelot but, on that day, another part of our optimism and innocence was irrevocably blown away.

* * *

The Vietnam War came with a whole new vocabulary list: *Vietcong, Da Nang, Ho Chi Minh, Gulf of Tonkin, hawks* and *doves, My Lai Massacre, napalm, Agent Orange.* If these words still evoke horror in me, what must they create in the minds of those who were there? As I went away to college at UC Davis, my parents said they would cut off my funds if I demonstrated against the war. At first, I complied with the letter of that law, but at the end of my first year away, even that became impossible.

On April 30, 1970, President Nixon announced the need for 150,000 more troops to expand the war and invade Cambodia. There were protests on campuses nationwide. Four days later, on May 4, 1970, National Guardsmen fired into a peaceful antiwar demonstration at Kent State University in Ohio, killing four students and wounding nine. Outrage was the emotion, and protest was the call to action. Universities were shut down for several days and we (most students and many professors) devoted ourselves full-time to marches in Sacramento and antiwar rallies on campus.

I remember deep anger and frustration and an awakening awareness of how easy it would be to resort to violence. But we didn't. Instead, my friends and I joined an antiwar information group; we educated ourselves and then went into the residential streets of nearby towns to knock on people's doors, hear their views, and speak ours against the war.

The year 1970 was an amazing one of triumph and tragedy, with the women's lib movement roaring like an avalanche in the background of it all. On April 17, the Apollo 13 crew safely landed in the South Pacific after an aborted mission to the moon. A week before President Nixon's announcement to escalate the war in Vietnam, the very first Earth Day was held on April 22, and twenty million Americans of all walks and persuasions celebrated and rallied for a clean, sustainable environment. The Beatles had already announced their breakup a month before, but their last album, *Let It Be*, was officially released on May 8, four days after the Kent State massacre. Jimmy Hendrix died of an overdose on September 18 right before I went back to college for my senior year.

The '50s and '60s were over, although the Cold War would last through the next two decades. 1970 was a watershed year of endings and new beginnings. It's trite to say *the world would never be the same again*, but it wouldn't, and it wasn't, and it never will be. Even so, for those of us who came of age in that era—and aren't we *all* always "coming of age"?—the words and images live on in deep visceral memory. That world within us remains forever vividly alive.

Don the Noose for Biscuits

Every childhood is replete with legions of misunderstood words, invented meanings, and big questions in little minds as to "just what are those tall people trying to say?" Anytime an adult speaks, there's high probability that children, always negotiating with what little they know of the world and its words, will fill in mental blanks with creative meaning-making. Adults take a lot for granted, having long forgotten how many dots must be connected for a single concept or act to be understood.

My mother was working on a project in the garden of our house on *V* Street in Bakersfield (I perceived it as a mansion on an expansive estate; I was only five), and she told me to run and get "a couple" of empty coffee cans. Anxious to be useful, I raced across the yard, through the house, out to the garage and to the shelf where—oops!—I realized I was missing an important piece of understanding. I retraced my steps at twice the speed back to the garden, and gulping air, asked, "Mommy, how many is 'a couple'?" I still hear impatient disbelief in the tone of her reply.

We went to Catholic Mass every Sunday, and it ultimately got to where I could practically speak Latin. But at that tender age, I didn't recognize it as a different language, and my brain was trying mightily and constantly to figure out its meaning by mentally searching out the closest word in the limited lexicon I *did* know. I just assumed the priest was pronouncing English badly, and it was up to me to compensate my way to some level of comprehension. Over and over in the Mass, he would say, "*Dominus vobiscum,*" and the congregation would respond, "*Et cum spiritu tuo.*" I hadn't yet learned that these phrases meant respectively, "The Lord be with you," and "And with your spirit," so my brain went to work on them: *dah-mu-nuus*: hmmm...something about "dominoes"? Unlikely, as I hadn't seen my favorite game played in church yet. Maybe something about a "noose"? But that *vobiscum* part must be about "biscuits." Is that what people get on their tongue when they go to Communion? Unanswered questions. Not so with the second phrase, *Et cum spiritu tuo*, whose meaning was obvious to me who heard it just as the priest said it, "Eh come spirit 2-2-0." It seemed neither magical nor wondrous, rather just totally practical that the Holy Spirit had a contact number. I assumed my parents phoned him a lot, and I hoped they were telling him mostly good things about me.

My grandmother emigrated from WWII-ravaged Holland and came to live with us when I was three or four. She and my dad conversed in Dutch, and my Italian mom learned to catch the gist of these unfamiliar utterances so she could follow what her hyper-critical mother-in-law was saying about her. My little sister, Margie, and I didn't understand anything of those chats between Mother and Son, but we soon made up nonsense sounds and insisted to Grandma that we, too could speak her language: *ownsee kownsee blamla floop*. She was neither impressed nor amused.

At the age of six, I started the first of twelve years of Catholic school at St. Francis Elementary and the rain of unfamiliar words turned into a deluge. We learned more prayers, in addition to the ones we already knew for reciting the Rosary. The nuns taught us "The Act of Contrition" to express penitence for our numerous and oft-repeated sins. It starts out, "Oh my God, I am heartily sorry for having offended Thee", and with true repentance and abiding fear of eternity in Hell, I prayed at least twice a day (after tripping Margie, or telling Karen she was a meanie): "Oh, my God, I am *hardly* sorry..." I was vaguely aware of the discrepancy between that mistaken adverb and my sincere intent, and I briefly wondered if God or the nuns had made a mistake. You just didn't question that sort of thing for fear of having yet another sin to do penance for.

In the second grade, we learned about this place called Limbo where the souls of innocent babies who died before they could be baptized were warehoused for all eternity, not to be tortured like the sinful ones damned to burn in Hell, yet forever denied the sight of God for lack of a sprinkle of water and requisite incantations. This affected me deeply, and I badgered parents, relatives, neighbors, and even strangers on adjoining blocks for donations to the St. Francis collection for pagan babies to get those innocents of Africa baptized and thus safe from the fate of being trapped in Limbo for all time. I recently asked a devout Catholic, "What ever happened to Limbo?" and she replied with firmness and finality, precluding further query, "They *closed* it."

In the third grade, my teacher announced that we were going to learn *homonyms* that day. I was in orbit with joy because I thought we were going to sing "harmonies" like Mom had taught us kids to do, as she fantasized we might become the next Lennon Sisters. (We never missed a Saturday night of the *Lawrence Welk Show*.) My sibs and I had been singing "You Are My Sunshine" in harmony for as long as we could remember. Back in the classroom with *homonyms*, it was a moment of intense excitement, followed by deep disappointment, though I admit to getting pretty interested in "two/too," "mail/male," "pail/pale," and so on.

Kids are little, literal meaning-makers. One boy, when asked if he knew the name of Mother Mary's husband, replied with confidence, "He's called 'The Verge.'" The *Verge??* "Yeah, you know— *The Verge n' Mary.*" Another child applied her best artistic skill to depicting Pontius Pilate coming in for landing outside the palace

where he was to condemn Jesus to death by crucifixion. It took
the teacher a minute of head scratching to make the connection.
When Bob was a fifth-grader, he took a note home to his parents
from his teacher that read, "Bobby has *outstanding* work in art."
He tells me how he remembers thinking, "Wow, how did *that*
happen? I never even turned anything in."

This anecdote isn't about a misunderstanding of meaning, but
perhaps just a misplaced context. When my baby sister Liz was
four or five years old, she would race past the bedrooms (I was
a teenager trying to ignore her), repeating just under her breath
the lines she was about to deliver to Mom when she reached the
kitchen. She did this regularly with speed, intensity, and accuracy.
Although at the time it just seemed like an annoying part of the
homescape, now I'm impressed with a language practice that was
training her for articulate verbal delivery. One day, after one too
many exposures to Betty Crocker biscuit mix commercials on
TV, she completed her rehearsal while racing through the hallway
and the living room, and arrived in the kitchen to announce with
enthusiastic affection, "Mommy, you're so moist, so light, so
flakey!" In adulthood, Liz is articulate and exceptionally clear on
what she means to say. For my part, perhaps I should have spent
more childhood time rehearsing lines in the hallway and less time
writing in my diary.

About to graduate from St. Francis after eighth grade and go
on to Garces Memorial High School, we had become cocky and
prone to making silly jokes about 1) *Ejaculations* 2) the *Diet of
Worms* 3) *Papal Bulls*, and 4) the seventh planet from the sun.* At
Garces, my vocabulary got bigger and more accurate; I memorized

---

* 1) A short prayer repeated throughout the day; 2) Assembly of the Holy Roman
Empire to which Martin Luther was summoned to renounce or reaffirm his heretical
teachings in Worms, Germany 1521; 3) An official letter issued by the Pope; 4) Uranus

soliloquies from Shakespeare, wrote reports on everything, and joined the Speech and Debate Club. Better late than never, I started learning my first foreign language in Mrs. Domínguez's Spanish 1 class and stuck it out through Spanish 4, partly because that was the only class at the high school that was co-ed (though the year I took it, we were twenty-five girls and Vincent). I wasn't obsessed about Limbo and pagan babies anymore and had most of my extracurricular attention focused on boys. To my knowledge, the Pope hadn't yet closed Hell or Purgatory†, and I was given to guilt and worry over where *my* eternity might be spent—useless concerns, but definitely formative as a rite of passage into the adulthood of erroneous beliefs that one must be very careful and/ or very good, and the misguided conviction that life is *serious* business.

---

† A place of suffering where souls go to atone for their sins.

All about Me (The Sequel)

There was a lot of linguistic history in my life prior to 1988, but I feel compelled to set the stage starting with that landmark year and reveal the rest in the *prequels*. That was the year I left the third-floor Victorian apartment in midtown Sacramento, assorted part-time teaching assignments, and my moonlighting job that had enabled me to weather the financial ups and downs (a profession some considered inappropriate for a college teacher. Hmmm, a prequel, yes...) and moved to Mendocino County for a full-time teaching position in Spanish at the community college. But I am already ahead of my story because first I had to venture into uncharted, northern territory to get to my interview.

I'd heard of Ukiah, even had a friend in Sacramento who had grown up there, but I hadn't a clue where it was located. To a majority of Californians, the cities named Ukiah, Eureka, Yreka, Yucaipa, and sometimes Yuba City thrown in as well, form a mystery map of vague, interchangeable, geographic generalities. I would tell friends from Sacramento to Southern California that I'd moved to Ukiah, and the conversation usually proceeded in one of these five directions:

A. "Wow! So you're all the way up there on the Oregon border?" (Yreka: 285 miles north)
B. "Are you going to teach part-time at Humboldt State, too?" (Eureka: 165 miles north)
C. "Can you walk to the beach from your house?" (Mendocino, the town: 57 miles west)
D. "Isn't that close to Chico? (Yuba City: 140 miles northeast)

E. "So you've become a desert rat!?" (Yucaipa: 600 miles south)

I'd say no, that Ukiah is on Highway 101 about two hours north of San Francisco, and I am met with glazed eyes as friend visualizes a complete topographical blank. I add that it's up in the wine country, and they knowingly nod: "Ohhhh! You mean Napa Valley." Well, skip it. I didn't want house guests, anyway.

But that was me, too, before the spring of 1988 when my dear friend, Liz G., who was my colleague and mentor at Sacramento City College, encouraged me to apply for a teaching position at Mendocino College. First, I had to find Ukiah on a map, contend with the fact that there is no simple and obvious way to get there from Sacramento, choose the most traffic-laden route (on 80 West, then through the wine country and up the 101—don't do it! Stay on the 5 and then Hwy 20), and...well, to make a long story short, I made it to the interview with little time to spare and had to rush back to Sac afterward for moonlighting in questionable profession.

Lucky me, I got the job. My brother offered to accompany me on a road trip to Ukiah (he chose an only slightly better route) to look for an apartment, and then the fun really began. We wanted to get off the freeway into downtown Ukiah, so I voted we should take Perkins Street. We passed up the Gobbi off ramp in part because we couldn't settle a debate as to the pronunciation of Gobbi. He thought it should be a long 'o'- as in "oh," and I disagreed with a lengthy argument about how that would be the same pronunciation as the Gobi Desert, and "Gobbi" with the double *b* surely rhymes with "knobby," like "globby" without the *l*. That seemed phonetically logical to me even though the idea of a major street pronounced *either* way was vaguely disconcerting. But I would deal with that later[‡] because soon enough,

---

[‡] As it turned out, my brother was right.

we were at the stoplight of Perkins and State. I looked at the store windows across the intersection, then over at my brother and said in amazement, "This must be a really progressive place. Just look at that—they have a Frederick's of Hollywood on the main street of downtown!" I wish I'd snapped a photo, but in my mind's eye, I still see a sensuous display of flimsy red lingerie-clad mannequins in the picture windows of what I later learned was the Palace Dress Shop.

So, it wasn't Frederick's of Hollywood on State and Perkins, but Ukiah continued to reveal surprises, and I have never forgotten my first impressions—those moments of elation and despair—as I tried to relate to my new home. The search for an apartment that was both desirable and available turned up zilch (I ended up renting one burg north in Redwood Valley), but driving around town was entertaining and even had its linguistically exciting moments. After seeing the name Yokayo pop up several times, I theorized that it must be a corruption of the Native American word *ukiah*. It wasn't long before I learned I had it backward: *ukiah* is the corruption of the Pomo word *yokayo* meaning "deep valley."

By day's end, we'd seen many of the neighborhoods in Ukiah, and despite my high degree of directional challenge, I was starting to get the lay of the land. My mind was excitedly racing ahead to the start of the school year in September as my brother made a left turn off Talmage Road onto South State Street and the big bright sign for the Ron-Day-Voo diner and cocktail lounge (now the site of Jalo's Mexican restaurant) came into view. I recall it as being garish hues of red-and-blue neon. It first struck me as entertaining, but then sunk me into deep doubt about the linguistic ambiance in the town where I was henceforth to teach foreign language.

Well, to make the long story of my career at the college short, that doubt was unfounded and I enjoyed twenty-five years of teaching thousands of enthusiastic and delightful language learners, many of whom today I count as friends. When I started my job in the fall of 1988, my first students taught me to pronounce the name of a nearby town "*CO-ve-lo*," not "*Co-VE-lo*"; and that the Mendocino College athletic teams were *not* named after those big black birds circling overhead, which, in fact, were turkey vultures and not the eagles I was rhapsodizing about.

It was easy to leave behind multiple part-time teaching jobs and freeway flying between Sacramento and Davis and move to the land of simpler life and fewer choices. For the first time ever, I had only one job full-time, and a monthly salary with no overtime pay but with benefits. And though there was no more need to moonlight in that "questionable" profession, it was the one thing I missed.

All about Me (Prequel I)

The sequel began as I left Sacramento to take a teaching position at Mendocino College in 1988. But my life in words started long before, perhaps even in the womb, because English was not the native language of either of my parents. Caterina Gambardella Crai, my Italian mother, was born in the Bronx to immigrant parents from Naples and Calabria. She started learning English in grade school through the unenlightened but very effective *sink or swim* method of "bilingual" education.

Friedjof Johannes Christie Janssen, my father, came from the Netherlands with the Dutch Merchant Marines during WWII. Since he was very good-looking (tall, blond, and handsome) and loved dating tall, blond, American girls when his ship was in US ports, he was highly motivated to learn the English language and adopt American ways. He wasn't prejudiced against darker-hued women, but understandably, he was attracted to and exclusively dated the ones who looked like the Dutch girls he'd grown up with and regretfully left behind at age seventeen.

So how did this tall, blond, handsome Dutchman cross paths with a short, dark, beautiful Italian *signorina*? Where else but in front of the church? His best friend and shipmate, Dirk, was getting married to her best girlfriend, Elsie. Caterina was running late for rehearsal—literally—and was crossing the street to St. Raymond's at a fast trot. Friedjof's eyes went dreamy and his stomach flipped as he said to Dirk with the certainty that only lovers at first sight can know, "Dat is du voman I am goving to marry." And so it was to be. They were engaged in two weeks and married within two months, despite the dire warning from Caterina's Italian cousins of the dangers of marrying a foreigner, and from Friedjof's Dutch shipmates about what happens to petite Italian girls after a couple of babies. (Neither prediction came true in the short or the long run.)

They came West to California, still a relatively sparsely populated land of cheap real estate and golden opportunity in 1946, where an elderly Dutch couple in Artesia outside of Los Angeles had agreed to sponsor Fred for citizenship. Yes, Friedjof became Fred, and Caterina became Kay, and they embarked wholeheartedly on American postwar life, leaving the ways of the old country behind and contributing regularly to the baby boom.

When Dad's mother immigrated in 1952, she was allowed to take only a small amount of cash—around $400—out of war-ravaged Holland. She had her household treasures packed and shipped in a 5'x4'x8' wooden crate (Dad added windows, door, and roof; voilà—playhouse), which arrived months later to US shores: grandfather clock, china cabinet, throne like chairs, assorted copper coal buckets and candle holders, an ancient spinning wheel, and a late 1800s vintage church pew.

What little English Grandma knew when she arrived improved only slightly during the decades of her life in the United States. Given to telling inflated stories of her circumstances and social position in Holland, she was haughty and of the opinion that the Netherlands sat at the top of the European hierarchy and Italy at the bottom. That should give you an idea of how she regarded my mother who, hungry for family roots and traditions, never failed to include Grandma for Sunday dinners, summer vacations, and every single religious or secular event this Catholic family could think to celebrate.

Dad and Grandma often spoke Dutch, so I grew up hearing a foreign language but not capturing a word of it. My sister and I used to mimic the phrases in babbly-baby bla-bla. Grandma was deeply insulted when she heard us carrying on in our invented lowlands language, not appreciating that we only wanted to sound like her. It seems ironic that I was exposed to so much Dutch in childhood but no Italian because Mom had no family to talk to in the West, yet it is Romance languages that are absorbed into my brain like water on parched earth. It's also worth noting that I gave up early on attempts to learn Dutch, because, though I traveled to Holland often, almost everyone there spoke English comfortably and enthusiastically. (And, I admit, I found it too hard to learn on my own.)

At Garces High School in Bakersfield, foreign language was a requirement, and the options were French, German, Latin, and Spanish. It's hard to believe, but in the mid-1960s, Californians still didn't think of Spanish as a very useful, let alone necessary, second language. The César Chávez farm workers' movement in nearby Delano was about to explode and would focus the nation's attention on the plight of exploited Mexican laborers. But in 1964, French would have been my path, except for one crucial factor: Mom's dear friend, Mrs. Domínguez from Puerto Rico, was the high school Spanish teacher. I started on my second language path through no clear selection on my part, but rather because of maternal insistence.

We lived on a street called Loma Linda (Spanish for "pretty hill"), and nearby lanes were named Pasatiempo (pastime), Alta Vista (high view), and Colinas (hills). We already knew lots of Spanish words—*enchilada, burrito, fiesta, siesta, tortilla*—so how hard could this be?? Well, I'll tell you: I barely survived the first few weeks of class with Mrs. D, and if it had been up to me, I would have quit altogether and taken anything other than Spanish. *Anything.* She was using a new methodology in which students could hear and repeat but never actually *see* words written in the language. So we were mired in frustration, parroting phrases day in and out (*escuche y repita* said the disembodied voice in my headphones: "Listen and repeat"), trying to decipher their meaning, and wondering all the while where one word ended and the next one began.

Second language acquisition changes dramatically around the time of puberty, and I was already past the stage of carefree unquestioning absorption, assimilation, and regurgitation of foreign sounds. So were the rest of the adolescent students in my freshman Spanish class, and I remember it as a kind of mass revolt, ultimately motivating Mrs. D to produce a handout with written words, leading to ah-ha moments as we connected the letters with the sounds with the meaning. (When a teacher myself, I could appreciate the value of her attempt at all-audio methodology as an approximation to how a child learns its first language.) My first foray into foreign language now took a turn for the better, and I sailed through four years with Mrs. D, earning straight A's but, in the predictable high school process and outcome of that era, never having actual conversations in Spanish, and graduating without even enough linguistic finesse to comfortably respond to the prompt, *Hola, ¿cómo estás?*

After that, it was two years of community college and more Spanish because it just seemed like the thing to do having already invested four years. I also took all the general education requirements, loving biology and botany but really struggling through math (a pattern well established in high school) and chemistry. By the time I transferred to the University of California at Davis, it was evident I would not cut it as a science major no matter how deftly I could pith and dissect the frog. I declared Spanish as my major, completed all the upper-division requirements in my junior and senior years, and hadn't a clue what would come next.

Maybe a K-12 teaching credential? The feminist movement had begun, but I could not think beyond traditional careers.

As I was applying for the fifth-year credential program, a totally unexpected event happened that sealed my future as a college Spanish teacher. I had continued to get good grades in my classes, never mind that I still couldn't actually carry on a conversation in Spanish because a perfect grade point average spoke louder than even rudimentary fluency in the foreign language. Along with my bachelor's degree, I was given the academic excellence award by the Spanish department accompanied by an invitation to the graduate program to work toward a Master's Degree in Spanish Literature while teaching one class per quarter. How convenient, since I was now to be severed from the parental financial feed bag and had no plan how I would manage. As it turned out, with a teaching assistant's salary, I could get by very nicely. Crazy as it sounds in this era of hugely inflated college costs and student loans into the tens of thousands, from 1971 to 1973 I earned something around $375.00 a month as a TA at the University of California and could pay for tuition, room and board, with a little left over for macramé supplies and a bottle of cheap Spañada wine for the Friday afternoon apartment house party.

Getting the award was the easy part. The reality I was to face in graduate school would prove to be the hardest test.

All about Me (Prequel II)

A s I was saying in "Prequel I," getting into graduate school was the easy part; the day-to-day reality of it was devastatingly difficult. I was one of only two non-native speakers of Spanish in the MA/PhD program at UC Davis. *Gringa* #2 had just returned from a year in Spain and spoke beautiful, lispy, peninsular Spanish as if she'd been born there. The other students in our graduate program were from Chile, Argentina, Bolivia, Mexico, España, Perú, and Uruguay, striving in their native language toward postgraduate degrees in Spanish and Latin American literature.

The fist of fate had plucked me from the top of the undergraduate ladder and flung me to the bottom of the graduate school barrel. Eight years into my second language study, I still could not comfortably carry on a conversation, and this was so painful that I would go up and down nine stories of stairs in Sproul Hall three to five times a day to avoid meeting up with professors in the elevator. All it took was their amiable invitation to small talk, *"Hola, ¿Cómo está usted?"*, and my throat would close up and I'd feel like I was going to pass out.

As painful and shaming as my experience felt, there was surely similar suffering going on at higher levels in this ivory tower of academia, and it too had to do with the fact that the conversational approach in foreign language teaching still had not become the favored methodology. It seems almost impossible to conceive of, but in those days languages were taught mostly to be read and written rather than spoken and heard.

When I peeked out from the bottom of the barrel, I noticed

that two of my grad school professors were perhaps suffering similarly. One was a well-regarded authority on the sixteenth-century Spanish novelist, Miguel de Cervantes, and his masterpiece *Don Quijote*; the other was equally established in the arcane field of the South American essay of the nineteenth century. They could produce flowing Spanish prose in the articles they wrote for publication, but were not at ease during casual conversation (I would meet them on the stairs to the ninth floor) because their academic training had never prepared them for something so mundane as chat-in-the-elevator Spanish. What a fate to be erudite but not comfortably conversant in a second language! I am forever thankful that fate was not to be mine.

The first year felt like it would kill me, but I hung on for dear life because I didn't have a plan B. First of all, there was no *assisting* in being a teaching assistant, for I was to solo teach an undergraduate class—starting immediately. I remember walking into the classroom on the first day of the fall quarter of my first year of grad school to teach my first Spanish I class. It consisted of a dozen or so freshman girls, one older female student, and half the college football team. The "how-to-teach-Spanish" graduate seminar hadn't yet begun, but forget about the fine points of methodology; the larger problem was my shaky grasp of the basic grammar and vocabulary I was to teach.

What I lacked in ability I made up for in sweat, many candles burnt out at both ends, and eventually, true enthusiasm. During that first year for my Monday through Friday one-hour-a-day in front of the class, I prepped for at least three hours daily. I didn't know the answers to most of my students' "How do you say..." and "What's the difference between..." questions, but I always came back informed the next day. You might be understandably shocked that someone as incompetent as I was teaching a university class.

I, too was in disbelief, but after a few weeks, I was more relaxed and started to truly enjoy the classroom experience.

My graduate literature classes were an even stiffer challenge. Since I couldn't competently speak the language, I sat in the back of the classroom taking reams of notes, afraid of being called on or even of being engaged in a chat with the professor before or after class. We were a small group of graduate students, around a dozen, all sharing the same large office, and there was no way to protect my torched ego or hide my sorry plight. The thing that terrified me the most—having to speak Spanish with all these native-speaker professors and students—turned out to be the very thing that nudged me toward fluency. Between teaching one class a day (plus prepping and grading homework), taking several seminars, studying, and writing papers, I was hearing/speaking/reading/writing Spanish for ten hours a day.

My *compañeros* were patient with my inadequacy and generous with their help; I was taken under a lot of wings, especially that first year. My new Chilean friend, Santiago, would sit with me for hours at a time correcting my writing before I submitted my papers. There were frequent group study sessions, constant conversations, and regular social mixers, often including the professors. It was like living total immersion in a Spanish-speaking country, and I came to feel moments of linguistic buoyancy. It became less like flailing just to tread water; I was starting to swim.

I learned more Spanish in that first year of grad school than in eight years of high school and college combined. I developed the knack of seldom making the same mistake twice, especially if motivated by embarrassment. Like the time at a party at the department chairman's house when I walked around the room of professors and grad students with a plate of cookies, offering them *gallinas*. Finally, someone quietly but pointedly thanked me for the *galletas*, and it was all I could do not to drop the plate and slap my forehead when I realized I had been offering not "cookies" but "barnyard chickens."

Despite linguistic missteps and mishaps, after two of the hardest years of my life, I received my master's degree, moved from Davis to Sacramento and launched into my new career as...a waitress?! Well, what's a girl to do? I had to make a living. At least I chose a Mexican restaurant, one of those upscale El Torito-type places. We had to wear short skirts with off-the-shoulder peasant blouses and greet each table in Spanish. I'll never forget the time I approached a table at lunch with my usual cheery ¡Buenas tardes!, and the girl's head shot up from her menu in shocked recognition of my voice. It was a former student from UC Davis, and she had heard me say those same words as I walked into the classroom every day for ten weeks.

Within a few months, I had been hired to teach part-time at Sacramento City College and had also been retained by UC Davis for similar assignments. These two jobs, plus waitressing shifts, and later, a five-year stint managing a health food restaurant, carried me from 1973 to 1988. It was a period of dearth in full-time teaching positions in the California Community College system given that many of the schools were fairly new and their faculty still young. I clung to my restaurant jobs as a way to "support my teaching habit," and in fact loved that the physical work balanced out the more cerebral life of academia. Though my family and colleagues thought it questionable that I taught college by day and waited tables nights and weekends, I was managing to support myself and Sacramento was a big enough city to allow for my two professions to remain mostly separate.

In the spring of 1988, Mendocino College was advertising for its first full-time Spanish teacher, the only such opening in the

California Community College system that year. Good fortune shined upon me (and not every under-employed Spanish teacher was willing to move to a small city in rural Northern California); I was hired and launched into the next twenty-five years of my career that September. It was a fantastic opportunity in a town I soon called my own, with people I easily came to know and love. It was a world away from Davis and Sacramento, but as I made friends among my new colleagues, students, and neighbors, I settled in with the warm feeling that we were all, in essence, speaking the same language.

Ez Dakite Euskaraz Hitz Egiten Duzu?

N o, I don't either—speak Basque, that is. Not a single word. I can't even pronounce that title. Seems a shame because I grew up in Bakersfield surrounded by Basque people, Basque food, and Basque sheep ranches. The big immigration from far Northwestern Spain and far Southwestern France had begun with the American Gold Rush of the mid 1800s, but most Basques didn't feel suited to mining and turned to what they knew best— ranching sheep—ensuring waves of immigrants well into the twentieth century. I went to Catholic school with kids named Ansolabehere, Echeverry, Etchechury, Eyherabide, Bidart, and Anchordoquy.

After our move from a tiny cottage in a Los Angeles suburb to an enormous (to my kindergartner eyes) house in Bakersfield, my parents became fast friends with the Anchordoquys who lived at the other end of *V* Street. My sibs (then only two) and I played with Tommy, Arnie, and Vivi every day—their house or ours: bikes, ball, Monopoly, Pickup Stix, and diving into piles of leaves my dad had raked up from the huge sycamore trees in front of our house. I remember gazing in spellbound horror at an enormous jar in the Anchordoquy's garage of some small animal's legs in liquid, hooves and all. Having an Italian mom had exposed me to a few unusual things on the fork, like raw clams on the half shell and the stomach lining of a cow (which, in a rolling boil, looked to me like a ruffly bathing cap), but I still could not fathom the culinary allure of pickled pigs' feet.

Our moms took turns driving us to St. Francis Elementary School every day. I loved riding in Rose's car because it was a brand-new big, red sedan with shiny upholstery and long, exotic finlike things out the back. Besides her car, I loved everything about her. She was pretty and stylish, gave only the gentlest of scoldings (at least to the neighbor kids), and spoke accented English with a sweet lilt from the French side of the Pyrenees.

Tom was a sheep rancher outside of Bakersfield, a barrel-chested man, the exact opposite kind of handsome as my tall, blond, blue-eyed Dutch father. Their shared experience of being immigrants from European countries must have forged friendship out of kinship. Not the types to bond over Friday night poker or Sunday beer and TV football, they were the kind of friends that simply and enduringly admired and respected each other and would always lend a needed hand. I remember Tom as a man of kindness but few words, though supplemented by the twinkle in his eye, inherited by his son Arnold. My dad admired the Basque as "the gentlest people in the world."

It's distant and blurred, but my earliest memory of a specific incident of life in Bakersfield is a visit out to the sheep ranch with Rose behind the wheel and all us kids tumbled all over the nauga-hyde (before the legislated advent of seatbelts). The excitement had been building for days because it was to be an adventure into the unknown and also because my parents would not be there to supervise. We arrived to flat, dry, ranch land, hot dust hanging in the air and clinging to our sweat, thousands of bahhhhhs in all directions. It was shearing day, and Rose joined the women leaning over big pots on open fires while we kids took off on an adventure that I can still replay with all five senses through the long lens of time.

My older sister and I tagged after Tommy and Arnie who were headed for the pen where tightly packed sheep waited their turn to be relieved of their wool. The boys climbed up the fence, and

Karen and I clambered to follow their lead. At the top of the barrier, they slid down to land their feet firmly on the backs of sheep, docile now with nowhere to bolt in the tight herd. We followed, found our footing, and flitted behind them over the thick wooly backs to the bleating of the animals and the shouts of the herders. I felt no fear, only the rush of excitement in one of those high adrenaline *is-this-really-happening?* moments.

Why was this ovine experience so unforgettable? Well, for one thing, I had a deep and abiding crush on both of the boys, and beyond that confessional detail, this was way more exciting than growing the award-winning giant radish in kindergarten or jump-skating the cracks on *V* street sidewalks. After our walkways of animals found their turn under the shears, I remember seeing nicks that drew blood and feeling sorry for the sheep now shorn of their protective coats.

That was my most dramatic memory, but the Basque way of life permeated my childhood in permanent and fortuitous ways. After the church ceremonies of First Communions and Confirmations, the celebrating families repaired to Noriega's restaurant on the other side of town. This was one of the several family-style Basque restaurants clustered around the old railroad station of East Bakersfield. My dad thought nothing of propping us little kids on stools at the bar while we waited to go in for dinner. I would sip my Shirley Temple, insisting that what I really fancied was a picon punch. The name sounded enchanting, and I didn't realize it had nothing to do with nuts.

Noriega's was the hands-down favorite restaurant among us kids because the grown-ups would excuse us from the table so we could romp around the three-walled ball court attached to the building. The Basque game this was built for is called *pelota* and is played similar to handball. The commercialized version of it, called *jai-alai* (billed as "the fastest sport in the world" because of ball speeds approaching 200 mph), used to be a popular gaming attraction in Las Vegas and still is in Florida.

All my family's big events were and still are celebrated at the Wool Growers or Noriega's, both legendary family-style Basque eateries whose renown has grown from local to national. The first course is minestrone soup with brown beans, spicy red salsa on the side, a simple green salad dressed with oil and vinegar, plus a tomato salad. It's hard not to eat multiple helpings of all of this from the big communal bowls, accompanied by fresh crusty bread and satisfying red table wine from an unlabeled bottle, and just call that dinner. It's tempting, but no one in my family would dream of passing up what comes next: thinly sliced, pickled beef tongue, which is so popular and addictive that refills at the Wool Grower's are no longer free.§ Along with the tongue, a vegetable plate, spaghetti, and french fries are served. And all that is just for starters. I remember taking some friends to a Basque restaurant in San Francisco and being so enthralled with the taste of home that I neglected to tell them to save room for the main course: your choice of pork chops, roast lamb, steaks, veal, chicken, halibut, scampi, or ox tail stew.

Francisco Franco, the dictator who iron-fisted Spain for forty years after the Spanish Civil War (1936-1939), tried mightily to obliterate Spain's secondary languages and regional customs. This suppression was particularly brutal against Catalunya (capital: Barcelona) and the Basque region, banning the languages and imprisoning those caught speaking them in public. Spain's return

---

§ My brother, Fred, sweet talks the waitress into an extra plate or two because he has "come all the way from Seattle" just to indulge his passion for their pickled tongue. He's been known to buy a pound or so of the delicacy from Luigi's deli and tuck it— very well sealed—into his suitcase when returning to Seattle from trips to Bakersfield.

to democracy in 1975 after Franco's death fueled a resurgence of interest in diversity and the preservation of ancient customs and linguistic variations from the dominant tongue.

Before that, the Basque language (officially named Euskara) was one of many feared to become extinct in our lifetime. Will it survive? As a world language, Basque is one-of-a-kind, not related to any of the Indo-European branches from which all but maybe five (Basque, Korean, Ainu, Sumerian, and Burushaski) of the world's languages evolved, and believed to have its roots much earlier in Stone Age Europe. There appears to be no link between Basque and any other known language, current or extinct. This is a linguistic phenomenon of mind-bending magnitude, leading to many theories of its origin, some remotely plausible and others downright fantastical, like the Lost Continent of Atlantis. The Basque people are proud, strong, individualistic, independent, and committed to preserving their history and heritage. Their language, no longer considered endangered, is on the "vulnerable" list, but hopefully headed back toward vibrant health through literacy and fluency among the younger generations.

*   *   *

With my sisters and our mom, we had a long-overdue reunion in the garden of Rose's care home with Arnold and Vivian when the matriarch was in her early nineties. I last saw her shortly after she celebrated her ninety-fourth birthday, and she even regaled me with a few phrases in her native Basque. Rose passed away in December 2015 at age ninety-six after having enjoyed visits from one or more of her kids and grandkids every single one of her days in assisted living.

Even though it evolved into an important part of my vicarious linguistic and cultural identity, Basque didn't mean much to my young mind way back then on *V* Street in Bakersfield. It was simply woven into the tapestry of childhood, and the Janssens just loved the Anchordoquys to pieces as dear friends and close kin. Still do, always will.

The Cure by Feeding of Earworms

'''ve had an annoying "earworm" in my head for over a week, and I am hoping that, with writing about it, the exorcism process will begin. But first, I wonder if you know what an "earworm" is because I didn't until recently when I came across a mention of it in something I was reading online. Eureka! This is a word we have needed for a long time to describe the universal phenomenon of our least-favorite line in a song we really don't like, perhaps espousing a sentiment we don't agree with, playing over and over through our head like, well, like a broken record.

As I was packing up the house to prepare for my big move to the "desirable" West Side away from the "undesirable" West Side, the Beatles kept my spirits high, my feet hopping, and my lips syncing while I loaded my life of accumulations into U-Haul boxes. But now I can't get Paul McCartney to stop singing in my ear, though in the listening I was transported to a time when I would have invited him to do just about anything in my ear. Over and over again, I am hearing the same line from the song, "You're Looking through Me" (*Rubber Soul*): "Love has a nasty habit of disappearing overnight."

They say, "What you resist, persists," and that may be a clue to the creation and persistence of earworms. Love is supposed to last forever, and I resist the possibility, but have had the experience—as we all have—of it "disappearing overnight." As the word suggests, the thing burrows in through the ear, and I theorize, goes deeper into the brain each time we "hear" our own mental replay and wish we hadn't, wish we could make it go away, or wish it were a perfect world in which love *does* last forever and always.

Meaning, however, is not requisite to being invaded by an earworm. After Manfred Mann sang, "There she was just a-walking down the street, singing *do wah diddy diddy dum diddy do*," well, I know I'm dating myself, but that nonsense still rattles around in my brain. My contemporaries may also remember with fond bewilderment, "papa-oom-mow-mow" (the Rivingtons, sometime in the past century), and also from ancient history, "supercalifragelisticexpialidocious, even though the sound of it is something quite atrocious."

Here's what I learned while opening the proverbial can of (ear) worms that I thought worth sharing with readers because the phenomenon is such a universal annoyance. Borrowed and literally translated from the German term, *ohrwurm* (pronounced, "oar-vorm"), it's now an American colloquialism according to the *Oxford English Dictionary,* and anticipating your next question, yes! you *can* use it in Scrabble play!

There has been scientific study and copious writing about these pieces of music looping endlessly through the brains of all but 2 percent of us. Some researchers offer remedies including brain work with Sudoku or crosswords, reading novels, listening to a different "cure" song (great, now I've got the "Karma Chameleon" ditty stuck in my head), taking OCD medication, or—the two universal cures for what ails—chewing gum and meditating (but not simultaneously).

I searched further for real people's experience with strategies on how to kill the pesky earworm. Melanie of Vancouver, Canada reports: "The cure we have tried—and this is dangerous, so we only use it when desperate—is to start singing 'New York, New York.' That will usually clear out the stuck song, but occasionally takes over like a dictator after a revolution." To follow up with another great metaphor, Anthony of Birmington, UK likens his years-long earworm (the theme from The Adams Family) to a screen saver in the brain because it pops in when his mind is blank. Other reader recommendations include doing long division in one's head and mentally "taking the needle off the vinyl." The problem with that last strategy is that an increasing number of folks have never actually seen a record player, let alone placed a large vinyl disk on a turntable and then a needle on top of it.

In a short story titled, "The Imp of the Perverse", Edgar Allen Poe penned about earworms: "It is quite a common thing to be thus annoyed with the ringing in our ears, or rather in our memories, of the burthen of some ordinary song, or some unimpressive snatches from an opera. Nor will we be the less tormented if the song in itself be good, or the opera air meritorious." Earworms have burrowed their way into the plots of books, films, sitcoms (notably, a *Seinfeld* episode, "The Jacket"), and legions of science fiction stories because of the viral nature of the worm and the possibilities for crazy making and mind control.

Long ago and far away, I learned that to make something unwanted disappear, the trick is to *consciously* create what is happening unconsciously. I have the habit of flexing the very powerful muscles between my eyebrows—also called frowning— sometimes causing people to think I am worried, upset, or mad at them. Of course there's Botox, but a noninvasive and totally cost-free procedure is to knit the brows purposely and repeatedly, perhaps even while looking in the mirror. Over time, the habit can be broken. After I saw the movie *Jaws*, I experienced visceral terror every time I went into a body of water larger than a bathtub. A wise friend counseled that I might watch the horrific flick over and over again, explaining that this was like pressing the shock button so many times that it finally loses its impact. I couldn't bear to actually do this, but I could see the logic behind his advice. It's simply a call to exercise the opposite of resistance.

If you're a chronic nail biter, perhaps you stress over it, searching for a way to break the habit once and for all. At one time, a straitjacket might have been attempted as a cure, but with the influence of Eastern wisdom, we are learning to surrender and embrace what *is* instead of fighting against it. I'm just theorizing here, but it seems very likely you could affect a major shift in that nail biting by standing in front of the mirror every day to knowingly, purposefully, and even creatively chew your fingernails to the nubs, until you don't anymore.

So my strategy for excising this Beatles earworm from my brain is simple enough: I will consciously and at the top of my lungs sing that particular line to extinction. I will be free of the earworm, but the couple next door to my uptown house may think their new neighbor has a screw loose or is having a nervous breakdown over love doing its "nasty habit of disappearing overnight." If that doesn't work, I'll try alternating song and dance rounds of the "Hokey-Pokey" and the "Locomotion" with chants of "bibbidi-bobbidi-boo." If my persistent earworm isn't vaporized by that interference, at least I'll have developed a more interesting looping repertoire. I'll let you know how it goes...

Wishing you a "Zip-A-Dee-Doo-Dah" day!

In Megahurtz but Notfurlong

For a very long time, I have been toying with the idea of getting a Dragon. No, not the fire-breathing kind, but the computer-dictation variety so that everything from e-mails to grocery lists to whole book chapters could roll melodically off the tip of my tongue to magically become print on the screen. The concept of computer dictation software is already obsolete, at least according to Mac users who have had this function built into their computers for years. Having failed to find the Mac so "very intuitive" as everyone rhapsodized, I cut my losses, sold the beast, and returned to the world of PC with a sigh of relief. Well, I'm just not very tech-savvy, OK?

In the best of circumstances, I type with four fingers, never taking my eyes off the keys, three typing classes between ages fourteen and forty-four notwithstanding. (Is "typing" still an extant word?) My colleague at the college tried her best with me in my third attempt at learning to type, and I passed her class by the skin of my fingertips at thirty-four words a minute, including *a, of, the, or, but*, and *oops!*, with accuracy at some percentage pretty close to the number I just mentioned. Keyboarding is something I just couldn't master, and this challenge badgers me daily, from two-word, e-mail responses (in which I commonly have a 100 percent error rate as in *Thakn yoou*) to this book you tenderly hold in your hands.

Grandma despaired when she gave me piano lessons for ten years, holding out a hope I would miraculously exhibit a burst of talent somewhere along the way, but *insisting* I look at the music book and not at my hands on the keys. I could not do it. I could not look straight ahead and know where my fingers were down below. I could not make that brain-hand connection. The resulting cacophony finally became too much, and Grandma finally became resigned to the fact that what I *didn't* possess was musical talent and what I *did* possess was some kind of a spatial-learning impairment. To this day, when I watch someone type or play piano without looking at the keys, I am in awe, wonderment, and confusion at how it is possible that they are doing what for me is impossible.

Keyboarding is not the only type of *boarding* at which I have failed. I also flopped (onto concrete and into ice banks) at skateboarding and snowboarding. Most recently, I proved my ineptness with fast-moving flat, slick surfaces by way of a running plant of my left foot on a 10"x14" piece of hard plastic (royal blue in hue) located where I had carelessly flung it on the stone step of my house while zippily carrying in items from those U-Haul boxes in the garage. In retrospective analysis, as the unintended sled took off, my left foot left the ground, and my body went airborne east-southeast. I picture myself suspended horizontally in mid-air for one bananosecond before plummeting to stone: heel of left hand, outer bone of left hip, inner right ankle, in that order of impact. Despite the megahurtz, it was only a compression fracture to my left wrist (and I'm right handed!) But for a time, I was challenged by everyday maintenance acts like washing my face (forget flossing!), opening a can of cat food, pulling my yoga pants all the way up to my waist, and other less mentionable acts.

And oh yes, about that limited-fingered typing: since three of the four *boarding* fingers belong to my left hand, can you picture what I did for weeks with the middle finger of my right hand? Yes, typing with a single finger was slow going and I'm feeling a bit beat up, but in my heart I am shouting *thank you* to the heavens. Though no longer a church-goer, I have a long ecclesiastical memory (as you might recall from the "Don the Noose for Biscuits") and now I keep recalling the verse from Psalm 91:12: "(Angels) will bear you up lest you dash your foot against a stone." Well, those angels still get top billing in my life because, although I *dashed* my wrist (and bumped bum and ankle) against that stone, they saved my head and let me off with a non-separated radial fracture, and nary a word of reproach for my careless fling of the plastic lid in the first place, accompanied by self-promise to retrieve it "before someone gets hurt." I hereby renew their contract through 2050.

That's it for one-fingered typing today. Harking back to the piece entitled "The US and Them View of the World" in which I explored America's way of making measurements and recording things, I want to share with you these wonderfully funny and delightfully clever definitions sent by a friend who makes it his business to keep me well supplied with laughs and lexical fodder. They not only make us smile (or groan), but they illustrate how very versatile, unpredictable, flexible, and risible our language can be when it falls into the "wrong" hands that chop it up and reassemble the pieces for our willing ears and eyes.

Useful English System Conversion Units

- Ratio of an igloo's circumference to its diameter = Eskimo pi
- Ratio of a jack-o-lantern's circumference to its diameter = Pumpkin pi
- 2000 pounds of Chinese Soup = Won ton
- Statute miles of intravenous tubing at Yale University Hospital = One I.V. League
- Weight an evangelist carries with God = 1 billigram
- Time it takes to sail 220 yards at 1 nautical mile per hour = Knotfurlong
- 365.25 days of drinking low calorie beer = 1 lite year

- Half a large intestine = 1 semicolon
- 1,000,000 aches = 1 megahurtz
- Basic unit of laryngitis = 1 hoarsepower
- 2000 mockingbirds = 2 kilomockingbirds
- 1 kilogram of falling figs = 1 Fig Newton
- 1000 cc's of wet socks = 1 literhosen
- 8 nickels = 2 paradigms
- 2 wharves = 1 paradox¶

This surely has multiple authors and I admire them all for their imaginative twists. Can you hear the sound of one hand clapping?

I'm still undecided about whether I'm going to get that word-breathing Dragon or just keep doing keyboard aerobics with the middle finger of my left hand.

¶ Bonus originals:
By me: Male instinct to periodically hole up in man cave = mens' troll cycle
By my lexi-fodder friend: Two crows hanging out with a raven = an attempted murder

A Girl (Not) Named Sue

Yes, it's true. I did make a unilateral decision (i.e., did not consult my parents) to change my name from Susan to Susanna for a couple of reasons I believe to be more defensible than reprehensible.

The name on my birth certificate is Susan Janssen. That's it—no frills. Just one first name and one last name. That has mostly simplified things throughout my life, except that people often think there must be a middle name lurking in the shadows that I'm embarrassed to disclose. My father had two middle names for a total of four that he had to write on official documents (Friedjof Johannes Christie Janssen), and my mother—well, those Italian names have enough syllables to fill several bowls of alphabet soup. After naming their firstborn Karen Mary, they quit the business of middle names, never to revisit the subject with their four more additions to the family.

I used to be kind of jealous of Karen getting something that I didn't. First, it was the middle name; then, it was braces in high school. Heaven knows I didn't want to go around looking like her with a horse bit of metal gear in my mouth and around the back of my neck, but in retrospect, it would've been a worthwhile investment of my suffering and my parents' money for the long-term esthetics of my teeth. (Okay, I'm glad I got that off my chest and out of my mind. Now, getting back to names…)

It used to be that many Catholic parents baptized their child with a saint's name. This was a custom that started in medieval France and Germany and was widely accepted and followed, though never a part of the Church's regulations (called Canon

Law). My parents were strict Catholics, and I theorize that my older sister got the middle name of Mary because they felt the need to compensate for the fact there is no saint named Karen (although it's a name derived from Catherine). Ah, but there *is* a Saint Susan—Santa Susanna, actually—the third-century virgin martyr whose story I won't even mention because it reads like a tabloid and may even be spectacularly fictional.

When my little sister was born two years later, Mom and Dad concluded that Marjorie was sufficiently close to (Saint) Margaret that the middle name could again be dispensed with. With the subsequent offspring, Frederick and Elizabeth, there was no doubt their names came directly from the official roster of saints. When I made my Confirmation, the saint's name that I and half the little girls in my sixth grade class chose was Therese ("The Little Flower") of Lisieux. A confirmation name is a devotional name, not a legal name, or one that is really ever used. That said, for years my mother addressed letters to me as Susan T. Janssen, perhaps regretting that no middle name had been bestowed at birth.

Nobody ever called me Susan until I was in college, except for maybe the parish priest when he came into our second-grade classroom to quiz us on the Catechism before we made our First Communion. I was Susie to everybody, and that was fine with me. My mother chose a personalized song from that era for Karen, Margie, and me, and mine was, "If you knew Susie" ("...like I know Susie, Oh! Oh! Oh, what a girl!") It was cute and catchy, and always put me in a happy mood. It wasn't until I was in high school that I became restless with my moniker and felt compelled to at least give it a bit of an edge by modernizing the spelling to Suzi. My friends caught on fast. The family was a harder sell. Mom still writes me letters, "Dear Susie..."

To everyone in the family and most of my friends from

Bakersfield, Davis, and Sacramento, I am Suzi (Aunt Suzi to a dozen or so of them), and I can't imagine it any other way. But in and after graduate school, it just seemed natural to transition to the more mature and professional Susan. By then, I was living a lot of my life in Spanish, and in that language, people usually called me Susana or Susanita.

I liked my given name, Susan Janssen, but found two faults with it. The first is that I never much cared for the monotonous quality of the repetitive schwa—you know, that *uh* sound that any one of the vowels can make. (As illustrated in "the Law of Schwa," whether we spell my name Susan, Susen, Susin, Suson, or Susun, it will be pronounced the same.) There's the second schwa at the end of my last name, so, altogether, it comes out "Su-suhn Jans-suhn," with a dull, rhyming quality. I know; it sounds silly to make a big deal over this, but I always longed for a three- syllable name— Samantha, Alexa, or perhaps Juliana, after a queen of Holland.

The second fault is both fun and fraught. In the 1950s, Susan was the fourth-most popular girl's name (after Mary, Linda, and Patricia) with close to a half million of us bearing it. The fun part is that when I first moved to Mendocino County, there was a Susan Club as well as a Susan Marching Band. The downside is that everywhere I go, there are legions of us. As an occasional visitor to the Mendocino coastal tango community, I am *Rita* because there are already four other long-term dancers in the group named— you guessed it. Preparing to go with friends to Tanzania a few years ago, there was another woman in our group named Susan, so I researched Swahili names and chose to be called Jamila (three syllables and a *JJ* alliteration) for the duration of our safari.

A few years ago, I started traveling to Italy and connecting with my mother's language and heritage. Now I teach basic Italian and have become comfortable with being called Susanna. This, by the way, sounds notably different from the Spanish Su-SA-na because in Italian, there is a *Z* sound that Spanish lacks, and also because whenever there is a double consonant in Italian, the voice must "rest" there for an extra fraction of a second—a significant amount of time in the pronunciation of a word—altogether to pronounce Susanna as Su-ZA-nnna.

In a single moment of early April 2016, I was suddenly galvanized to alter my appellation. I was just a few days from leaving for New York to attend Steve Harrison's National Publicity Summit. I got an e-mail saying something to the effect that *today is the last day to submit/change your personal information for nametags, directory, etc.* In a sudden bolt of clarity, I saw one hundred nametags arranged on the welcome table, and the name Susan jumping out at me from at least a half dozen of them. I emailed the organizers to change mine and became the only Susanna in a group of attendees that included, yes, a half dozen Susans.

And it's worked out just fine. Except for the time or two when someone called out "Susanna" and I didn't respond, or I looked behind me to see who they were calling to. Except for some friends writing me e-mails and not knowing *what* to call me. Except for my fellow newspaper columnist, TWK, asking me in the middle of our respective morning walks, "So what's the deal with Susan here and Susanna there?"

The simple answer is that you can call me anything, but please don't call me Sue!

Behind Closed Classroom Doors, Part I

O ver a Japanese lunch with Joanne and Esther, two of my former students—now dear friends—we were laughing about a memory one of them brought up of my telling a story in class involving a perfectly ordinary word in Spanish (*bicho*: "bug") that means something quite out of that ordinary in Cuban slang (I leave it to you to look up). We then joked about what would be revealed if I did a survey asking, "What do you remember best from señora Janssen's Spanish class?" With a mixture of fear and delight, I suspect it might be one of these incidents in the following pages. Along with the language learning that went on in my college classrooms over the years, here are some entertaining moments I'll never forget.

It isn't surprising how many memorable experiences involved food. We did a lot of eating in Spanish classes: salsa competitions, holiday burrito buffets, flan, Spanish tortilla-making demonstrations, and end-of-semester potlucks. Of course, there was always Dove dark chocolate passed around on Mondays, before tests, and whenever else the energy level needed a lift.

* * *

I never actually cleaned a squid in class, but I have this great diagram of how to do it, and sometimes I passed it out while describing the famous dish, *calamares en su tinta*. Wednesday's class ended with a particularly enthusiastic response of mostly, "Eeww, gross!" On Monday at 8:00 a.m., I walked back in to greet the same group of students, and my "*Buenos días, clase!*" caught in my throat when I saw a plastic baggie on my desk containing something dark and squishy. Not accustomed to pranks in college classrooms, I tried to remain calm and cheerful as I gently poked the watery black blob (now noticing there were white, fleshy things floating in it) and asked, "¿Qué es esto?"

The whole class was in on the answer to "What is this?", and the perpetrator came forward and proudly announced he had found a recipe for the squid-in-its-ink we were talking about last Wednesday. He'd bought the ingredients, cleaned the squid, carefully emptied the ink sacs to make the sauce, cooked it all up and served the dish to his friends, thoughtfully setting aside a portion for *la profesora*. That night, I prepared white rice, heated up the contents of the plastic baggie, and had an unforgettably authentic supper of *calamares en su tinta*. In the following class, I gave the dish a glowing review, and the baseball player-cum-chef a dollop of extra credit.

* * *

Half the final exam in conversation classes was an oral report that students gave as a presentation on a subject of their choosing, trying to stick to known vocabulary and structures as much as possible. For the beginning classes, it was to be one to three minutes; for the intermediates, three to five minutes. They moaned at the anticipated impossibility of speaking Spanish for X minutes straight *in front of an audience*, and then usually went on for ten minutes or more when their turn came. There was often food involved, especially in levels I and II: *cómo preparar guacamole*, my *abuela*'s recipe for salsa, the world's best flan. (My favorite flan recipe that I have been preparing for over thirty years came from Crystal's final exam presentation at Sacramento City College.)

In one memorable presentation, Sheryl used full-color illustrations to talk about hunting for wild mushrooms. Of course, the audience of students wanted to know how to tell the difference between the edible ones, the ones that make you violently ill, and the ones so lethal that you drop dead in the forest. Sheryl pointed out differences in the photographs, however, to many uninitiated in the art of foraging for fungi (teacher included), the toxic and the table-worthy were indistinguishable.

At the conclusion of her talk, she presented me with a plastic bag full of wild mushrooms—large and small, smooth and swarthy— the names of which I don't now recall. The other students had a field day: "You're not going to eat those, are you? I wouldn't if I were you. If you're not here for the written final on Tuesday, we'll know what happened. It could be a plot to make sure you don't come back!" Sheryl and I had already become fast friends and I knew her experience of the natural world was informed and profound. That night at home, I sliced, sautéed, and savored that whole assortment of mushrooms, and my taste buds have never forgotten.

* * *

From ancient history in the Sacramento City College days, there was an oral final involving food that had a not-so-happy but unintended funny ending. The young man was doing a presentation on how to prepare the Spanish omelet called *tortilla*. In addition to the perfectly browned and set version he'd made at home, he had all the ingredients arrayed on the table as he described the process: *huevos* (eggs), *cebolla* (onion), *papas* (potatoes), y *aceite de olivo* (and olive oil.) Everything went just fine until, at the very end, he picks up the three eggs and theatrically announces that he

will now *hacer malabares* (juggle). I'm just being laissez-faire in
the back of the room when, sure enough, a second later three eggs
fly into the air and splat onto the classroom carpet. We cleaned
up as best we could, but for the rest of my years at Sac City, I
pretended to know nothing about the mysterious omelette-sized
stain on the floor in front of my desk.

* * *

Students often went all out with these presentations and took
to heart my encouragement to use props and engage audience
participation. My colleague Skip had everybody up practicing the
tennis serve. A lovely lady fashioned a time capsule out of card-
board and presented the *what* and the *why* of the assortment of
twentieth-century items to be shot into outer space. The lawyer
instructed the class on the how-to of a basic will. A grape grower
demonstrated the art of pruning vines. One very large dog was
smuggled through the side door of MacMillan Hall and its owner
delighted everyone as it obeyed her commands in Spanish to sit,
roll over, and shake hands.

* * *

I just ran into Yvonne at the local bookstore and we again
shared a laugh over how, in my first-semester class, she shot down
my romantic naiveté about the big birds circling overhead: "Those
aren't eagles, they're *turkey vultures!*" That's what I remember
about my first class at Mendocino College—oh, and sweet Marge
in the front row wearing adorable little lady bug earrings, and
Cheryl announcing $99.00 fares to Mexico on Alaska Air, which
resulted in my first of twenty trips to Oaxaca and a study/travel
program for the college.

I should have taken better notes in my classes because there must be many incidents I've forgotten. But my memory is still darned good, and I haven't yet told all. That's right, you've only heard the third of it. Turn the page for part II and an end-of-semester toast that turned unexpectedly alcoholic, an (almost) fist fight, and a whole lot of smoking going on.

Behind Closed Classroom Doors, Part II

While we were students at UC Davis, in addition to working hard for our graduate degrees, participating in antiwar activities, and enjoying great camaraderie among professors and students, we smoked in the classrooms. I know—it's unthinkable now, just as it's unimaginable that there were ashtrays in clothing store fitting rooms (and lots of clothes that went on the sale rack with cigarette burns in the fabric).

It was the '70s, and you could light up anywhere. Professor Rogers walked into classes with a mug of coffee in one hand and a cigarette in the other. Professor Scari was an Argentine romantic whose good looks were distracting enough, but what really caused us not to remember anything he lectured about was his habit of drawing a cigarette from the pack and then spending the next fifteen minutes lighting match after wasted match that burned down while he talked, gesticulating with the unlit cigarette, and flinging spent matches from his singed fingertips.

Unlike the dressing rooms at Macy's and J.C. Penny, our classrooms did not have ashtrays. Professors and students lit up, flicked ashes on the floor, then stamped out the butts and left them for janitors to sweep up at night. I never taught my classes with a cigarette in hand, but I do recall lighting up when my students were taking tests. I cringe even as I write this because I think of how awful that smelly environment must have been for the nonsmokers and how unimaginable this must seem to anyone who didn't live through that era, and even those of us (now, hopefully, ex-smokers) who did.

* * *

On dozens of occasions, I dragged the two burner stovetop from my office into the classroom to heat the tortillas for our burrito buffet or to whip up Mexican hot chocolate. On the study/travel trips to Oaxaca, Mexico that I led, I had discovered *the* best brand of chocolate for making the drink, and would return every summer with at least ten pounds of Mayordomo in my suitcase for the next school year. Once or twice I made a Spanish tortilla (egg, potato, and onion omelet eaten an appetizer or a light supper), but I never attempted a paella only because the timing and number of ingredients in this spectacular Spanish rice, sausage, chicken, seafood, and vegetable dish was too daunting for in-class preparation.

* * *

Before finals week, my students and I always wrapped up the semester with a party that included food and beverages. At the end of a particular Sacramento City College class, everyone had chosen a potluck item to bring, and one woman had volunteered to bring drinks for the group. On the evening of the in-class party, she arrived with six chilled bottles of what she thought was sparkling apple cider, so proud to have chosen the perfect beverage for the Spanish class party because it was *from Spain*. Yes it certainly was!—hard cider from Asturias in Northern Spain. Hmmm... teacher dilemma: what to do? It was either alcoholic beverages or the drinking fountain. Since I'm more pragmatic than pure (and they were all over twenty-one), I swore them to secrecy and invited the beverage hostess to pour her cider enthusiastically, but not liberally, into the plastic cups. Then we toasted: "¡*Salud, amor, dinero, y tiempo para disfrutarlos, amigos!*" ("Health, love, money, and time to enjoy them, friends!")

* * *

At Mendocino College, I remember a particularly lively Spanish II class that, within the first month of the semester, had developed as a wonderful multi-age group community of highly communicative people. As was my pattern, every class started off in a stand-up exchange with students circulating around the room asking each other a specific question. I don't recall what the question was on this particular day, but my memory is crystal clear about the fact that, while the students were moving about on foot, our college president was seated as an observer in the back of the room.

Suddenly, I realized some sort of altercation had broken out in the middle of the activity because I heard one young woman yell, "It was *you*!" and then I saw her haul off and hit the guy standing in front of her. She wacked him pretty hard in the shoulder and continued to berate him while he was shrinking backward with a sheepish look of half-amusement, half-guilt. We didn't have to pull them apart, but it did take some unraveling to get to the story. They had been happy classmates for the first several weeks when suddenly a chance exchange in their second language clued the woman that this was the knave who, at the stop sign exiting from campus to State Street, had braked, accelerated, then braked again, resulting in her rear-ending his car and having to pay for the damages. I thought I had chosen the perfect class to showcase for the president, and instead he witnessed a near brawl.

* * *

Nearly every semester, there was an auction day in my classes, *una subasta*. The evening before the big day, I assembled stacks of paper money that my student assistant had made for me (before that employment category became extinct in the succession of budget cuts during the '90s) in color-coded denominations of $500, $100, and $50. Although they bore photocopied images of Antonio Banderas, Pablo Picasso, and Penelope Cruz, these were *dólares* and not *pesos* because ironically, Americans find the name of both our country (*Los Estados Unidos*) and our currency (el dólar) to be among the most challenging words in Spanish to pronounce. (***Dólares*** would usually come out sounding like *Dolores*, the feminine name, also the word for aches and pains.)

The students received their stack of bills and immediately counted their money to make sure they had the full $30,755 and not a *dólar* less. They'd been instructed to bring a belonging they were willing to sell that others might want to buy. Those who had forgotten to bring something beat a path to the vending machine for Snickers, Skittles, or M&Ms, popular auction items that incited serious bidding wars into the thousands. Of course, the whole point was to practice saying larger numbers in Spanish, and the student auctioning an item had to repeat the number each time a bid was shouted out.

When the bidding slowed, they said, "$1,565 *una vez...dos veces...tres veces....* ¡Se vende!" ($1565 once...twice...three times.... Sold!) The money changed hands as did the book, vase, mug, baseball cap, candy bar, colored-pencil set, or mini stapler. One student auctioned off an intact wasps' nest (minus insects) that another bought as a work of art for his office. A real estate agent had the winning bid for a transparent, green plastic watch and wore it daily for years. I was afraid I'd have to stop my winemaker student from auctioning off the bottle in his hand, but it turned out to be a gift for the teacher and was accepted graciously.

It all sounds so clean, neat, and perfectly orderly in the telling, doesn't it? Maybe it started out that way, but about halfway through any given auction, when a few students had a towering stack of bills and most had too few to buy anything else, things started to deteriorate. With the wink of an eye and the nod of a head, wads of money started passing across the classroom, and purchasing cartels spontaneously formed to acquire that coveted bag of M&Ms (which could be shared) or the baseball cap (which couldn't), more for the sake of sport and strategy than actual attainment. These were delightful days when I just sat in the back row, coached them on their use of higher numbers, and laughed as one by one they took to the front of the room to extol the virtue and value of a used shopping bag, a Beanie Baby, or a Disney character Christmas ornament.

The *subastas* sure didn't teach anything about the value of money, but numbers came alive and, after all that practice, they could begin to imagine themselves in an open air market somewhere in Mexico, holding their own with the vendor as they negotiated the price of a wool poncho and a pair of huarache sandals. Mission accomplished.

Behind Closed Classroom Doors, III

F ourth semester Spanish class at Mendocino College wasn't a literature class per se, but I finally gave up on following textbook dictates, and designed conversation-based learning activities that included culture and literature, and *didn't* involve buying a $120 book. These classes were unique and delightfully unpredictable because students at that level were capable of so much linguistic creativity.

In a turn of the century spring class, we had read several pieces of prose and poetry by Latin American writers living under repressive regimes. Students learned about *los desaparecidos* ("the disappeared ones") of Chile and Argentina in the seventies. They watched a film about the mothers who marched every Thursday, from 1977 through 2006, in the Plaza de Mayo of Buenos Aires to demand that the military dictatorship of Rafael Videla reveal what it had done with the thousands of sons and daughters who were summarily detained between 1976 and 1983 and never seen again. We read heart-rending first person accounts of those who had survived imprisonment and torture by the regimes, and poetry by dissidents against the Cuban Revolution imprisoned for years or for life with no legal recourse.

I had never intended an extended course on such an emotionally wrenching subject, but once we started pulling the thread of the "Dirty War" in Chile, one thing kept leading to another. With all of this weighty material, even past subjunctive verb conjugations became a jovial topic. But, in truth, we were all moved deeply by the experience and, when it came to the final assignment, they were inspired. Each took the viewpoint of one imprisoned by a dictatorship for their beliefs, and poured their thoughts and experiences into a poem. I was awed, humbled, and deeply moved. I still am after all these years.

* * *

In mid-December of 1999, we were reviewing before final exams when there was a campus-wide blackout. Our classroom had one south facing window which didn't provide enough light to see either textbooks or the board. I was going to cancel the class and let them join the streams of students headed for the parking lot, but the electrical failure spawned a spontaneous conversation about Y2K (Year Two Thousand), and in their foreign language at that! Soon we were creating a list of the items everyone thought should go into a survival kit when or *if* the worldwide computer systems enabling most aspects of our lives crashed at 12:01 a.m. on January 1 because maybe they weren't programmed to recognize the zeros of 2000. In the daily business of prepping lessons and correcting homework and compositions, I hadn't given this possibility a lot of my attention. However, many of my students *had*, and this sparked a provocative conversation in Spanish during which I wrote in huge letters on the board the items they recommended for our hypothetical survival box.

Though the Y2K angel of doom has long since passed over us, I still keep a student-inspired box of emergency supplies, *en caso de que...* (just in case): *botellas de agua* (bottles of water), *comida enlatada* (canned food), *un abrelatas* (a can opener), *cobijas* (blankets), *una almohada* (a pillow), *curitas* (band-aids), *velas y cerillos* (candles and matches), etcétera. ¡Ah! y *una botella de cognac* (for medicinal purposes only, of course.)

* * *

I often had colleagues sign up for my evening Spanish conversation classes at Mendocino College. In this particular semester, I had the chemistry professor in my class, and he was now the last student of the evening to take the stage for his final presentation. What came next was explosive, unprecedented, probably illegal, and had consequences. Forgive my memory lapse of the technical details, but I do recall he faced his audience with a rolled up newspaper in one hand and a glass bottle in the other. He lit the end of the newspaper wad, all the while talking in Spanish about the exchange of gases, combustion, and I-don't-know-what because I was watching the torch burn down towards his hand as he waved it around to make his points.

I had no idea how this was going to turn out, but it had to end soon because that torch was over 50% ash and cinders. Then he drew our attention to the glass bottle and put flame to whatever was inside of it. A sudden second later, there was a loud, sharp *bang!* We all jumped two inches off our chairs. I was thinking, "Should I stop this now or let him go on?" He was, after all, a professor of chemistry and had a decade and a half more tenure than I. Surely he knew what he was doing with gases, fire, and whatever else he had up his sleeve. As it turned out, he did, and two seconds before the torch flame reached his hand, he doused it in a bucket of water hidden beneath the desk. The grand finale over, we all started breathing again. We applauded him with relief and admiration, and the evening of presentations ended with ¡Chido! ("Cool!") and claps on the back. After rounds of ¡Felicidades! ("Congratulations!") and *abrazos* (hugs), we called that semester class a wrap and exited for the parking lot.

End of story? Ohhh no—at least not for teacher who found

out through college email first thing the next morning that the maintenance and security personnel had searched all of MacMillan Hall the previous evening after several staff reported smelling smoke in the offices and classrooms. They found nothing to account for the worrisome odor, but the fire department was called in to go through the building again, just to be on the safe side. It was determined that smoke had circulated through the ventilation system of the building, but the source could not be identified. This occasioned much shrugging of shoulders and scratching of heads, but luckily no investigation into the shenanigans in the service of learning foreign language behind the closed doors of room 1260.

CHAPTER SEVEN

Marking Moments in the Year

High Notes on Highway 99

Christmas always finds me driving south to family, and at New Year I'm plying the same highway back north to redwoods and wine country. Here I share with you some memorable slices of the central California valley culture as expressed through its billboards, road signs, place names, and rural geography. Hold on for a fast and fun ride!

May Your Days Be Merry and Bright

Whether it's December or May, this chapter should put you in high holiday spirits, especially if accompanied by a slice of fruit-cake and a favorite libation. As for the reindeers, no matter the month of the year (but *especially* in spring), they would want you to know the truth.

Have a *Feliz Navidad* and a "Diglot" New Year!

Maybe like me you resonate with that Spanish phrase in the title more readily than the English word *diglot*. Following a brief discussion of *diglotism*, you will be treated to a bilingual poem (with a glossary of words) that's meant for December, but might even provide cheer in August.

And the Word of the Year Is...

Lexophiles wait breathlessly for the annual announcement of the Words of the Year by various dictionary companies and academic societies. Here is the background and the history of the American Dialectical Society's selections since 1990.

"Reach Out" and "Open Your Kimono": A Lexical Review of 2015

There is yet more to be said about those Words of the Year. I am interested not only in how far you *open your kimono*, but also in knowing if the kinds of news items about words and language that I gravitate to are also the ones that grab a big share of your attention.

The Secret to Everything, Part I

It's the key to realizing your dream of *you-name-it*, and it will come as no great surprise. Then why is it that that over 95% of us don't do it?

The Secret to Everything, Part I

Herein are the four sub-secrets and an inspirational true story that will help us ride the rough times and finish with the elite few who *do* make their dream come true.

Mary and the Merry Month of May

We count on spring to bring flowers and rebirth, but snake parades and cheese racing?? We'll glance at some seasonal rites from around the world, then look more deeply into the Christian celebrations of Mother Mary in the month of May.

The Yodeling Dutchman, a Father's Day Tribute

This is a story of my father, with my mother in a supporting role, though in reality it was a pretty equal partnership in parenting, education, and discipline. Since this book is dedicated to them both, it seems a most fitting chapter with which to conclude.

High Notes on Highway 99

I love road trips. No talk radio, no iPod tunes, no recorded books, just the thoughts in my head and the scenery before my eyes. It's a long drive from Northern California to Bakersfield in the Central Valley to visit Mom for Christmas, and I usually break it up by stopping in Sacramento to see friends from the old days. After merriment and gift exchange, I leave the capital city with three hours down and four and a half to go.

Some folks say taking Highway 5 instead of 99 will shave off a few minutes. Could be, but the 5 has way too many big trucks and far too little entertainment for this connoisseur of California roads. Sure, Highway 99 presents the inevitable proliferation of chain retail with towering signage for endless iterations of Bed Bath & Beyond, TJ Maxx, Michael's, and Ross Dress for Less, making every city look alike when viewed from the freeway, but focusing beyond big corporate cookie-cutter clutter, things start to get more interesting. Past the slick urbanity of Sacramento, and coming up on Merced, I almost choked on my Triple Threat Power Bar at the sight of Lou Rodman's Barstools and Dining billboard inviting me to, "Come in and check out our stool samples." A neighboring billboard read, "We want your junk!", and yet another proclaimed, "We buy ugly houses."

On the food scene (though it was hard to consider such so soon after Lou Rodman's beckoning words), IHOP looks to have made a big comeback with pancakes in the heartland, and Black Bear Diners are leaving a big footprint. Jack-in-the-Box kept coming on to me with "MMMM-eaty!", but I stayed with my carrots and apple slices. On down the road, I'm as charmed as ever by signs for cafes named Apple Annie's and Blueberry Hill. (I can just hear Fats Domino finding his "thrill.") I was tempted by a juicy plate soaring in billboard sky for Salazar's Grill n' Bar, but figured there was no telling what they'd serve up at Joe Bob's Barn' Grill. Was that just an error in spacing?

It was Christmas Eve, with one of the few heavy rains in the fourth year of drought, and the FedEx trucks were out in full force to land those packages on their designated porches. The Walmart fleet was racing from store to store to fulfill their promise to America: "Save money—Live better." The jewelry stores had amped up their ad campaigns for the holidays, for what better time to shower that special one with diamonds?! The Roger's Jewelers billboard sparkles and purrs, "Stoke the fires." A local purveyor promises that with the gift of a glittery rock, there will be, "A great day for her. A better night for you." Another billboard of bling opts for a fear and jealousy pitch: "Your girlfriend wants me. Bad." That one still disturbs me. Also unsettling were the numerous signs by 1-855-FOR-TRUTH (by GospelBillboards. org): "If you die tonight? Heaven or Hell." Soon enough. I found welcome distraction and immeasurable cheer in a long lineup of bare-chested Chippendales inviting me to experience "50 Shades of Men." Suddenly, the Valley didn't seem so sleepy anymore.

The Central Valley is still California's premier food-producing region, with 230 different crops including tomatoes, almonds, grapes, cotton, apricots, and asparagus, and providing 8 percent of the value of US agricultural output. South of Fresno, livestock operations and huge dairy farms are frequent sights. The land extends eastward perfectly flat toward the Sierra Nevada mountains, which, due to valley smog, I can't usually see too clearly. Billboards abound for tractors, harvesters, and pesticides ("Stop this bug from killing California citrus!").

Back in 2005, there were forests of billboards up and down the entire valley promising everyone an easy mortgage with "No down payment!" for a home under $150,000. Those are all gone now except for one brave and perhaps exaggerated claim in Kingsburg just north of Fresno: "If you can dream it, we can finance it." All the rest noiselessly disappeared in the disastrous real estate market implosion of foreclosures on the American Dream.

The ubiquitous theme these days is water, and the signs of stress and divisive interests caused by the drought are everywhere: "Irrigation matters!" and "Is growing food wasting water?" After four years of drastically low rain and snowfall, the UC Davis Center for Watershed Sciences reports that the drought cost California $1.84 billion and 10,100 jobs in 2015. With El Niño dangling its promise of winter rains, new billboards exhort, "Build water storage now!"

The farmers may be struggling, but it appears the personal injury/defense lawyers are on a roll. With every trip, I see an increase in the number of outraged but confidence-inspiring male faces promising me they can fight the system, and together, we can win: "Been fired or harassed? Fight back!"; "Fix that ticket!"; "DUI, crash, injury? We are here for you."

Meanwhile, the economy beer and wine industry entices with billboards every mile or two: "Raid the state of celebration!" (Budweiser); "Go long. Finish light." (Coors); "Stella Rosa: your favorite tailgate wine" and "California loves to Stellabrate" (under $10 a bottle; heavy on the pinks and peaches.) A plumbing company promises, "We fix any leak... (photo of a toddler in diapers sagging to the floor) Well, almost any." What with Coors, Bud, Stella, the plumber, and of course, Rodman's stool samples, Central CA looks like one big party with a couple of trips to the bathroom.

Years ago on the drive south Susan, my passenger from San

Francisco commented on the cutesy names of towns and roads in the Valley. I was so used to growing up near Buttonwillow, Terra Bella, and Pumpkin Center that I was embarrassed to say I'd never even noticed. Plus, I felt like a hick around my friend from "The City." Now, I revel in the folksy charm of towns named Gustine, Snelling, and Chowchilla. I nod at the faded sign that still heralds Selma as the "Raisin Capital of the World," and drive on past off-ramps for Dinuba, Goshen, Tipton, Pixley, *Conejo* (rabbit in Spanish), Earlimart, and Alpaugh. The Elmo Highway to McFarland is a sign that Bakersfield is near. The Lerdo Highway to Shafter means I'm getting warmer. Then there's Kimberlina Road, and finally the sign that tells me *I have arrived*—at least to the northernmost end of greater Bakersfield: Oildale. There's still Merle Haggard Drive and Buck Owens Boulevard to navigate before I reach Mom's.

Fast forward five days: Santa and his little burros have come and gone; the roast beef was cooked and consumed; the gifts have been torn from their wrappings; the fourth Wise man was turned away for bringing a fruitcake; I've picked as many grapefruit from the family tree as I could fit in the car; and I'm on my way back north on Hwy 99, immensely grateful for the intermittent 70 mph limit that lets me fly.

On the first fast stretch toward Fresno, I strain my eyes to the east for Madame Sophia, in her fourth or so decade of reading palms in a rundown little house along the side of the highway. I always think I might stop to meet her someday. A little farther north around Modesto, I see she has competition: "Hermana Milagrosa" (Miraculous Sister) is obviously in the business of palm reading as well with a two-story sign along the 99 beside an equally dumpy little house topped by a huge hand sporting a long and promising life line.

Approaching Sacramento, and just about the time I think the roadside entertainment has played out, a billboard for Planet Fitness in Stockton renews my faith in the power of remodeling the hackneyed phrase to provocative effect. The gym promises that, if you sign up for a new membership in January, you'll "Pay diddly for your squat."

Comparing the North Valley to the South, the fields are greener, the sky is bluer, K-12 recesses aren't cancelled due to intense smog, and I can often see the mountains on both sides of the freeway. I admire the views but miss the entertainment and already anticipate a future foray through California's heartland to feel the pulse of this great state and sample what they're serving up on Highway 99.

May Your Days Be Merry and Bright

I f it's February or August, best save this read for December when you can imagine that Bing Crosby is again and forever dreaming of a "White Christmas," Paul McCartney is "Simply Having a Wonderful Christmas Time," and Andy Williams keeps reminding us that "It's the most wonderful time of the year." At the moment, I'm only convinced that it's the most expensive, stressful, and high-maintenance time of the year. As the "shoppers rush home with their treasures," they're already imagining what the credit card company will bring in January.

I can't be the only one who just occasionally gets ever so slightly crabby as the shopping days before Christmas dwindle, the pressure mounts, and I face the fact that my annual resolution to *simpli-fy* has again met with failure. If you *ever* experience a moment like that, I recommend building a snowman and engaging him in a game of catch with a fruitcake, singing carols to the neighbors then lobbing what's left of said fruitcake over the backyard fence, or roasting some chestnuts on an open fire, then throwing in last year's fruitcake for a spectacular burn.

Speaking of an open fire... Christmas was a much simpler affair when my father was a boy in Holland. He and his siblings put out their little wooden shoes, and in the morning, were ecstatic to find that *Sinterklaas* had left each one an orange. Infantile ecstasy over a piece of fruit is hard to imagine unless you lived in a cold, rainy, flooded country in the early twentieth century, ate boiled potatoes and cabbage every day, and regarded an orange as more precious than a Fabergé egg.

Dad told us stories from his early childhood, like the time he was chased around the yard by a giant rooster and fell into the family cesspool. I don't think this had anything to do with Christmas, but it always comes to mind along with the story about how his wonder got the best of him one late-December evening, circa 1925, and his hair caught fire when he leaned in too close to the tree, which was illuminated by *real* lighted candles tied to the branches of a *real* live tree. It makes one wonder how folks survived the "olden days," but I'm sure the number of house fires and hair fires accelerated the invention of the string of electrical lights and boosted product liability as a prime new area of specialization for lawyers.

My Italian mamma, along with being a pro at Scrabble, is a legendary cook and produces loaves of old-fashioned fruitcake every year—the rich, moist kind that many people actually eat. Last year, I got one for Christmas, another for the Fourth of July, and a third for my birthday in November because she always stores an extra few loaves in the freezer. She knows I'm going to tell her the same joke every Christmas Eve when I land on her back porch, road-weary but holly-jolly, after seven to eight hours en route from Ukiah to Bakersfield. (And somehow, her curiosity always kicks in before her memory of last year's telling does.)

Suzi: Mom, did you know that an ancient Dead Sea scroll has revealed the existence of a fourth Wise man?

Mom: Really?! Why didn't we hear about that in church?

Suzi: Because he was turned away for bringing a fruitcake.

Mom rolls her eyes and laughs as she hands me my first slice.

Before I share this recipe with you, let me be very clear: It's not Mom's. She hasn't yet given me hers, but promises not to take it to the grave. I found this one on the Internet as I was trolling around for "The Best Fruitcake Ever." You never know what you'll get with Internet recipes, but this one intrigued me and I thought it worth sharing with you for the holidays:

Ingredients: 1 cup butter; 1 cup sugar; 4 large eggs; 1 cup assorted dried fruit; 1 tsp baking powder*; 1 tsp baking soda; 2 cups flour; 1 tbsp lemon juice; 1 cup brown sugar; 1 cup nuts; 1-2 quarts aged whiskey.

Preparation (Time: between 20 and 120 minutes, and plan on the next day for recovery.)

- Measure 1 level cup of the whiskey into a clear glass to check for color. It should be light to medium golden-brown. Taste a bit to test its quality. Drink the rest of the glass to ensure it possesses the depth and character worthy of "The Best Fruitcake Ever." Repeat this step if you are not 100 percent convinced.
- Now, with an eclectic mixer, beat one cup of butter in a large, fluffy bowl.
- Add 1 teaspoon of sugar and beat the dickins out of it again. Meanwhile, at this parshticular point in time, make sure that the whixey hasn't oxshitized since offening the bottle. Open second quart if nestessary.
- Add two large leggs, 2 cups of fruit, and beat til high. If the fruit gets shtuck in the peaters, just pry the clods loosh with a drewscriver.
- "Example" the whikstey again, shecking confistancy, then shift two cups of floor or Cashcade or whatever—like anyones give a woot. Chample the whitchey shum mor.

---

* W*o*W* (Word of Wisdom): Beware of abbreviations! My little brother, Freddie, was helping in the kitchen, and when Mom's pancake recipe called for 2 tsp. of bp, he sprinkled two generous teaspoons of black pepper into the batter and fired up the griddle for the family's Sunday breakfast.

- Splurt in some lemming zhoosh. Foold in chopped splutter and strained nuts.
- Add in 100 babblespoons of brown booger and shumma dat shoda and mix well.
- Greash ubben and turn the cakey pan to 350 degrees.
- Now pour the whole blarn mesh into the dwyer and shpin on pertinent presh til dinnerstime.
- Sheck dat whixney wunsh more and pash ou.

Continuing in a more scientific, but no less festive, vein we shall now explore the gender distribution of Santa's reindeer, always depicted guiding the sleigh in sleek and graceful pose with beautiful racks of antlers. A popular "urban" legend of the past decade enlightens us with information attributed to the Alaska Department of Fish and Game:

"While both males and females of the species grow antlers in the summer each year, male reindeer drop their antlers at the beginning of winter, usually late November to mid-December. Female reindeer, however, retain their antlers until after they give birth in the spring. Therefore, according to every historical rendition depicting Santa's reindeer, every single one of them, from Rudolph to Blitzen, had to be a female. "

Every year Alaska F&G gets more queries than Santa gets letters about the sex of Dasher, Dancer, Prancer, Vixen, Comet, Cupid, Donder, and Blitzen—arguably unisex names in the main, but then there's Rudolph of the foggy nights. The Department informs that, yes, the majority of male reindeer do shed their antlers before December 24 while the females don't shed theirs until they calve in the spring. Therefore, it is highly probable that most, if not all, of Santa's reindeer were, are, and always will be, female. The urban legend says in conclusion: "We should have known. Only women would be able to drag a fat man in a red velvet suit all around the world in one night and not get lost." I say, *you go, girls!!*

Finally, words of advice for this holiday season: don't stick your head in the Christmas tree (even if the lights are electrical), don't accept a gift from the fourth Wise man unless you fancy fossilized fruitcake, keep Grandma out of the path of Dasher and Vixen, keep the cap tightly screwed down on her "whishkey" bottle, drink smart, and buy local!

Have a *Feliz Navidad* and a "Diglot" New Year!

That's a new word I learned the other day: *diglot*. In the absence of context, when I first spotted it in the title of a book, I thought it had something to do with a "dig" and a "lot." Whoa is me!—I was way off the mark. We are perhaps more familiar with the word *polyglot,* referring to one who speaks, reads, and writes several languages. Besides English, I can converse in Spanish (well) and Italian (passably), but I am flummoxed to read about someone who is fluent in those two languages plus English, German, Arabic, and Farsi. *Mon Dieu!*

In the United States, we're impressed by people who are bilingual (or *diglot*) because most Americans aren't, though a great number had enough experience in a second language high school class to appreciate the challenges of acquiring *lingua* #2, let alone #3. My aunties in the Netherlands were fluent in German and English besides their native Dutch, and dedicated travelers that they were, they devoted themselves to learning Spanish, French, Italian, and a smattering of the local language in whatever country of the world they were going on holiday. In over a dozen trips to Holland, I never picked up any Dutch because almost every Netherlander speaks, reads, writes, and watches TV in (usually American) English. I consider my Italian friend who lives in Barcelona a true polyglot. Ludovica has mastered English, Spanish, French, and Catalan (the language of Catalonia of which Barcelona is the capital), and on the job, she translates in all five of her languages. I am ever in awe of her mastery and fluency, but, as an American, I feel fortunate to have at least more than one language on the tip of my tongue. And I will always prefer the mellifluous flow of the Latin-origin word *bilingual* over the Germanic guttural thud of *diglot*.

To celebrate the season as well as our second-most spoken language in America, I would like to share with you my personal version of an anonymous diglot poem that never ceases to delight:

> 'Twas the night before Christmas
> and all through the *casa*
> not a creature was stirring...*¡Caramba! ¿Qué pasa?*
> The stockings were hung by the chimney *con cuidado*
> in hopes that 'Ol Santa would feel *obligado*
> to leave a few *cosas aquí y allí*
> for *toda la familia* but especially *para mí.*
> While *mamá* worked late in her big *oficina,*
> *papá* was shopping at the corner *cantina,*
> buying milk and Doritos and a can of *cerveza,*
> for Santa to find on the dining room *mesa.*
> Now the *niños* are snuggled all safe in their *camas,*
> some in their 'chones and some in *pijama.*
> Those little *cabezas* are filled with sweet dreams—
> they're all *esperando lo que* Santa will bring.
> Then out in the yard, there arose such a *grito*
> that I jumped to my feet like a frightened *gatito.*
> I ran to the window and looked *para afuera,*
> and who in the world do you think *¿quién era?*
> —St. Nick in a sleigh and a big red *sombrero*
> came dashing along like a crazy *bombero.*
> And pulling his sleigh, instead of *venados,*
> were eight little *burros* approaching *volados.*

And holding the reins was a quaint little *hombre*
shouting and whistling, calling them by *nombre:*
"*¡Panchita y Pepe! ¡Nacho, Lupita!*
¡ey Beto y Chata!, ¡Nieto y Flaquita!
¡Adelante! ¡Arriba! ¡Abajo! ¡Y vamos!
We'll park it right here on the lawn *donde estamos.*"
Then standing up straight with his hands on his *pecho,*
he flew to the top of our very own *techo.*
With his big round *panza* like a bowl of *jalea,*
he struggled to squeeze down our small *chimenea.*
Then huffing and puffing at last in our *sala,*
with soot smeared all over his red suit *de gala,*
he filled all the stockings with lovely *regalos,*
for none of the *niños* had been *muy malos.*
He nibbled *galletas,* took a sniff of *cerveza,*
and cleaned his round *lentes* with the cloth on the *mesa.*
Then, chuckling aloud, and feeling *contento,*
he turned like a flash and was gone *como el viento.*
And I heard him exclaim, and this is *verdad,*
"Merry Christmas to all! ¡Feliz Navidad!"

Whether you're reading this in July or December, may all our days be merry and bright, may we support the local economy with all our might, may all our credit card bills be light, and may we all sleep tight tonight!

Glossary of Spanish Words

abajo	down
adelante	forward
afuera	outside
arriba	up

aquí y allí	here and there
bombero	fireman
cabezas	heads
'chones	undies
como el viento	like the wind
con cuidado	with care
cosas	things
donde estamos	where we are
esperando	waiting
gala	festive
galletas	cookies
gatito	kitten
grito	shout
jalea	jelly
lentes	eyeglasses
mesa	table
muy malos	very bad
niños	children
nombre	name
panza	belly
pecho	chest
¿quién era?	who was it?
regalos	gifts
sala	living room
toda	all
techo	roof
venados	deer
verdad	true
volados	flying
¡Y vamos!	And let's go

And the Word of the Year Is...

E very year's events, trends, scandals, and tech advances are fertile ground for a new word or phrase to be born, capture our imagination, bounce from our brain to our tongue, and go verbally viral into the vibrant and volatile realm of words and the images they conjure. In many cases, an original term *must* be coined to allow us to refer to the new thing at all, or at least do so in a word or two rather than a half dozen or more. "To smoke an electronic cigarette inhaling nicotine through a vaporized solution" mercifully simplifies down to the verb *to vape*. No need to suffer the lengthy awkwardness of writing on your Christmas wish list, "I want one of those collapsible monopods to attach to my camera or cell phone to take better selfies" when you can just say, "Dear Santa, bring me a *selfie stick*!"

The Word of the Year (WotY) isn't just one contest but several, with widely recognized players including the Oxford University Press, Merriam-Webster, and Global Language Monitor presenting their selections. But the most prestigious choice of a year's winning word is that of the American Dialect Society, thus distinguished because it is the oldest such contest with its WotY determined by a vote of linguistic experts independent of commercial interests. The yearly selection made by these linguists is also unique and eagerly awaited because it is the last one announced—in January—after all the delights and disasters of the year have been consigned to history.

Here are the ADS picks since the tradition began in January 1991:

- **1990:** *bushlips,* similar to "bullshit" – stemming from President George H. W. Bush's 1988 "Read my lips: no new taxes" broken promise.
- **1991:** *mother of all...,* as in Saddam Hussein's foretold "Mother of all battles."
- **1992:** *Not!,* meaning "just kidding."
- **1993:** *information superhighway*
- **1994:** *1. cyber; 2. morph;* "to change form."
- **1995:** *1. web; 2. (to) newt;* to "act aggressively as a newcomer," like Speaker Newt Gingrich during the Contract with America.
- **1996:** *-mom,* as in "soccer mom."
- **1997:** *millennium bug,* the fear that computers' inability to distinguish 1900 from 2000 would create international havoc.
- **1998:** *e-,* as in "e-mail" or "e-commerce."
- **1999:** *Y2K*
- **2000:** *chad,* from the 2000 presidential election controversy in Florida.
- **2001:** *9/11*
- **2002:** *weapons of mass destruction (WMD)*
- **2003:** *metrosexual,* "heterosexual male into beauty treatments and fashionable clothes."
- **2004:** *red state, blue state, purple state,* from the '04 US Presidential election.
- **2005:** *truthiness,* quality of a "truth" that a person claims to know intuitively because it "feels right" without regard to evidence, logic, or facts, popularized on *The Colbert Report.*
- **2006:** *plutoed,* "demoted or devalued," as happened to the former planet Pluto.

- **2007:** *subprime*, describes a risky or less than ideal loan, mortgage, or investment.
- **2008:** *bailout*, in the specific sense of the rescue by the government of companies on the brink of failure, including large players in the banking industry.
- **2009:** *tweet*, a short message sent via Twitter.com; the act of sending such a message.
- **2010:** *app*, abbreviated form of application, a software program for a computer or phone-operating system.
- **2011:** *occupy*, verb or noun, inspired from the Occupy movements of 2011.
- **2012:** *hashtag*, a word or phrase preceded by a hash symbol (#), used on Twitter to mark a topic or make a commentary.
- **2013:** *because*, abbreviated phrase introducing a noun, adjective, or other part of speech, (e.g., "because reasons," "because awesome")
- **2014:** *#blacklivesmatter*, hashtag used as protest over blacks killed at the hands of police (especially Michael Brown in Ferguson, Mo. and Eric Garner in Staten Island).
- **2015:** Singular *they*, as a gender-neutral pronoun to avoid he/she. Example: Each student has to provide *their* own email address. (More on this selection in the next chapter.)

Here are some of my favorites that were in the running but didn't get the blue ribbon for their year:

- **2006:** *climate canary*, a species that serves as an early warning system because it is affected by an environmental danger before other species.
- **2007:** *Googlegänger*, a cross between "Google" and "Doppelgänger" (in folklore, the double of a living person); a person with your name who shows up when you google yourself.

- **2011:** *FOMO*, an acronym for "Fear of Missing Out."
- **2012:** *YOLO*, an acronym for "You Only Live Once."
- **2014:** *bae*, a sweetheart or romantic partner, from "before anyone else."

In addition to the "Word of the Year," the American Dialect Society also selects words in other categories that can vary from year to year. I have taken massive editing liberties to present you the ones I found most useful, creative, fun, or outrageous.

Most Useful

- **2008:** *Barack Obama*, specifically, the use of both names as combining forms, as "ObamaMania," "Obamacare," "Barack n' roll."
- **2011:** *humblebrag*, expression of false humility, especially by celebrities on Twitter.

Most Creative

- **2008:** *recombobulation area*, an area at General Mitchell International Airport in Milwaukee where passengers who have passed through security screening can get their clothes and belongings back in order.
- **2009:** *Dracula sneeze*, covering one's mouth with the crook of one's elbow when sneezing, seen as similar to popular portrayals of the vampire Dracula, in which he hides the lower half of his face with a cape.
- **2010:** *prehab*, preemptive enrollment in a rehab facility to prevent relapse of an abuse problem.
- **2011:** *Mellencamp*, a woman who has aged out of being a "cougar," named after John Cougar Mellencamp.

Most Unnecessary

- **2010:** *refudiate*, blend of "refute" and "repudiate" as used by Sarah Palin on Twitter.
- Most Outrageous
- **2012:** *legitimate rape*, type of rape that Missouri senate candidate Todd Akin claimed rarely results in pregnancy.

Most Euphemistic

- **2010:** *kinetic event*, Pentagon term for violent attacks on troops in Afghanistan.
- **2013:** *least untruthful*, involving the smallest necessary lie, used by (at the time) US Director of National Intelligence James Clapper.

Most Likely to Succeed

- 2013: *binge watch*, to consume vast quantities of one show or series in a single sitting.
- 2014: *salty*, exceptionally bitter, angry or upset.

Least Likely to Succeed

- **2012:** *phablet*, midsized electronic device, between a smartphone and a tablet.
- **2013:** *Thanksgivukkah*, confluence of Thanksgiving and the first day of Hanukkah that will not be repeated for another 70,000 years.

At this writing in 2016, the most up-to-date Words of the Year are those of 2015. I promise to update with a new report every January, but for now, let the next chapter open wide the kimono to reveal the naked truth about an exciting and controversial year in lexical history.

"Reach Out" and "Open Your Kimono": A Lexical Review of 2015

ometime prior to 2015, a corporate talking head or two decided that it was crass to "contact." The taboo spread like "wordfire," and now professionals everywhere are (all touchy-feely like) "reaching out" to colleagues, clients, students, and associates. Many find this usage weird, yet the verb *to contact* (which was controversial in the early '60s) is gathering dust in professional-speak circular files everywhere.

Sample memo: "Bob, it's time we *reach out* to the managers at Acme Excavations and Cronuts, Inc., and see if they're amenable to *opening their kimono.*"

The phrase *open kimono* appears to have first surfaced in the eighties with international business dealings between the West and Japan. To be *open kimono* or to *open one's kimono* means to reveal plans and share information freely; to be "transparent." The term is laughable and "kind of creepy" in the words of Bruce Barry, a professor at Vanderbilt University's Owen School of Business. But it was a top contender for Australia's word of the year in *Macquarie Dictionary* for 2015, occasioning chuckles over visualizations of kimonos in the Outback. In the end, *open kimono* was edged out by *captain's call*, a cricket term that has invaded the world of business and politics to refer to a decision made without consulting one's colleagues. Not very sporting, eh, mate? It's interesting how the two terms represent opposite tactics in the business world: "We hoped he would *open his kimono*, but he made a *captain's call* instead."

* * *

Here is the rundown of the Words of the Year (WotY) for 2015, revealed in January of 2016: The Oxford University Press WotY is not even a word but an emoji, the one of a smiley face with a big fat tear dripping from each eye. One might be moved to ask how this symbol best encompasses the ethos and preoccupations of 2015, and might then conclude that English speakers are doing less actual verbalizing and more point and click. Like, why articulate the emotion we are feeling when we can just find something suitable on the emoji menu? It's easy to relate to laughing and crying at the same time—a reaction often elicited during presidential debates—but this particular emoji is called "joy." What went on in 2015 that Oxford thinks we were mass-emoting tears of joy over? (I wonder if that verb *emote* still exists or has it joined *contact* in the lexical dustbin, to be replaced by *emojiate*, after the model of *conversate,* which many people will bet you money is in the dictionary.)

Merriam-Webster's selection for 2015 isn't a word, either, but rather the suffix *-ism.* It was chosen because there are 2733 English words ending in *–ism* in the *Merriam-Webster Unabridged Dictionary*, and seven of these were among their site's most popular searches during the year: *socialism, capitalism, racism, communism, sexism, terrorism, and fascism.* Important topics for our time, yes, but *–ism* as the WotY is lacking in, shall we say, "slexical" appeal.

Global Language Monitor's WotY is *microaggression*, defined as "everyday verbal, nonverbal, and environmental slights, snubs, or insults, whether intentional or unintentional, which communicate hostile, derogatory, or negative messages to target persons based solely upon their marginalized group membership." This is certainly recognizable as a relevant societal preoccupation, especially in the context of worldwide refugee crises and racial prejudice, as well as the move toward extreme political correctness on college campuses.

The American Dialect Society's choice is last though anything but least, because in addition to carrying the highest prestige, it resolves a long-standing grammatical problem in the English language. It is (drumroll...) the word *they*, and I say "Yay!" Specifically, this is the personal *they* used as a gender-neutral *singular pronoun.* This is no grand preoccupation like terrorism or fascism, but before you roll your eyes or throw up your hands, consider this: Do you ever wonder if you *must* go through the rigmarole of writing, "The applicant should be told how much he/she will have to pay for his/her loan"? Or could you just simplify things and write, "The applicant should be told how much *they* will have to pay for *their* loan," which is what you would verbalize anyway. Okay, so it's not a moral dilemma or a defining ethos, but this bold move by the ADS, with precedents in Chaucer, Shakespeare, and Jane Austen, is a logical step toward resolving a linguistic gap in our language. In 2015, *they* singular was blessed by the *Washington Post* style guide, and *WP* copy editor Bill Walsh called it, "The only sensible solution to English's lack of a gender-neutral, third-person-singular personal pronoun." Insensible solutions have included *s/he* and *'e*.

* * *

In worldwide lexical news from the past year, Rome's city council approved a new regulation to phase out and ultimately eliminate the Roman numerals on street signs, official documents, bills, and identity cards and replace them with numbers written in words. Many Italianos are understandably upset because these numerical symbols have named sites and ordered lives in the Eternal City for about thirty centuries. For example, Corso Vittorio Emanuele II, the boulevard that runs east-west through Central Rome and is named after the first king of united Italy (1861-1878), will now be Corso Vittorio Emanuele Secondo. Mario Ajello, a commentator for *Il Messaggero*, voiced the sentiment of many of his countrymen: "Is it easier and simpler to have no link to the past? Maybe, yes: but it is cultural suicide." Fortunately, all the MDCLXVIIIs chiseled into stone will remain. Fueling the backlash, the city's new principal branding slogan is in English: "Rome and You," replacing the elegantly straightforward "*Roma Capitale.*" Meanwhile, the Marina Militare has adopted the slogan, "Be Cool, Join the Navy," in the hopes of attracting more recruits via English than Italian.

The year 2015 also saw major linguistic upheaval on the continent of Africa. Ghana, Tanzania, and Zimbabwe are "casting off the language of the colonizer" in the words of Charles Mubita in *New Era* and installing plans to discard English as the principal language of instruction and replace it with native languages.

In the political arena, Trump said it was "stupid" for Jeb Bush to speak Spanish and that he should "set the example by speaking English while in the United States." Carly Fiorina agreed, asserting that English is the official language of the United States (which it isn't). And Sarah Palin, who can always be counted on for quotable contributions to any discussion, said we should all just "speak American."

To conclude with a thrillingly upbeat lexical item from 2015: New Zealander Nigel Richards won the French-language Scrabble World Championship in July, not because he is well-versed in French (he doesn't speak the language), but because he memorized the words in the French dictionary. At least one expert on the game has called him, "The greatest Scrabble player of all time, hands down." It's nothing short of amazing, and you don't even have to be a word geek to be jaw-dropping awestruck.

*   *   *

In keeping with some of these lexical revelations, here are my resolutions for the future: In the professional arena, more contacting but no reaching out; on the personal front, choosing to express true emotions over *emojions*; in entertainment, playing Sudoku using only Roman numerals; and in life in general, never going out and about with my kimono flapping in the breeze.

The Secret to Everything, I

These next two chapters might be an inspiring read around January 1, though it seems New Year resolutions have become unfashionable of late. Lest you think my title hyperbolic, I will caveat that the secret I am about to reveal will not breathe life into the garage door that suddenly and completely shut down yesterday afternoon. It will not magically disappear the dings in the car door, banish gray hairs, or materialize gold coins in our pockets. But it *can* provide the ticket to a flat belly, make you a great swing dancer, unlock the mysteries of becoming bilingual, and maybe even allow you to read your cat's mind. It really is the *secret* to learning *anything,* and, even more importantly, to not losing the mastery you gain. So simple, even obvious; not mysterious, just elusive. Although I discovered this "secret" for myself through life experience, it is a fundamental principle of how things work that has been around for all time. It will not come as a surprise to you.

As a kid, did you ever take lessons to learn to play a musical instrument? Do you still play that saxophone, guitar, or violin? I took ten years of piano lessons from my Dutch grandmother (very strict: all classical, no movie tunes, and certainly no improvisation), practiced every day by parental decree, and progressed steadily until, despite very limited musical talent, I could play "Unchained Melody," "O Sole Mio," and "Hard Day's Night" (oops, I mean Bach, Beethoven, and Bartók) with acceptable accuracy and even some passion. And now...I can't even read music.

The highly talented concert pianist, Elena Casanova, started lessons a couple of years earlier in life than I. World-class guitarist Alex de Grassi took up his instrument on his own at about the age I quit studying music. Look where they are today! Obviously, these two legendary musicians possess musical talent that Grandma noticed was lacking in me, but the "secret" reveals there is an essential element without which all the talent in the world cannot manifest and develop.

My brother turned up his nose at piano lessons and insisted on guitar. Now, fifty years later, he plays for an audience of God and hundreds of the faithful every week at his church in western Washington. Our dear family friend, Enrique Henao from Colombia, is an amazingly versatile and accomplished guitarist whose long career spans the globe. He plays regular gigs in Seattle-area restaurants and wineries. For money? No.† Enrique says he does it for practice and "to maintain the discipline of my concentration despite noise and distraction around me." Enrique adds, "Sometimes I compose musical pieces in those conditions, something I can't do in concerts when the audience is in total silence." Is *practice* the "secret"?? We're getting warm, but haven't quite unearthed the whole treasure.

In my years of teaching Spanish, I have heard many a student say, "I'm not good at languages," and too many people refer to that mysterious "flair" for learning foreign language as if it were some magical potion seeped into their brain. Or not. I actually do think I had a slight advantage for learning a foreign language because I grew up hearing one even though Dutch wasn't remotely close to the language I (my mother, actually) decided I should study. And yes, I do see that some of us have more affinity for mathematics and others lean more toward language. But the bottom line is this: The real difference among people who set out to become bilingual is that *the ones who persist, do; and the ones who stop, do.*

---

† The money that does come in from Enrique's gigs is donated to children's medical and educational funds around the world.

That's not the kind of satisfyingly earth-shaking, life-changing, wave-the-magic-wand answer we all hope for, but it's the truth. As my coach Tris said to me, "If spiritual progress were fast and easy, we'd all be enlightened by now, God would get bored, and the game would be over." The same goes for—you name it—becoming bilingual, learning a musical instrument, getting in shape, painting a masterpiece, and improving relationships. *What* to do is so very simple; *doing* it is where over 95 percent of us fall short. But don't lose heart because now our shovel has struck the chest of buried treasure, and we have only to dig a bit more to release it.

During my last years of teaching college, I began to learn Italian, first from dear Emma of Ravenna, Italy, then on my own and during short stints at the Dante Alighieri Institute in Tuscany. Experiencing myself as a struggling foreign language learner after having taught one for decades was humbling, but I thought I was immune to the most common of pitfalls. I came back from Italy full of pasta, gelato, and the inspired commitment to break through to higher levels of mastery. I organized my notes, made flash cards, created a fat binder for my future work, and then...I got distracted, busy, harried, overwhelmed by life and work. And I stopped.

As the fall semester ended, the good news was that most of my students were planning to continue to the next level of Spanish; the *downslide* was the five weeks of winter break when they would lose proficiency simply from lack of contact with Spanish—my exact experience in Italian. I devised a contract, as much for my benefit as theirs, and we committed to do *something* in our target language every single day, beginning immediately. What did that word *something* in the contract mean? It meant *anything*. Sure, they could practice irregular verbs every day, but just as valid (and probably more fun and engaging) was learning the words to a song, ordering lunch at local Mexican eateries in Spanish, writing an e-mail, flipping through flash cards, even opting for Spanish at the ATM. The length of time invested was not part of the contract, but frequency, consistency, and challenge mattered. Eureka! The "secret" is revealed, and yes, we *have* known it all along.

Daily contact with a foreign language (tennis ball, paint brush on canvas, piano keys, exercise mat) has a dramatic effect on body (physiology) and mind (imagination). So does daily absence. Every day separated from our dream makes it harder to return and easier to give up altogether. We *imagine* that we "don't remember a thing" from those old Spanish classes or piano lessons because the learning isn't readily accessible anymore. Physiologically, the only way to keep that learning center in the brain refreshed and "lit up" is to plug it in every day.

That's it. That's the "secret" to success in foreign language, sports, art, fitness, finance, writing a book, playing the castanets, *everything*—even relationships with loved ones: *consistent* (usually meaning *daily*) practice.

There will be subsecrets to the secret in the next chapter, but for now, I propose this first step in the contract: name something you've always wanted to get good at, dust off an important but neglected dream, or pick an area of your life where you'd like to create improvement. Just hold it in your heart and mind while you turn the page to read a few more lines about "The Secret to Everything."

The Secret to Everything, II

You have taken the first step to mastery of a skill or realization of a dream by choosing what you'll focus on and holding it in heart and mind. I decided to practice the "secret" I preach with a daily program of CBS: core, balance, and stretching. Now, after 30 early mornings of twenty minutes on the floor, I have six-pack abs, can walk a tightrope, and have regained the inch of height I lost somewhere in the last decade. Actually, no; but I can hold a plank for three times as long, do double the crunches, move with less pain in my lower back and neck, and brush my teeth standing on one foot. Imagine where I'll be in another 30 or 365 days!

There are dozens of things I want to get really good at: tango, Italian, meditation, using eBay, singing opera (okay, some things really do require talent; maybe next lifetime...), bicycling, throwing a party, playing the castanets, and multiple etceteras. So why did I choose CBS as my daily practice to illustrate the "secret to everything"? Because taking on all the aforementioned learning curves at once is a recipe for failure (witness my past lists of New Year resolutions); because fitness is what we all (intend to) practice in some form; and especially because of the age thing. If you're under forty, you may not relate to this now, but just try, because you eventually *will*.

You know how people age? We're young, strong, and invincible...and then, like suddenly, seams are unraveling, joints ache, the middle is spreading, bones are thinning, and we've got an appointment with the orthopedic surgeon to talk new knees. By the time this happens, we're way behind the eight ball and more likely to opt for meds and surgery than a CBS program because...well, because we're too busy to exercise, and besides, this is the era of "pharma-surgical" flash miracles, not daily sweat equity for the long haul. We know we've let it go too long, but—look around, America!—everyone is in the same (sinking?) boat—except for those two to five people out of a hundred who made a different choice.

The "secret to everything" is to practice every day what we want to master in the future. That sounds so seductively simple, but it is dastardly difficult because we want the end result—the tight-rope balance, the virtuosity at the piano, the fluid brain-tongue connection in a foreign language—and we want it *now*. I chose core strength, flexibility, and balance because I am looking twenty years into the future when I want to be a) alive, b) upright and walking, c) as pain-free as possible, and d) moving with stability and a bit of zing. Oh, and did I mention living independently?

Let's dig into the treasure chest for four subsecrets to "the secret to everything."

Subsecret #1: Not only does it not happen overnight, but don't expect to see positive results day-to-day or even week-to-week. You replace bagels and donuts with broccoli and kale and start drinking eight glasses of water a day. What if in a month you still look and feel the same? The human body is miraculously resilient and finely responsive, but like the Titanic, it doesn't have a tight-turning radius, so hold that new course and change *will* manifest. Becoming bilingual is not something you can accomplish quickly (despite ads like "Learn Spanish in a Weekend"). You're taking a class, studying online, practicing faithfully.... A month or a year goes by, and you're just not very fluent. You get disheartened; you give it up, thinking, "I wasn't really getting very far, anyway." No! It's not about short-term *results*. The point is to stay the course, gaining small—even imperceptible—but incrementally compounding, benefits day by day.

Ever hear the expression, "The darkest hour is right before dawn"? Sometimes I do the crossword puzzle in the newspaper instead of reading before bed. It's entertaining, but here's what I *really* get from it: There's often a moment when I think to myself, "This one is too hard. I can't do it. I should give it up." But I don't, and I keep training myself over and over that if I persist, there *will* be a breakthrough. Funny how it always comes when I'm feeling most convinced I'll *never* get it, and I might as well quit. Nothing manifests without persistence. A dream stuffed in a corner of the basement gathers dust, goes dormant, but never really dies.

Subsecret #2: You're exercising daily, eating well, sleeping seven to nine hours, practicing Spanish ten minutes a day, tickety-tock like a fine-tuned clock, and then...life happens: an unplanned trip, a demanding project, a bad cold, final exams, a family emergency, and your successful practices fall away *precisely when you're under stress and need them the most.* "It's only for a day or two," but somehow, weeks, months, even years go by before you get them back again. Simply stated, when the going gets tough, we *can* choose to hang in with good choices that propel us beyond just surviving into *thriving.*

Discipline can become our default. The achiever of the dream is the one who did the small incremental actions over time to make it happen, consistently, wholeheartedly, and with an abiding sense of purpose. How familiar we all are with overwhelm, breakdown, and nonstop life under high-level stress, but this approach cuts to the ultimate chase in personal responsibility. The mind screams, "No, no, I'm just too overloaded. It's not my fault!" And we spend our days trying to get that elusive "round tuit," unable to countenance that "overwhelm" is an excuse for not pursuing what we *really* want and need. I say that without any self-righteousness because it is precisely my biggest challenge in life. It comes as no surprise that the going *always* gets tough, yet we can come prepared with our own personally devised strategy to help us stay the course when it does.

Subsecret #3: Take Nike's advice and *Just do it!* Throughout years of teaching adults, many of my students felt they shouldn't actually try to *speak* Spanish with anyone until they were "better" at it. I should keep taking tango classes and going to practice sessions to improve my skill before I venture out to a real dance where someone might actually lead me onto the floor. You won't play your ukulele at a party until you learn more chords. This is one of the deepest and most seductive pitfalls to achieving real progress because we perpetuate the status of beginner to stay safe. Stepping up to the plate is scary, and the temptation is to settle into the fleecy comfort of low-level challenge, long-term infancy, and easy forgiveness for being a "novice."

Spanish has a wonderful folk saying: "An ounce of practice is worth more than a pound of grammar." Ten minutes of sweating bullets in conversation with a Spanish speaker will move you further than a week of silent study. An evening of dancing with good leaders will test my nerves but take me further than ten hours of online tango classes. I have to keep telling myself, "So what if my palms sweat, if I don't follow well, even if someone says, 'She's not a very good dancer.'—So what?" There is no dress rehearsal. Get out there and just do it already! and often! while making mistakes! –daring ones, audacious ones, stellar ones, unforgettable ones. Who cares?! People will remember you for enthusiasm and willingness, not for slip-ups. *Being* precedes *doing*. Own yourself as a _____, then go out and do what a _____does.

Subsecret #4: Install a rear-view mirror. If you are looking forward to that time when you will be fluent in Spanish, formidable on the tennis court, pain-free when walking, or a ragtime virtuoso at the piano, you'll never feel you've "arrived." If you train yourself to look back to where you were and acknowledge that you *have* come a ways, you'll be more likely to persist in the project because you will be viewing your progress rather than gazing dazed and downhearted at an endless road ahead. There *is* no final destination, only the path and the sometimes imperceptible 1 percent increments. *No hay destino, sólo camino.* ("There is no destination, only the path.")

*   *   *

In Sonoma County, California, Steve Brumme offers a course for individuals who have no art training and perhaps even the belief they have no talent. He has them practice under his guidance for fifteen minutes a day with the *promise* that by the end of his course, they will have recreated "a painting by any master that ever lived" and have a life they love in the areas of health/fitness, relationships, and careers. His students recreate masterpiece paintings by Vermeer (*Girl with a Pearl Earring*), Frida Kahlo, or Michelangelo, and change their lives in the process.

You are understandably dubious, but let me add that Steve is not only an accomplished painter but also a gold medal martial artist in multiple disciplines, an inspirational speaker, language learner, rock climber, horse rider, traveler, author, and master storyteller. He recently completed a nine-hundred-mile bike ride to "End Polio Now" (and wrote a book about it called *Moving Fast, Sitting Still*) while pedaling with his arms because he suffered that illness at age one and has never had the use of his legs. Steve is an inspiring example of one who keeps his dreams alive by nurturing them and practicing them daily *against any odds.*

So now—yes, *right now*—take one thing you care deeply about and have a breakthrough year getting better at it one percent at a time by investing at least five minutes a day. Those daily increments may be imperceptible in producing visible results, but they translate into over 300 percent improvement at realizing your heart's desire in just one year's time. And at that 365-day anniversary, you will either be saying, "I'm glad I did", or "I wish I had."

Mary and the Merry Month of May

Spring's beauty unfolds as wildflowers delight woodland walkers, new foliage glistens on trees, and another wave of blooms graces backyard shrubs. May is the month for patio parties, the dilemma of having to choose from six music and fund-raising events on the same weekend, and colorful festivals all over the world. What follows is a short list of them that you just might consider for your bucket list.

In Cocullo, Italy, a tiny village in the Abruzzo province, the first Thursday in May is the Feast of Saint Domenic, for which snakes have been collected in the environs for the previous six weeks. On the big day, the snakes are festooned over the head and shoulders of the larger-than-life statue of San Domenico, and the writhing assemblage is then paraded through the streets of the hamlet, promising to believers immunity from snakebites for yet another year. In olden times, they then cooked and ate the snakes, but these days they release them (de-fanged) back into the forest.

Jerez de la Frontera in Andalucía, the Spanish capital of sherry, flamenco, and horses, celebrates the annual Feria del Caballo (Horse Fair) in which a million people converge to indulge their love of all three for seven days of parades, horse competitions, flamenco dancing, and the kind of revelry that Spaniards are famous for.

In France the glitterati make their May pilgrimage to the Cannes Film Festival. In Hong Kong, revelers climb sixty-foot towers covered with sacred buns to grab and eat one for good luck during the Cheung Chau Bun Festival on Buddha's birthday. In India, a procession of elaborately decorated elephants and their riders goes on for thirty-six hours with drumming and fireworks.

In Brockworth, England, a seven-pound wheel of cheese is set in motion down the very steep Cooper's Hill, and hundreds of people race or tumble down after it. *Lonely Planet* says, "It's like a spin-dry cycle to the bottom." The first to grab the cheese gets to keep it, and all get to nurse their bruises and scrapes. There are five cheeses rolled at twenty-minute intervals in this now-international competition that grows in popularity every year despite the number of cheese fans who end up in the hospital. (The ambulances are parked at the bottom of the hill, always at the ready.)

Belgium holds its annual dragon-slaying festival with St. George on his black steed daring onlookers to get close enough to pull the dragon's tail. It's all great fun and games as humanity celebrates the new flowering of life and the resurgence of hope and hormones.

The sense of rebirth and renewal comes from a deep, spiritual well. For Christians, the resurrection of Christ on Easter Sunday (between late March and early April) holds the promise of redemption, and in the Catholic traditions, the month of May is dedicated to Mother Mary. In St. Francis Elementary School, each one of us kids in the class got to bring a tiny wreath of fresh flowers on our assigned day in May to place on the head of the statue of Mary, which prayed for us sinners from the back of the classroom. It was a big honor that kids, parents, and the nuns took quite seriously, and woe to the child who showed up empty-handed on their assigned day. Some of the crowns of flowers were so large they slipped straight down to circle the statue's feet, and Sister Mary Irene had to raid a couple of lunch boxes in the cloakroom for tin foil to mold a headpiece inside the twined stems. Some were so small, they sailed off the ceramic brow at the first breeze through the windows. I was sure we sang a special song each day to accompany the crowning and also sure I didn't remember it, but quite miraculously, it popped into my head as I was writing this, and an online check tells me that indeed it *is* the May crowning song: "Hail holy Queen enthroned above, Ohhh Maa-rii-a..."

In the Catholic Church, Mary has dozens of titles: Blessed Mother, Queen of Heaven, Advocate of Sinners, and on for a list of about 250 according to *Wikipedia*. My true motive for interest in and exploration of all this is to trace the source of traditional female names in Spanish. Why would parents name their baby Dolores if it means "pain and sorrows," or Soledad, signifying "solitude and loneliness"? Because these names and many others belong to Mary as in *Our Lady of...*: *Nuestra Señora de la Soledad, Nuestra Señora de Dolores*, and more to come in the next paragraphs.

The Virgin Mary has many manifestations in history and the hearts of the faithful, and several famous apparitions that have long been popular female names like *Lourdes* (France, 1858), *Fátima* (Portugal, 1917), and *Guadalupe* (Mexico, 1531). Our Lady of Guadalupe is the Patron Saint of Mexico and countless Mexican women, as well as some men, carry her name. I didn't realize this latter fact until, in a citywide teachers' conference, the chairperson called upon *Lupe*, and my head whipped around when a deep male voice replied from the back of the room. In Spanish-speaking countries, men might be given *María* as a second name: *José María, Jesús María, Alberto María*, and so on. I remember being deeply puzzled as a child to come across a book in my father's collection authored by Bohemian Austrian poet Ranier Maria Rilke. My mind was unable to grasp how he could possibly have a girl's name.

Dolores, then, is *María de Dolores*, usually officially by baptism but at least conceptually; *Soledad* is *María de la Soledad* (perhaps shortened to *Marisol*); *Mercedes* comes from *Nuestra Señora de las Mercedes* (Our Lady of Mercies); the beautiful name *Nieves* is from Our Lady of the Snows; *Rocío* is from *La Virgen del Rocío*, the Virgin of the Morning Dew.

Mary is also the Patroness of Spain, invoked by the name of *Nuestra Señora del Pilar*, our Lady of the Pillar. On my first trip to Spain, the daughter of the family I stayed with was named María del Pilar, or "Maripili," or just "Pili" for short. The popular name, *Carmen,* comes from *Nuestra Señora del Carmen* (Our Lady of Mount Carmel), and the number of Spanish women named María del Carmen, or "Maricarmen" for short, is legion. Other titles for the Virgin Mary have given us the traditional Spanish names (with or without "María de") *Socorro* (help), *Refugio* (refuge), *Remedios* (remedies), *Imaculada* (immaculate), *Concepción* (immaculate conception), *Consuelo* (comfort) , *Rosario* (rosary), and *Luz* (light). A woman I knew in Sacramento named *Amparo* (shelter) was unfortunately nicknamed "Umpy" by her friends who couldn't pronounce that beautiful word.

In her many guises as Our Lady of…(so many different manifestations), Mary is honored worldwide and year around, but especially in the lovely month of May. My mother continues a lifelong devotion to her "Mother Mary," having lost her own mom early in life. In the month of May and every day, love to her and all the mothers of the world.

The Yodeling Dutchman, a Father's Day Tribute

In the nationalistic mood of the postwar fifties, neither my mother nor my father even considered teaching us their native languages. Mom learned English when she started school in her Italian neighborhood in the Bronx. Dad wanted only to become all things American and leave everything Dutch behind. Despite this zeal, it took him years to learn to like avocados, and he never did lose his accent. With the advance of technology in the sixties, he heard a recording of his voice for the first time and was appalled to discover he didn't sound like a native of his adopted country. "Vell, der was just no vay around dis and dat."

When I was twelve, the budding linguist in me decided to write his birthday card in Dutch. I found his well-worn dictionary and started my search for words. *Dear. Father.* Easy enough—I thought this was coming together quite nicely. On April 12, I presented it to him with confident excitement, watching his face carefully to see his reaction. He read it aloud: "*Duur Vader...*" I can still see his furrowed brow in a moment of confusion, and then he laughed at being saluted as "Expensive Father." It was my first lesson in the pitfalls of language lost in translation. I think he enjoyed it all the more for my gaffe.

I loved him fiercely and feared him enough. And now with him gone over twenty-five years, I miss him still. I admire the person he was and feel proud of all he did. I love to tell the story of how he lied about his age so he could join the Dutch Merchant Marines a few months before his eighteenth birthday in 1940. As the Nazis advanced in early May, his was one of the last ships to leave free Holland, carrying Queen Wilhelmina to safe haven in England. He spent the war years in the boiler rooms of transport ships carrying troops and supplies for the Allies. I know from snatches of conversations not meant for my ears that these ships with my future dad on them took torpedo hits, but he never once told us kids a "war story."

It seems serendipitous that his ship docked in New York toward the end of the war because that's where he met a nineteen-year-old Italian girl named Caterina Crai. We never tired of hearing his account of how, in front of the church for the wedding rehearsal of their respective best friends, Dirk and Elsie, the tall, blond, and blue-eyed best man (who had never even considered dating a girl who didn't share the same palette) took one look at the petite, black-haired, dark-eyed maid of honor and announced to the bridegroom-to-be, "Dat's du voman I'm goving to marry." It's hard to thumb your nose at destiny when you're the progeny of a story like that.

Though I had always felt close to him, at his funeral, I was stunned to hear people talk about a man it suddenly and irrevocably seemed I'd hardly gotten to know. Bob Kerry, former US Senator and recipient of the Congressional Medal of Honor said, "A hero is someone who over and over does the right thing even though no one is there to witness it." That was my dad. People he'd worked with at the company and in the service club to which he gave lifelong loyalties *had* witnessed some of it, and they spoke of all those he had helped with open hand and heart.

My dad lived what some might call a small-time life. He passed up a transfer to a more high-powered job that would have meant moving us back to Los Angeles, and stayed with a family-owned company in the Central California Valley, convinced it was a better place to raise kids. He provided well, but never got rich. His dream of a family trip to the European homeland never materialized. Instead, we had homey vacations camping in Yosemite or renting a beach bungalow in Southern California. On winter weekends, we went for drives to the snow and in spring to see the wildflowers. In summer, Mom packed picnic lunches and Dad hooked the sailboat trailer to the family car for Saturdays at Lake Woolomes in nearby Delano where we practiced port and starboard, close haul and tack. He taught us how to ice skate and delighted us with his yodeling. I've never known anyone else in my life who could yodel, and wonder if anyone practices this vocal art anymore. I remember a camping trip in the Sequoias when he yodeled for us little kids until he was hoarse as we tried to figure out the magic of his melody echoing back from the facing mountains.

Dinnertime was always at 6:00 p.m. sharp and that meant no TV, no answering the phone, and active participation in the family conversation. My parents had plenty of friends, but company at dinner was a rarity, and they almost never spent an evening out. One night a week, though, Dad left after dinner to pick up one of the several "little brothers" he had over the years and take him bowling or to a movie. Only his own experience of losing his own father too early in life could have motivated a man with five kids at home to become a Big Brother. A boy who had grown up in a foster home in Holland, and a girl who was taken in by an Italian aunt after her mother died when she was only twelve, became parents who cherished their family above all else. It was a simple life in which we were always loved and always cared for. Nothing small about that. It is the greatest gift parents can give the children they bring into the world.

In my teen years, it all seemed so strict, stifling almost, and way too old-fashioned. Why *couldn't* I go to a drive-in movie? And why does the music always have to be that classical stuff? We laughed at Daddy for being such a worry-wart that he kept wind chimes hanging from the ceiling right above his bed, giving him what he calculated was a five-second advantage to save his family in case of a major earthquake. Suddenly, Dad's yodeling concert from our front porch at midnight on New Year's Eve seemed a little too quaint, even if it was accompanied by the years-long tradition of Mr. Lemucchi shooting off his pistol, and Mr. Nicolletti banging assorted pots and pans. Those were the breakaway years, a time when I knew I had all the answers and even thought I'd invented the questions. Now I feel ever thankful for a childhood woven of stable love and firm convictions from the two people who raised us without benefit of parental models of their own.

Dad lingered long enough in his last illness to put family and personal affairs in order. I was the only duck not quite lined up in that row of attempted stable security since I didn't have a husband to look after me and was still creating my own financial turbulence. When I was visiting for the holidays of 1990-91, Dad was in the same hospital bed he had been confined to for two years since the cancer had rendered him paraplegic. On a sunny winter afternoon, I answered a knock at the front door and hadn't a clue who this tall, handsome young man with a big yellow dog on our front porch could possibly be. The holidays were over, I was getting ready to drive home, and we weren't expecting visitors. In one of the most serendipitous and touching events that I still cannot talk about without choking up, this young man who had been one of my dad's little brothers in Big Brothers just happened to stop by with his dog over ten *years later* to say hello to the man who had showed up to be his friend when his own dad could not. He had no idea Dad was on his deathbed, but I have always wondered what deep knowingness drew him to our door.

I was all packed up and ready to start the long drive to Bakersfield when I got the call that Sunday morning that he had passed. Dad died on Easter Sunday of 1991 having already passed through the valley of the shadow of death and fearing no evil. I'd had a phone call with him a few days before, and in luminous words and voice, he had told me so. I think he knows through all these years since that I am okay and that my life is good, if not to the letter of his vision for me, certainly to the spirit. I meet him often while listening to Rachmaninoff and Beethoven, under sail on open ocean, or painting a room in my house. In my memory's imagination, he still yodels to the mountains at his beloved cabin in the woods.

Despite many visits to Dad's sisters in Holland and Belgium, I never did learn more than a phrase or two in Dutch. But now I can navigate a bilingual dictionary confidently enough to attempt that salutation to my dad again in closing:

Lief Vader,

Happy Father's Day.

Love always.

AN AFTERWORD OR TWO

In my home office, there are books, binders, and dictionaries on the three walls that surround my desk. A friend has just called to say he's gifting me two boxes of volumes on words and language. I can't pass them up but wonder where I'll shoehorn dozens more books into this crowded space. Hmm...has anyone yet invented book storage that hangs from the ceiling? At Mendocino College, my tiny office had books shelved seven feet high on the walls behind my chair and in front of my desk. Colleagues and I used to joke about how and *if* they would dig us out in the event of an earthquake.

What there aren't a lot of on my shelves are novels. I love them, and the few I indulge in are memorable. But nonfiction always beckons irresistibly and the wisdom, humor, and self-revelation of writers like Phil Cousineau (*The Art of Pilgrimage*), Lynne Truss (*Eats, Shoots and Leaves*), Richard Lederer (*Anguished English*), Bill Bryson (*The Mother Tongue*), John McWhorter (*The Power of Babel*), and so many more I would love to name, sing the siren song I must follow.

I deeply admire authors like Elizabeth Gilbert, Anna Quindlen, and Neil Gaiman who write best-selling novels as well as unforgettable nonfiction. I'm well convinced I don't have a novel in me, though I've learned from life's unexpected turns to *never say never*. A short story at least? I don't think so, and neither is there a book of poetry about to burst from my breast. But I'm still brimming with ideas and musings on words, language, and cultures, and these chapters of *Wordstruck!* are just the first yellow pad of thoughts and ideas fully fleshed out. Grateful for the discipline that deadlines provide as well as feedback from readers near and far, I'll keep "fleshing" in my bimonthly column in the *Ukiah Daily Journal*.

There's a growing pile of scribbled notes atop the filing cabinet waiting to find their way to a fresh yellow pad and from there, eventually, into print. The umbrella theme of words and language still holds, but the subjects are, like those of this book, all over the boards and the world. There's also a notebook of travel stories begging to be told, mostly because they are stranger than fiction. Yet another fat file will soon become a handbook for intermediate and advanced Spanish learners.

No, I don't think I'll produce a novel in this lifetime any more than I think I'll write a symphony, pilot a jet, or sing my opera at the Met. That said, the possibilities are unlimited and I will *still* never say "never".

Acknowledgements

In wonderment over how I got from there to here, I say thank you to the Ukiah Daily Journal and editor K.C. Meadows for publishing my column which has given me the opportunity and the discipline to produce a few thousand coherent words a months.

To Tris Thorp, I have deeply appreciated your coaching, wisdom, and guidance in helping me envision and achieve the steps to turn dreams into reality. I continue to be guided.

Thank you to Madalyn Stone, not only for your professional skill as an editor, but for the patience and equanimity you generously emanate.

To Jerry Dorris and AuthorSupport.com, I appreciate your exterior and interior design work as well as, once again, the calm and patience you have exercised with a tech-challenged author prone to making frequent changes.

To Jack Canfield and Steve Harrison: your Bestseller Blueprint covers it all and is a valuable and inspiring guide.

Thank you again to Steve Harrison for the Quantum Leap Program, all the amazing coaches, and my fellow "leaper" authors who have lent support, feedback, and camaraderie.

To Jonathan Dooley: What would I do without you? Not only have you given me hours of help with my tech issues, but your judgment and attention to detail are invaluable.

Deep gratitude to my family, friends, and readers for following my newspaper column, tuning in to my Facebook blog, and offering cheer, appreciation, and ideas for new forays into uncharted territories of words, language, and cultures.

Reaching back in time, forever thanks to the nuns at St. Francis Elementary and Garces High School; to Mrs. Domínguez, my first Spanish teacher; and to my dear graduate school *compañeros* to whom I owe my bilingualism and, especially to Liz Ginsburg, my career.

Thank you Wikipedia for the ease and accuracy of readily-available information. I'll keep sending an annual donation in appreciation for all the information I access throughout the year.

Finally, I beam gratitude to powers and energies *beyond* words and the five senses where intuition, inspiration, and endless possibility dwell.

REFERENCES

CHAPTER ONE—Life and Language in the USA

The Tower of Scrabble Babble

CBS DC. "New Scrabble Dictionary to Include 5,000 new Words." August 4, 2014. http://washington.cbslocal.com/2014/08/05/new-scrabble-dictionary-to-include-5000-new-words/

Roeder, Oliver. "The New Scrabble Dictionary Disrespects the Game." FiveThirtyEight. October 18, 2014. http://fivethirtyeight.com/features/new-scrabble-dictionary-disrepects-the-game/

You Say Goodbye and I Say Hello

Online Etymology Dictionary. "hello", "goodbye." Accessed January, 11 2015. http://www.etymonline.com/index.php?allowed_in_frame =0&search=hello

Grimes, William. New York Times. "Great 'Hello' Mystery Is Solved." March 5, 1992. http://www.nytimes.com/1992/03/05/garden/great-hello-mystery-is-solved.html

Wikipedia. "Terminator 2: Judgment Day." Accessed January 11, 2015. https://en.wikipedia.org/wiki/Terminator_2:_Judgment_Day

Carly Googles. "How do People Answer the Phone in Different

Countries?" Accessed January 11, 2015. http://carlygoogles. com/2009/10/how-do-people-answer-phone-in-various.html

The US and Them View of the World

Wikipedia. "Metrication in the United States." Accessed May 15, 2015. https://en.wikipedia.org/wiki/Metrication_in_the_United_States

Minding the Metaphor, Part I

Hirschfield, Jane. "The Art of Metaphor." TedBlog Accessed October 17, 2015. http://blog.ted.com the-best-of-ted-ed-the-art-of-the-metaphor/

The Oxford Companion to the English Language (1992) "Metaphor." pp 653-655.

Minding the Metaphor, Part II

The Washington Post. "How 'Texas' Became Norwegian for "crazy."" Accessed October 29, 2015. https://www.washingtonpost.com/news/ morning-mix/wp/2015/10/26/how-texas-became-norwegian-for-crazy/

McClelland, Nancy Harris. Adobe House Artists. Accessed October 20, 2015. Quotes reprinted from her website with permission. http:// www.adobehouseartists.com/

Van Praet, Douglas. "Why Metaphors Beat the Snot Out of Facts When It Comes to Motivating Action." Co.Create.com. Accessed October 27, 2015. https://www.fastcocreate.com/3048817/why-metaphors-beat-the-snot-out-of-facts-when-it-comes-to-motivating-action

Carlton, Jim. "My Favorite Mixed Metaphors." Accessed October 27, 2015. http://www.jimcarlton.com/my_favorite_mixed_metaphors.htm

The Russler. "Mixed Metaphors." Accessed October 27, 2015. http:// therussler.tripod.com/dtps/mixed_metaphors.html

Pants on Fire

Benjamin, Kathy. "60% of People Can't Go10 Minutes Without Lying." Mental Floss. May 7, 2012. http://mentalfloss.com/ article/30609/60-people-cant-go-10-minutes-without-lying

Basu, Tanya. "It's Almost Weirder if You Don't Lie on Your Online-Dating Profile." Science of Us. February 26, 2016. http://nymag. com/scienceofus/2016/02/its-almost-weirder-if-you-dont-lie-on-your-online-dating-profile.html

White, Natalie. "10 Verbal and Non-Verbal Signs to Spot a Liar at Work." Stanford Graduate School of Business. Accessed April 1, 2016. http://stanfordbusiness.tumblr.com/post/54109702521/10-verbal-and-non-verbal-signs-to-spot-a-liar-at

Way of the Mind. "Signs of Lying: How to Catch a Liar." Accessed April 1, 2016. http://www.way-of-the-mind.com/signs-of-lying.html

You Tube. "Bill Clinton Lies About His Affair with Monica Lewinsky." Accessed April 2, 2016. https://www.youtube.com/watch?v=JUDppdVXeMw

Politifact. "Donald Trump's File." Accessed April 2, 2016. http://www.politifact.com/personalities/donald-trump/

Politifact. "Pants on Fire." Accessed April 2, 2016. http://www.politifact.com/truth-o-meter/rulings/pants-fire/

CHAPTER TWO—Whence These Words?

The Herd Mentality

Wikipedia. "List of English Terms of Venery, by Animal." Accessed July 13, 2014. https://en.wikipedia.org/wiki/List_of_English_terms_of_venery,_by_animal

Wikipedia. "Book of Saint Albans." Accessed July 13, 2014. https://en.wikipedia.org/wiki/Book_of_Saint_Albans

Collective Nouns. "Collective Nouns for People." Accessed July 14, 2014. http://www.collectivenouns.biz/list-of-collective-nouns/collective-nouns-people/

Shakespeare: The Legacy in His Lines, Part I

Autenrieth, Georg. A Homeric Dictionary. Focus Publishing/R. Pullins Co., Inc. Massachusetts. 2001. Preface, page vi. https://www.amazon.com/Homeric-Dictionary-Georg-Autenrieth/dp/1585100285

Wikipedia. "Shakespeare's Influence." Accessed August 8, 2014. https://en.wikipedia.org/wiki/Shakespeare%27s_influence

Shakespeare Online. "Words Shakespeare Invented." Accessed August 8, 2014. http://www.shakespeare-online.com/biography/wordsinvented.html

Shakespeare: The Legacy in His Lines, Part II

e notes. "Knock, knock! Who's there?" Accessed August 22, 2014. http://www.enotes.com/shakespeare-quotes/knock-knock-whos-there

William Shakespeare Quotes and Quotations. Accessed August 22, 2014. http://www.william-shakespeare.info/william-shakespeare-quotes.htm

Anglophenia. "45 Everyday Phrases Coined by Shakespeare." Accessed August 22, 2014. http://www.bbcamerica.com/anglophenia/2014/04/45-phrases-coined-shakespeare-450th-birthday

Learn English. "Idioms from Shakespeare." Accessed August 23, 2014. http://www.ecenglish.com/learnenglish/lessons/idioms-shakespeare

Create Your Own Shakespearean Insults. Accessed August 23, 2014. http://www.dl.ket.org/humanities/connections/class/medren/insults.htm

Mr. William Shakespeare's Insult Generator. Accessed August 23, 2014. http://insult.dream40.org/ (Author note: Great fun, it works kind of like a slot machine.)

The Washington Post. "Wordplay Masters Invitational." Accessed July 27, 2014. http://www.washingtonpostsmensainvitational.com/

Brechlin, Jeff. "The Hokey-Pokey, Shakespearean Style." Reprinted with permission from the author.

On the Trail of Word Origins, Part I, Part II, Part III

Online Etymology Dictionary. Accessed March 7, 2015. http://www.etymonline.com/

Almond, Jordan. Dictionary of Word Origins: A History of the Words, Expressions, and Cliches We Use. New York: Kensington Publishing Corporation, 1985.

Espy, Willard R. O Thou Improper, Thou Uncommon Noun. Clarkson N. Potter, Inc., 1988.

Jowett, B. The Dialogues of Plato. "Alcibiades I". P. 512. Charles Scribner's Sons. New York. 1897.

Bryson, Bill. The Mother Tongue, English and How It Got That Way. New York: Avon Books. 1990.

The Familiarity of Foreign

"toodeloo." Wiktionary.org. Accessed March 19, 2014. https://www.google.

com/webhp?sourceid=chrome-instant&ion=1&espv=2&ie=UTF-8#q=Wiktionary+toodeloo

"mayday." Wikipedia.org. Accessed March 19, 2014. https://en.wikipedia.org/wiki/Mayday

"poppycock." Online Etymology Dictionary. Accessed March 19, 2014. http://www.etymonline.com/index.php?allowed_in_frame=0&search=poppycock

The Scholar's Ink and the Martyr's Blood

Wikipedia. "Moors." Accessed June 27, 2015. https://en.wikipedia.org/wiki/Moors

Wikipedia. "Arabic Language Influence on the Spanish Language." Accessed June 27, 2015. https://en.wikipedia.org/wiki/Arabic_language_influence_on_the_Spanish_language

Oxford Words Blog. "Which Everyday English Words Came from Arabic?" Accessed June 26, 2015. http://blog.oxforddictionaries.com/2014/08/which-everyday-english-words-came-from-arabic/

The Metaverse. "English Words from Arabic." Accessed June 26, 2015. http://www.zompist.com/arabic.html

Elmasry, Mohamed. IslamaCity. "The ink of a scholar is more holier than the blood of a martyr." Accessed June 27, 2015. http://www.islamicity.org/3137/ink-of-a-scholar-is-more-holier-than-the-blood-of-a-martyr/

Isamweb.net. "Seeking Knowledge." (Accessed June 27, 2015) http://www.islamweb.net/en/article/167239/seeking-knowledge

Snelling, Nick. "What did the Moors do for us? a history of the Moors in Spain." Culture Spain. (Accessed June 27, 2015) Quoted with permission from the author. http://www.culturespain.com/2012/03/02/what-did-the-moors-do-for-us/

CHAPTER THREE—Grammar Grievances, Malaprop Muddles, and Pronunciation Pickles

Inconstant Consonants and Sudden Vowel Movements

Wikipedia. "Norman Conquest of England." Accessed February 6, 2016 https://en.wikipedia.org/wiki/Norman_conquest_of_England

Wikipedia. "Anglo Norman Language." Accessed February 6, 2016.
https://en.wikipedia.org/wiki/Anglo-Norman_language

AVKO. "Could /fish/ be spelled "ghoti" or "-fici"?" Accessed February 6,
1016. http://avko.org/free/articles/george-bernard-shaw-ghoti.html

Grammurder in the First Degree

McWhorter, John. "Freedom from, Freedom to: Yes You Can
End a Sentence in a Preposition." New Republic. Accessed
September 20, 2014. https://newrepublic.com/article/113187/
grumpy-grammarian-dangling-preposition-myth

Wikipedia. "Preposition Stranding." Accessed September 20, 2014.
https://en.wikipedia.org/wiki/Preposition_stranding

Oxford Dictionaries Blog. "Can You End a Sentence with a Preposition?"
Accessed September 20, 2014. http://blog.oxforddictionaries.
com/2011/11/grammar-myths-prepositions/

"No Man is an Island" by John Donne
(Italics added by S. Janssen)

No man is an island,
Entire of itself,
Every man is a piece of the continent,
A part of the main.
If a clod be washed away by the sea,
Europe is the less.
As well as if a promontory were.
As well as if a manor of thy friend's
Or of thine own were:
Any man's death diminishes me,
Because I am involved in mankind,
And therefore never send to know *for whom the bell tolls;*
It tolls for thee.

http://www.poemhunter.com/poem/no-man-is-an-island/

The Abdominal Snowman on the Cal-Can Highway

Fun-With-Words.com. "Famous Malapropisms." Accessed June 13, 2015.
http://www.fun-with-words.com/mala_famous.html

Wikipedia. "Bushism." Accessed June 13, 2015. https://en.wikipedia.
org/wiki/Bushism

Snopes.com. "Quayle Quotes." Accessed November 2, 2016. http://www.snopes.com/politics/quotes/quayle.asp

City-Data.com. "GED Test (Actual Answers)." Accessed June 13, 2016. http://www.city-data.com/forum/other-topics/1013936-ged-test-actual-answers-funny-but.html

Lederer, Richard. Fractured English. New York: Pocket Books, 1996. page 14.

Into the Prepositional Fray

Ethnologue. "List of Romance Languages and Dialects." Accessed August 14, 2016. http://www.orbilat.com/General_Survey/List_of_Romance_Languages.html

CHAPTER FOUR—Windows on the World

It's All Bubble and Squeak to Me

Bartleby.com. "Preface to Pygmalion." Accessed April 16, 2016. http://www.bartleby.com/138/0.html

TheBrits.com. "Famous Cockneys." Accessed April 15, 2016. http://www.thebrits.com/famous-cockneys/

Cockney Rhyming Slang. Accessed April 16, 2016. http://www.cockneyrhymingslang.co.uk/blog/what-is-cockney-rhyming-slang/

The Anglotopia Magazine. "Language: Top 100 Cockney Rhyming Slang Words and Phrases." Accessed April 16, 2016. http://londontopia.net/londonism/fun-london/language-top-100-cockney-rhyming-slang-words-and-phrases/

EF English Live. "The Ultimate Guide to Cockney Rhyming Slang." Accessed April 17, 2016. http://englishlive.ef.com/blog/the-ultimate-guide-to-cockney-rhyming-slang/

Google.com. "Learn the Cockney Accent with Jason Statham." Accessed April 16, 2016. https://www.google.com/webhp?sourceid=chrome-instant&ion=1&espv=2&ie=UTF-8#q=learn%20the%20cockney%20accent%20with%20jason%20statham

Lost (but Not Forgotten) in Translation

Boyle, Justin. "Interpreters and Translators Salary and Career Outlook." Schools.com. July 31, 2014. http://www.schools.com/news/interpreters-and-translators-salary-career-outlook.html

Snopes.com. "Don't Go Here." Accessed November 14, 2015. http://www.snopes.com/business/misxlate/nova.asp

Farago, Robert. "Ten Most Unfortunate Car Names." The truth About Cars. July 14, 2009. http://www.thetruthaboutcars.com/2009/07/ten-most-unfortunate-car-names/

Qualman, Eric. "13 Marketing translations Gone Wrong." Socialnomics. net. Accessed November 14, 2015. http://socialnomics. net/2011/03/29/13-marketing-translations-gone-wrong/

Vehr, Nick. "Selling Across Cultures Can Be Treacherous Business." Vehr Communications. May 14, 2014. http://www.vehrcommunications. com/selling-across-cultures-can-be-treacherous-business/

Bored Panda. "35 Hilarious Chinese Translation Fails." Accessed November 14, 2015. http://www.boredpanda.com/funny-chinese-translation-fails/

We Don't Have a Word for It, Part I

Rheingold, Howard. They Have a Word for It. Kentucky: Sarabande Books, 1988.

Mather, Katie. "45 Beautifully Untranslatable Words that Describe Exactly How You're Feeling."

Thought Catalogue. Accessed January 24, 2015. http://thoughtcatalog. com/katie-mather/2015/07/45-beautiful-untranslatable-words-that-describe-exactly-how-youre-feeling/

NPR Books. Review and excerpt of In Other Words by Christopher J. Moore. Accessed August 21, 2016. http://www.npr.org/templates/story/story.php?storyId=4457805

We Don't Have a Word for It, Part II

Wikipedia. "Duende (art)" Accessed February 8, 2015. https://en.wikipedia.org/wiki/Duende_(art)

News from the World of Words

Pimsleur Approach. "Foreign Language Syndrome, Is It Real or a Hoax?" Accessed May 30, 2015. http://www.pimsleurapproach. com/resources/language-research/special-needs/foreign-language-syndrome/

ABC News. "Texas Mom Wakes Up From Surgery with a British

Accent." Accessed July 2, 2016. http://abcnews.go.com/Health/texas-mom-wakes-jaw-surgery-british-accent/story?id=40065999

USA Today. "Tenn. judge: Parents can name their baby 'Messiah.'" September 16, 2013. http://www.usatoday.com/story/news/nation/2013/09/18/tenn-parents-baby-name-messiah/2830999/

BBC News. "French court stops child from being named 'Nutella.'" Accessed May 19, 2015. http://www.bbc.com/news/world-europe-30993608

McWhorter, John. The Power of Babel. New York: HarperCollins, 2001.

BBC News. "Who, What, Why: Why do some countries regulate baby names?" February 1, 2013. http://www.bbc.com/news/magazine-21229475

Ostler, Rosemarie. "Disappearing Languages." Whole Earth Catalogue, Spring 2000. Accessed May 30, 2016. http://www.wholeearth.com/issue/2100/article/138/disappearing.languages

DATABLOG. "Endangered languages: the full list." Accessed May 30, 2016. http://www.theguardian.com/news/datablog/2011/apr/15/language-extinct-endangered

Wikipedia. "List of Last Known Speakers of Language." Accessed May 30, 2015. https://en.wikipedia.org/wiki/List_of_last_known_speakers_of_languages

Rivas, Anthony. "7th Grader Builds 'Braigo,' a Braille Printer Made out of LEGOS." Medical Daily. February 25, 2014. http://www.medicaldaily.com/7th-grader-builds-braigo-braille-printer-made-out-legos-270004

Pigments of Our Imagination

Psychology.com. "Cultural Meanings of Color and Color Symbolism." Accessed August 1, 2015. http://www.empower-yourself-with-color-psychology.com/cultural-color.html

The Huffington Post. "What Colors Mean in Other Cultures." Accessed August 1, 2015. http://www.huffingtonpost.com/smartertravel/what-colors-mean-in-other_b_9078674.html

Web Designer Depot. "Color and Cultural Design Considerations." Accessed August 1, 2015. http://www.webdesignerdepot.com/2012/06/color-and-cultural-design-considerations/

Color Wheel Pro. "See Color Theory in Action." Accessed August 1,

2015. http://www.color-wheel-pro.com/color-meaning.html

Roach, John. "In Sports, Red is Winning Color, Study Says." National Geographic News. Accessed August 1, 2015. http://news.nationalgeographic.com/news/2005/05/0518_050518_redsports.html

Language Police

Real Academia Española. Accessed July 9, 2016. http://www.rae.es/

NDSU Libraries. "The 'High' and 'Low' of the German Dialect." Accessed July 9, 2016. https://library.ndsu.edu/grhc/articles/newspapers/news/dialect.html

Ethnologue "Languages of the World." Accessed July 9, 2016. https://www.ethnologue.com/

Wikipedia. "Languages of China." Accessed July 9, 2016. https://en.wikipedia.org/wiki/Languages_of_China

Wikipedia. 'List of Language regulators." Accessed July 9, 2016. https://en.wikipedia.org/wiki/List_of_language_regulators

BBC News. "Italian Call to Use Less English." September 10, 2008. http://news.bbc.co.uk/2/hi/europe/7608860.stm

Daily Mail. "French say 'non' to the term hashtag in battle to stop English words violating their language." January 26, 2013. http://www.dailymail.co.uk/news/article-2268722/Zut-alors-The-French-banned-world-hashtag—email-blog-English-intrusions-beloved-language.html

Badcock, James. "Spain Launches Anti English Campaign to Drive out Foreign Words." The Telegraph. May 25, 2016. http://www.telegraph.co.uk/news/2016/05/25/spain-launches-anti-english-campaign-to-drive-out-foreign-words/

La Semana. "La RAE contra el inglés." Accessed July 9, 2016.http://www.semana.com/cultura/multimedia/la-real-academia-de-la-lengua-espanola-lanza-una-campana-contra-el-uso-excesivo-de-anglicismos/474200

Rum and Revolution, Part I

Daily Mail. "Dissidents Say As Many As 200 Arrested in Cuba." February 23, 2015. http://www.dailymail.co.uk/wires/ap/article-2965891/Dissidents-say-200-arrested-Cuba.html

Rum and Revolution, Part II

Romey, Jared. Quick Guide to Cuban Spanish. Presented by SpeakingLatino.com.

Gitau, Beatrice. "The US to Begin Commercial Flights to Cuba: How soon Can You Go?" The Christian Science Monitor. December 17, 2015. http://www.csmonitor.com/USA/USA-Update/2015/1217/US-to-begin-commercial-flights-to-Cuba-How-soon-can-you-go

U.S. Department of the Treasury. "Frequently Asked Questions Related to Cuba." Updated July 25, 2016. https://www.treasury.gov/resource-center/sanctions/Programs/Documents/cuba_faqs_new.pdf

Section II Travel. Page 2: Travel-related transactions are permitted by general license for certain travel related to the following activities, subject to the criteria and conditions in each general license: family visits; official business of the U.S. government, foreign governments, and certain intergovernmental organizations; journalistic activity; professional research and professional meetings; educational activities; religious activities; public performances, clinics, workshops, athletic and other competitions, and exhibitions; support for the Cuban people; humanitarian projects; activities of private foundations or research or educational institutes; exportation, importation, or transmission of information or information materials; and certain authorized export transactions.

Wikipedia. "Wet Feet, Dry Feet Policy." Accessed July 27, 2016. https://en.wikipedia.org/wiki/Wet_feet,_dry_feet_policy

Leogrande, William M. "A New Crisis of Cuban Migration." The New York Times. December 4, 2015. http://www.nytimes.com/2015/12/05/opinion/international/a-new-crisis-of-cuban-migration.html?_r=0

CHAPTER FIVE—The Wonders of the Bilingual Brain

Riding the Silver Tsunami

Alzheimer's Association. "The Search for Alzheimer's Causes and Risk Factors." Accessed July 11, 2015. http://www.alz.org/research/science/alzheimers_disease_causes.asp

Clark Boyd and Rob Hugh-Jones. "Melting Down Hips and Knees: The Afterlife of Implants." BBC News. February 21, 2012. http://www.bbc.com/news/magazine-16877393

Freeman, Shanna. "Top 10 Myths About the Brain." How Stuff Works. Accessed July 11, 2016. http://science.howstuffworks.com/life/ inside-the-mind/human-brain/10-brain-myths9.htm

Brain HQ. "Brain Myth: Drinking Alcohol Kills Brain Cells." Accesses July 11, 2016. http://www.brainhq.com/ brain-resources/brain-facts-myths/brain-mythology/ brain-myth-alcohol-kills-brain-cells

Dovey, Diana. "How Learning Languages Affects Our Brain." Medical Daily. November 24, 2015. http://www.medicaldaily.com/ pulse/how-learning-new-language-changes-your-brain-and-your-perception-362872

Carper, Jean. 100 Simple Things You Can Do to Prevent Alzheimer's. New York: Little, Brown and Company, 2012.

Science Daily. "Language learning makes the brain grow, Swedish study suggests." Published October 8, 2012. https://www.sciencedaily. com/releases/2012/10/121008082953.htm

The Best Brain Elixir

Sarich, Christina. "6 Herbs to Help Boost Your Brain Power." Natural Society. December 2, 2014. http://naturalsociety. com/6-herbs-boost-brain-power-genius/

Alban Dean. "12 Brain Foods that Supercharge Your Memory Focus and Mood." Be Brain Fit. Accessed May 14, 2016. http://bebrainfit. com/brain-foods/

Godman, Heidi. "Regular exercise changes the brain to improve memory, thinking skills." Harvard Health Publications. April 9, 2014. http:// www.health.harvard.edu/blog/regular-exercise-changes-brain-improve-memory-thinking-skills-201404097110

Dam, Robina. "Why a walking workout is good for your body." Daily Mail. Accessed May 14, 2016. http://www.dailymail.co.uk/health/ article-122898/Why-walking-workout-good-body.html

Stone, Dan. "The Bigger Brains of London Taxi Drivers." National Geographic. Accessed April 27, 2016. http://voices.nationalgeographic.com/2013/05/29/ the-bigger-brains-of-london-taxi-drivers/

Drummond, Katie. "Baby talk: newborns recall words heard in the womb, research shows." The Verge. Accessed May 14,

2016. http://www.theverge.com/2013/8/26/4661368/
newborns-recall-words-heard-in-the-womb-research-shows

Skwarecki, Beth. "Babies learn to recognize words in the womb." Science
AAAS. Accessed May 14, 2016. http://www.sciencemag.org/
news/2013/08/babies-learn-recognize-words-womb

Morin, Amanda. "At a Glance: 8 Key Executive Functions."
Understood.org. Accessed May 14, 2016. https://
www.understood.org/en/learning-attention-issues/
child-learning-disabilities/executive-functioning-issues/
key-executive-functioning-skills-explained

McCarthy, Laura Flynn. "What Babies Learn in the Womb" Parenting.
Accessed May 14, 2016. http://www.parenting.com/article/
what-babies-learn-in-the-womb

Daily Mail. "Bilingual children ARE smarter: Babies who grow up listening
to two languages have better problem-solving skills even before they
can talk." April 5, 2016. http://www.dailymail.co.uk/sciencetech/
article-3524180/Bilingual-babies-smarter-Children-grow-listening-
two-languages-better-memory-problem-solving-skills.html

McElroy, Molly. "Bilingual baby brains show increased activity in
executive function regions." University of Washington. April 4,
2016. http://www.washington.edu/news/2016/04/04/bilingual-
baby-brains-show-increased-activity-in-executive-function-regions/

The Blooming Brain

Ferjan Ramirez, Naja. "Why the Baby Brain Can Learn Two Languages
at the Same Time." The Conversation. April 15, 2016. https://
theconversation.com/why-the-baby-brain-can-learn-two-languages-
at-the-same-time-57470

Flaherty, Colleen. "Not a small World After All."
Inside Higher Ed. February 11, 2015. https://
www.insidehighered.com/news/2015/02/11/
mla-report-shows-declines-enrollment-most-foreign-languages

The Tongue May Stumble, But the Brain Purrs

Grosjean, François. Blog: Life as a Bilingual. "Who is Bilingual?"
October 21, 2010. https://www.psychologytoday.com/blog/
life-bilingual/201010/who-is-bilingual

Garrett, Mario D., PhD. "Brain Plasticity in Older Adults." Psychology

Today. Accessed June 2016. https://www.psychologytoday.com/blog/iage/201304/brain-plasticity-in-older-adults

CHAPTER SIX—A Life in Words

Make Love, Not War

History.com. "Kent State Incident." Accessed July 8, 2016. http://www.history.com/topics/vietnam-war/kent-state

Ez Dakite Euskaraz Hitz Egiten Duzu?

Wikipedia. "Basque Americans." Accessed February 13, 2016. https://en.wikipedia.org/wiki/Basque_Americans

The Cure by Feeding of Earworms

Wikipedia. "Earworm." Accessed August 28, 2015. https://en.wikipedia.org/wiki/Earworm

BBC News. "Ten Readers' Cures for Earworms." Accessed August 29, 2015. http://www.bbc.com/news/magazine-17302237

In Megahurtz, but Not Furlong

Cool Science. "Math jokes." http://www.coolscience.org/CoolScience/CoolJokes/MathJokes.htm

A Girl (Not) Named Sue

Canon Law Made Easy. "Do Catholic Children Have to be Given Saints' Names?" Accessed July 30, 2016. http://canonlawmadeeasy.com/2011/10/25/do-catholic-children-have-to-be-given-saints-names/

Wikipedia. "Saint's Name." Last modified June 15, 2016. https://en.wikipedia.org/wiki/Saint%27s_name

Social Security. "Top Names of the 1950s." Accessed July 30, 2016. https://www.ssa.gov/oact/babynames/decades/names1950s.html

CHAPTER SEVEN—Marking Moments in the Year

High Notes on Highway 99

Wikipedia. "Central Valley (California)." Accessed January 2, 2016. https://en.wikipedia.org/wiki/Central_Valley_(California)

May Your Days Be Merry and Bright

"Fruitcake recipe." Accessed December 6, 2014. http://indigo.org/humor/fruit.html

Snopes.com. "Reindeer Games." Accessed December 6, 2014 http://www.snopes.com/holidays/christmas/santa/reindeer.asp

Have a Feliz Navidad and a Diglot New Year

Garg, Anu. The Dord, the Diglot, and an Avocado or Two, The Hidden Live and Strange Origins of Common and Not-So-Common Words. South Africa: Penguin Books. 2007.

NPR. "The Night Before Christmas, Latin Style." December 24, 2005. http://www.npr.org/templates/story/story.php?storyId=5068774

And the Word of the Year Is...

Wikipedia. "Word of the Year." Accessed December 21, 2014 and January 2, 2015. https://en.wikipedia.org/wiki/Word_of_the_year

Reach Out and Open Your Kimono, A Lexical Review of 2015

BBC News. "Australia Makes 'Captain's Call' on Best Words of 2015." January 20, 2016. http://www.bbc.com/news/world-australia-35368063

NPR Code Switch. "Why Corporate Executives Talk About Opening Their Kimonos." November 2, 2014. http://www.npr.org/sections/codeswitch/2014/11/02/360479744/why-corporate-executives-talk-about-opening-their-kimonos

Wikipedia. "Word of the Year." Accessed January 15, 2016 https://en.wikipedia.org/wiki/Word_of_the_year

Oxford Dictionaries. "Word of the Year." Accessed January 16, 2016. http://blog.oxforddictionaries.com/2015/11/word-of-the-year-2015-emoji/

Merriam-Webster. "Gallery: Word of the Year 2015." Accessed January 16, 2016. http://www.merriam-webster.com/words-at-play/word-of-the-year-2015

Global Language Monitor. "Microagression Is Top Word." Accessed January 16, 2016. http://www.languagemonitor.com/category/word-of-the-year/

American Dialectical Society. "2015 Word of the Year is singular 'they.'" Accessed January 16, 2016. http://www.americandialect.org/2015-word-of-the-year-is-singular-they

Guo, Jeff. "Sorry, grammar nerds. The singular 'they' has been declared Word of the Year." The Washington Post. January 18, 2016. https://www.washingtonpost.com/news/wonk/wp/2016/01/08/donald-trump-may-win-this-years-word-of-the-year/

Philipson, Alice. "Rome finally abandons 'too complicated' Roman numerals." The Telegraph. July 23, 2015. http://www.telegraph.co.uk/news/worldnews/europe/italy/11758563/Rome-finally-abandons-too-complicated-Roman-numerals.html

New Era. "Indigenous languages are fundamental to development." October 30, 2015. https://www.newera.com.na/2015/10/30/indigenous-languages-fundamental-development/

Fox 32. "Donald Trump tells Jeb Bush 'speak English,' not Spanish if he wants to be president." September 3, 2015. http://www.fox32chicago.com/news/dont-miss/16108564-story

Huffington Post. "Carly Fiorina Thinks English Is the Official Language. It's Not." September 3, 2015. http://www.huffingtonpost.com/entry/carly-fiorina-english-official-language_us_55e85f23e4b0c818f61ae02d

Willsher, Kim. "The French Scrabble champion who doesn't speak French." The Guardian. July 21, 2015. https://www.theguardian.com/lifeandstyle/2015/jul/21/new-french-scrabble-champion-nigel-richards-doesnt-speak-french

The Secret to Everything, Part II

Brummé, Steve. Moving Fast, Sitting Still. http://www.movingfastsittingstill.net/

Mary and the Merry Month of May

Lonely Planet. "Festivals of the world: where to go in May." Accessed April 23, 2016. https://www.lonelyplanet.com/travel-tips-and-articles/77164

Roman Catholic Saints. "Titles of Mary." Accessed April 24, 2016. http://www.roman-catholic-saints.com/titles-of-mary.html

INDEX

ABOUT THE AUTHOR

SUSANNA JANSSEN is a foreign language educator and newspaper columnist who writes extensively about words, language, and culture. In her life as a author, speaker, and teacher, she is dedicated to contributing to the linguistic culture of America and advocating for learning a foreign language at *any* age. She resides in Northern California where magnificent redwood trees, legendary wines, a rich culture of all the arts, and great friendships are a source of wonder, inspiration, and joy.

For more information about Susanna Janssen
and her work, contact the author:

Email: susannajanssenauthor@gmail.com
Blog: https://www.facebook.com/SusannaJanssenAuthor/
Twitter: https://twitter.com/susannajanssen
Website: http://www.susannajanssen.com/

See website for:

Free special reports:

"How to parlay your current language
skills into your dream job"

"The disastrous flaw that prevents fluency in most
foreign language classrooms of America"

"The top ten languages to learn now and why"

and more!

Consulting: How you can work with Susanna Janssen
as your Spanish language coach
Speaking engagements and interviews

For book purchases from the website:

Special gift included with each book, plus author signature
Volume discount for purchase of 10 or more copies